THE LEGENDARY CRICKET GENIUS

Sydney F. Barnes

(1873-1967)

J.L. Nicholls

Editing, design, typesetting and publishing by UK Book Publishing
www.ukbookpublishing.com

ISBN: 978-1-912183-53-1

To the Nicholls family
- Stephen, Jenny, Jessica and Sam

Contents

CONTENTS

Acknowledgements

A special thanks to Peter Barnes, the grandson of Sydney Francis Barnes, for providing information and family photos. I am especially indebted to his co-operation, encouragement and support throughout the research.

My sincerest thanks to David Frith, the famous cricket author and journalist, and Keith Plant both of whom permitted me the right to use their works. David's fascinating article of his meeting with Mr Barnes at his home in 1967 when the great man was 94 years-old and Keith's wonderful script of the play he wrote of the 'life and times' of the Staffordshire man.

I would also like to thank two Welsh compatriots, David Parry (Colwyn Bay) and Dr Andrew Hignell (Glamorgan) who helped in the research of Barnes' time spent in North Wales.

Not forgetting a good friend of mine, Angela Middleton, a well-known local Genealogical Researcher.

A special thanks to the team at UK Book Publishing and the support from Ruth Lunn (Editor) and Jason Thompson (Designer) who worked so well together to produce this book.

The book is richer for their contributions.

The Staffordshire Lad

A cricketing hero who attracted large crowds
Who did seeth the man, in starch white and so proud
Hard-driven, tall, upright and arm outstretched,
Turning the ball who can ever forget.
All were proud of him, the Staffordshire lad
An English bulldog all batsmen were glad
Age doth wither as time goes by
Below the Staffordshire grass lies
Our champion, to forget him would be a sin,
One day there might well be a school boy akin.
Let's not forget the northerner who wore the coat of arms,
Three Kings with pride, a brave heart, the man, Sydney F. Barnes.

J.L.Nicholls

Foreword by Peter Sydney Francis Barnes

It was a day in January 2017 when I met Jeff for the first time at a pre-arranged meeting at the Bell Inn, near Shifnal, a market town in the county of Shropshire. He had phoned me two weeks earlier to explain that he was researching the life of Grandad for a book he was hoping to get published and asked me if I had any material of interest which I would be willing to let him use to include in the book.

I was immediately struck by Jeff's intense enthusiasm, determination, firmness of purpose and acquired knowledge already obtained about Grandad. So much of it I was not aware of both on and particularly off the field. There was no doubt in my mind I was very keen to meet this man, Jeff, and soon realised, deep in my heart, he was the person I was wanting to help by providing interesting memorabilia I was treasuring including family photographs as a means of sharing far beyond, into the public domain.

We met and 'hit it off' immediately. Over a very nice well-cooked pub lunch we spent over two hours talking about Grandad and his fantastic life on and off the field. Since then we have become great friends and I am so pleased that he has eventually published this book about Grandad and of his eventual rise from the Victorian slums and poverty to have become a great cricket 'star' and a legend of his time.

My grandad has been described as amazing with his bowling feats at all levels of the game. Comments made recently by some of today's influential former cricketing greats and cricket journalists, that he was a "once-off" freakishly great bowler who has certainly not yet been emulated in style. It has been said any bowler of great accuracy capable of swinging the ball, or swerving it in his case, and then be capable of moving it away off the wicket glancing the bails off on its journey would have dismissed any batsman in any era. Many admirers considered him to be a must-see champion bowler who would in his prime attract thousands to the cricket grounds of England just to watch him play.

Cricket was in his blood when at 15 years of age he became involved playing matches with a small club that had its ground at the back of the Galton Hotel, Smethwick and it wasn't long before becoming associated with the town club shortly afterwards. His career in the game spanned more than 40 years later when his last professional engagement at 69 was cricket coach at the Harrison Colliery, Little Wyrley, Staffordshire. Looking back I now appreciate fully what a good player he must have been.

My family and I today are immensely proud and honoured that Grandad's portrait by the artist Harry Rutherford is hanging in the famous Long Room at Lords with other cricketing greats. He was a world-class player who achieved a lot but to me he was just Grandad.

I never actually saw him in action but I did have 17 years with him before he died and can remember him as a very kind and modest man, unselfish and caring, independent, a private man with a subtle sense of humour. I spent a lot of my times as a youngster especially in his later years keeping him company in his room. He liked a 'tipple' but not much and he did enjoy a smoke, either a pipe or a cigar. His favourite was

St Bruno tobacco flake and he would sit in his armchair next to the fire listening every night to the 'Archers' on his radio.

He certainly lived a very active lifestyle and continued working for the Staffordshire council well into his 90s. As a skilled calligrapher he was asked to present a handwritten scroll to Queen Elizabeth II to commemorate her visit to Stafford. Something else my family and I are so proud of him for.

I was with him when he died. St. Luke's Church, Cannock, is where he chose as his resting place. I remember there were so many people at the funeral the town was brought to a standstill. The event was televised. It was then that I began to realise that Grandad was, and had been, someone special to lots of people.

Portrait of Barnes at Lord's

There is a full length painting of Sydney Barnes in the Long Room at Lord's. The picture is the one shown in the photograph below. The artist Harry Rutherford is also in the picture standing on the right just behind Barnes.

Members of the Staffordshire County Cricket Club who attended the Annual General Meeting at the Swan Hotel, Stafford on 27th April 1954 had the opportunity to view the portrait of Barnes, which was presented to the MCC in London on 1st May 1954.

The portrait, an oil painting by Harry Rutherford of Hyde Cheshire, shows the bowler in the England touring sweater he wore when on tour in Australia. He is also wearing the Staffordshire County cap with pride. The portrait was presented by the President of the club, Bernard Meakin, at Lord's where it is hung in pride of place in the famous Long Room in company with portraits of other cricket celebrities, among them Dr W.G.Grace, Sir Pelham Warner and Sir Donald Bradman.

Introduction

It is a fact that very little is known of Sydney Francis Barnes of his time spent when he resided in North Wales and that he represented Wales in first-class matches. He was unique in that he should have qualified to represent two countries (England and Wales) during his 45-year long career in the game. This book features his life and times he proudly spent in Wales and the achievements, honours and rewards he gained as a member of a team representing Wales. Some questions were asked how it was that he had qualified to play for Wales. The answer was simple: He had a residential qualification having lived in Colwyn Bay for many years. There is evidence to suggest that he was living in Colwyn Bay as early as 1913 and perhaps off and on until 1930. Records do show that he participated in a fund-raising match at a public school in Colwyn Bay in September 1913. The game at Rydal Mount had been arranged to raise some funds for a local hospital and was played on the cricket pitch of the well-known public school. His involvement in such a venture may well have been that the move to North Wales was indeed likely because of his wife's health.

It was remarkable that his performances on the cricket field in 1927 at the age of 54 were considered to be of the highest esteem, and would deserve well-earned notice for him to be chosen to play first-class cricket again. He played 9 times for Wales between 1927 and 1930. In 1928 he took 49 wickets which included the formidable figures of 7 for 51 and 5 for 67 in an 8 wicket win against a West Indies touring side.

Most of the matches were played in North Wales at The Oval, Llandudno and at the Colwyn Bay club's Penrhyn Avenue ground at Rhos-on-Sea. His appearances included matches against South Africa, New Zealand (twice), West Indies, MCC, Lancashire, South Wales (twice), and a team representing the Minor Counties. It is difficult to speculate on his motives for moving and taking up residence on the North Wales coast and especially Colwyn Bay. Perhaps he was like others at the time looking to cash in on the property boom in the area round Colwyn Bay and Llandudno. Indeed, many people from the North-West of England had made money through the financing of properties in these thriving and genteel resorts. Alternatively, his move to the area may have been because of his wife's health, or indeed, the chance to become involved in a new business venture. In fact the latter was a step he actually took when in 1923 he ended his contract with Saltaire in the Bradford League to take on the job as resident Licensee of the Royal Hotel, Colwyn Bay. It was thought at the time, and might well have been his intention, to retire from the game. However, quite unexpectedly, due to a scrape with the law which required an appearance in the dock at the local Magistrates Court, he suddenly resigned from his job at the Royal Hotel after only 11 months and immediately signed professional terms with Castleton Moor of the Central Lancashire League.

Barnes was regarded, and still is, as one of the greatest bowlers ever to have set foot on a cricket field. For many years he gave pleasure to thousands of followers of the game with his unique pace bowling from medium to fast with the ability to make the ball both swing and break from leg or off.

Barnes was unusual in that, despite a long career as a top-class player, he spent little more than two seasons in first-class cricket, playing for Warwickshire and Lancashire. For mostly professional reasons he preferred league and Minor Counties cricket. Between 1895 and 1934 he played for several clubs in the Lancashire, North Staffordshire, Bradford and Central Lancashire leagues. He played for Staffordshire in the Minor Counties. Between 1901 and 1914 he played Test cricket for England in 27 matches and will always be remembered for one of the lowest Test bowling averages ever achieved. He helped England win the Ashes in Australia taking a mammoth 43 wickets in the 1911-1912 series and in his final Test series against South Africa in 1913-1914 he took a world series record at the time recording a magnificent 49 wickets.

His final appearance in first-class cricket was for Wales against the MCC in 1930.

Barnes, at the age of 90, was named by Wisden Cricketer's Almanac in its hundredth edition as one of its ' Six Giants of the Wisden Century'. The other 5 players chosen were Sir Donald Bradman, W.G. Grace, Sir Jack Hobbs, Tom Richardson and Victor Trumper.

He died peacefully in 1967 at the age of 94 at his home in Chadsmoor, Cannock, Staffordshire.

A full length painting of him by the artist Harry Rutherford hangs in the famous Long Room at the Lord's cricket ground which was presented to the MCC in London on 1st May 1954.

In 1973 a large plaque was erected outside one of the main gates at the famous Edgbaston ground in recognition of his very first county match and also inscribed that he was universally acknowledged in later years 'as the greatest bowler of them all'. In 2008, he had the highest rating among bowlers in the ICC Best-Ever Test Championship Ratings and in 2009 he was inducted into the ICC Cricket Hall of Fame.

He is the only man ever to be picked for England while not playing first-class cricket – that is, while only playing Minor Counties and league cricket. Indeed, despite an astonishing Test record – 189 wickets in 27 matches at an average of 16.43, with no fewer than 24 five-wicket hauls in the 50 innings in which he bowled (9 for 103 being his best analysis), and 9 ten-wicket matches (a best of 17 for 159), including a world-record 49 wickets in a series against South Africa (at the age of 40, despite pulling out of the fifth game due, typically, to a dispute over disbursements) – Barnes played relatively little first-class cricket. Only 133 games, in fact, over a 36-year span (intermittent, of course), in which he bagged the small matter of 719 wickets at an average of 17.09 runs.

The relatively scarce appearances in county cricket (just 44 games) were more the product of his own economic hard-headedness and prevailing market forces than any lack of opportunity. Warwickshire had been reluctant to offer him a contract despite impressive results in the Birmingham League. As a teenager, the son of a Black Country metal-beater, he decided he would become a professional bowler, wherever the highest bid took him. A living had to be earned; all other rewards would come or go as they may. He was a man with a keen sense of his own value as a cricketer and realised he was becoming a commercial attraction. If you paid, he bowled. And he sure did some bowling, playing league cricket up and down the country – in his native Staffordshire (Smethwick, Porthill Park), the Bradford League (Saltaire, Keighley) and the Lancashire Leagues (Rishton, Burnley, Church, Rawtenstall, Rochdale, Castleton Moor) – while of course enjoying a long career for Staffordshire, for whom he took the small matter of 1,441 wickets at 8.10 each, on the way bagging 26 of the 30 best innings analyses for the county. Barnes finally hung up his boots in 1940, aged 67, after a season spent with Stone in the North Staffordshire Wartime League.

As for the man, he was, by all accounts, a remote and cussed soul off the field and temperamental on it, where he was remorseless and hard-driven in the pursuit of wickets and sharp-tongued toward captains who placed unnecessary obstacles in the way. Cardus said that "a chill wind of antagonism blew from him even on the sunniest day", and his slightly pitted eyes, prominent brow, and cheekbones like onions no doubt added to his severe, forbidding aura. Yet beyond his lack of affability and general disdain for social niceties, what was it that made him such a fearsome proposition, so good that he not only made Cricinfo's all-time England XI but also Richie Benaud's Greatest XI?

Standing an inch over six feet and with long arms, he was, according to John Arlott, noted for his stature:

"{his] High delivery gave him a lift off the pitch that rapped the knuckles of the unwary and forced even the best batsmen to play him at an awkward height".

In addition, his large hands and spidery fingers gave him a grip on the ball that often made facing him a question of when, not if... Most intriguingly, his style of bowling has been described, variously, as cutters, medium-pace, fast-medium, fast spin, even leg-spin. Consensus is that it was all of this, with the leg-cutter his stock ball, mixed with fast off-breaks, in-and out-swingers and constant, subtle changes of pace. One can only guess how effective he'd have been on covered pitches. Certainly, one imagines he'd have been a revelation in limited overs cricket, with batsmen having to attack him. And whatever it was he bowled, there is no doubting he was a genius, a freakishly consistent wicket machine whose final balance sheet showed no fewer than 6,225 wickets in all forms of cricket at the puny average of 8.31.

Sydney Barnes must have been amazing and seems to have been a "one-off" freakishly great bowler who has not been emulated in style. Any bowler of great accuracy capable of swinging the ball in (or "swerving" it in his case) and then moving it away off the wicket to hit top of off would have dismissed any batsman in any era. He could move the ball the other way too and obtained lift off the pitch. A one off champion bowler. A cricket admirer.

Life and Times

It was such a memorable occasion when in 2017 and on a typical cold and wet winter's January day I had, for the first time, the privilege of meeting Barnes' grandson, Peter. He was keen to meet me after I had explained to him over the phone that I was researching the life and times of his grandad and that I was looking for any material of interest he could recall for me, not previously reported in the media, about the famous man, most especially the period in the 1920s when he and his wife, Alice, and son, Leslie, were residing in Colwyn Bay, North Wales. We arranged to meet that day at The Bell Inn, Tong, near the market town of Shifnal, in the county of Shropshire. It was there we spent a pleasant couple of lunch-time hours in a warm cosy atmosphere enjoying a highly recommended English meat pie pub lunch, washed down with a strong cold beer, and in conversation, both very enthusiastic, of the great man. Peter had brought with him a host of treasured memorabilia (including family photographs) to show me. It was amazing! He very kindly offered to loan me whatever I wanted to use, for the purpose, and the choice I made included: The photo of the portrait of Barnes hanging in the Long Room at Lord's; the letter from Buckingham Palace from the Queen; the two mounted balls presented to him by the South African and Australian Cricketing Associations; and other interesting cricket and family photos not been seen publicly before.

Peter told me that when he was very young he was aware that his grandad was a famous sportsman cricketer but to him in those days he was just Grandad whom he doted on. He could recall as a 7-year old at the family home, then at Coppice House in Penkridge, when he stood on the lawn with a cricket bat in his hand waiting for his grandad to bowl at him. They used three iron railings as the wickets on a lawn which was big enough to hold an entire cricket pitch. Peter went on to say that his grandad was already in his 80s at the time but Peter never forgot seeing his tall frame coming at him with a hard cricket ball in his hand and letting it go at a speed his grandad considered suitable for a 7-year old.

"I didn't have a hope of hitting the ball he bowled and it made me appreciate what it must have been like for a batsman facing him during his playing career. Tough would have been the answer."

Peter went on to say:

"I obviously never saw him in action, but we have lots of memorabilia from his playing days and was also told so many wonderful things about him it makes me feel very proud that he was my grandad especially as time goes on. I think he was a self-taught cricketer, never seriously coached, but was the right build to be a bowler. When he was in his 80s I remember he could get his fingers two-thirds of the way around the cricket ball because they were that long. I couldn't get mine half-way round. Mind you, not expected to at 7-years old. He must have been born with a cricket ball in his hand. From speaking to people the Aussies had a bit of bashing from Grandad and not many people liked facing him."

Peter recalled that his grandad was the head of the family who lived with him, his sister Penny and parents Leslie and Mary at Coppice House.

"I had 17 years with Grandad before he died and he was a very modest, private man," explained Peter, who now lives with his wife Rita in Great Wyrley near Walsall. *"I wasn't ever into cricket and only played at school, so I can't remember chatting to him about the game. He never pushed me to play either. I used to spend a lot of my night times as a youngster keeping him company in his room. He'd have his tea, which usually consisted of a lamb chop and some bread, accompanied by a yellow whisky jug full of warm water and a cup of tea. It was all laid out on an oval drop-leaf dining table, which I've still got, with a tablecloth on it. Grandad didn't drink much, but he did smoke, either a pipe or cigars. After his meal, I'd help him flake his St Bruno tobacco for his pipe and he'd sit in his armchair next to the*

fire and listen to the Archers on the radio. He also liked to have a bath in cold water to get the circulation going. I'm not sure what benefits it had, but he must have done something right because he lived until he was 94."

Barnes certainly led an active lifestyle and continued working into his 90s. He worked at Staffordshire County Council and became a skilled calligrapher. In 1957, he was asked to present a handwritten scroll to Queen Elizabeth II to commemorate her visit to Stafford.

"His copper plate writing was something to behold," added Peter, who worked as a truck driver and latterly with the Air Ambulance before retiring earlier that year.

"Grandad was very independent and even in his 90s he would travel by bus to go to work. What was remarkable, at 92 he was working a 3-day week and was travelling a 20-mile round trip to and from work changing buses on the journey. You could never miss him because he was always dressed in a mac and trilby. And along with his stature, he certainly stood out in a crowd. The bus conductor would always say to him 'Morning, Mr Barnes' and they never dreamed of taking a fare off him because of his cricketing fame."

Peter told me that his fame did spread well beyond the confines of Staffordshire after his exploits on a cricket pitch. He recalled the 27 Tests for England, he managed to take 24 five-wicket hauls, and he was inducted into the ICC Hall of Fame in 2009. His record for Staffordshire was just as remarkable – if not more so. We both agreed that five-wicket hauls are a fine achievement at Minor Counties level.

"Grandad did it on 159 occasions. Taking all 10 wickets in a match is even rarer, but astonishingly, he managed to achieve the feat 9 times."

It is little wonder the cricketing world was eager to pay its respects when Barnes died, at the age of 94, on Boxing Day 1967 at the family's home in Chadsmoor, Cannock, where they had moved the previous year.

"I was with him when he passed away," recalls Peter. *"The funeral surprised me. It was at St Luke's Church in Cannock and the town was brought to a standstill. The police were there stopping traffic and the funeral was televised, which brings it home to you that he wasn't an ordinary person. I'm sure there had never been a televised funeral in Cannock before! I feel certain that there were several cricket people in attendance, but over time you forget these things. At a funeral you are locked into your own little world and you are concentrating on the family."*

Playing cricket hasn't continued down the Barnes family line, with interest from Peter, his wife, sons Simon and Michael and daughters Angela and Fiona, confined to the other side of the boundary.

"Cricket was in his blood and he was very proud to represent Staffordshire," Peter added. *"Looking back you can now appreciate fully what a good player he must have been. He was a world-famous cricketer who achieved a lot, but to me he was just Grandad."*

Peter with his grandad

The author (left) with Peter Barnes

BUCKINGHAM PALACE

8th November, 1955.

Dear Mr Barnes,

       The Queen much appreciated the gift
of the beautifully inscribed copy of the records
of a visit by Queen Elizabeth I to Stafford in
1575, which you presented to The Duke of Edinburgh
at the County Buildings last week.   Her Majesty
is very much impressed by the beautiful writing,
of which you are still a master, and is very glad
to have this account of the visit of her predecessor
and namesake to Stafford.   I know how much His
Royal Highness enjoyed meeting you and accepting
this document on Her Majesty's behalf.

       I am commanded to express The Queen's
sincere thanks to you and her hope that you may
be given many more years to practise your skill in
this craft.

             Yours sincerely,

             Edward Ford

S.F. Barnes, Esq.

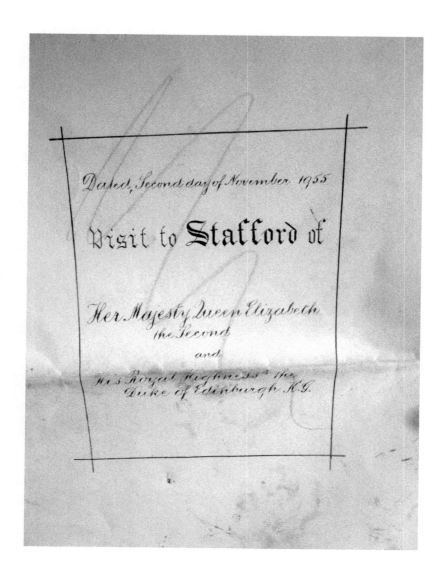

This is a Copy of the Records of a

Visit of Queen Elizabeth 1.

to Stafford in 1575

This Year Queen Elizabeth came in progress from Chartley (where Her Majesty had lain ten days)

And before Her Majesty came to this town each man's house was new painted, the streets gravelled, and the croft which then stood where the Shire Hall now standeth, was repaired and set on fresh rollers.

The Bailiffs accompanied with the brethren went on foot to meet Her Majesty upon the East Gate Dam, over against Crabbapennies' Croft where the Bailiffs presented Her Majesty with a Cup, being two cups in one, closed in the mouth in height two foot or more in value Thirty pounds, which she most lovingly received using most gracious favourable words saying to the Bailiffs and the brethren "Alas! poor souls! other towns give us of their wealth, and you give us of your want. But if you can devise any manner way how we may do you any good speak now and we will further you"

After this William Lamb Schoolmaster made an oration unto Her Majesty which being ended the Bailiffs stood up and delivered unto Her Majesty their maces which she received and delivered the same back again commanding the said Bailiffs to bear them, which they receiving having the horses ready with the foot clothes mounted upon them and rode next before Her Majesty's sword bearer. So passed Her Majesty in at the east gate and so along the street until she came unto the Market Place where she stood still and bid them speak to Her Majesty that they were in any need.

Her Majesty commended the situation of the town and asked what was the cause of the decay of the same And answer was made that the decay of capping was

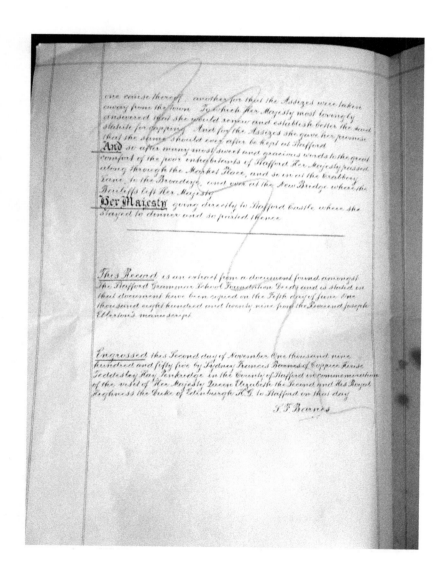

Alice's divorce and marriage

Barnes was happily married to Alice for more than 41 years. They had a very happy and fulfilling life together. He was Alice's 2nd husband and it was in 1903 they "tied the knot" after she experienced a tough and difficult divorce from George Taylor the year before. Barnes was the co-respondent in the divorce suit brought by Taylor who at the time was a clerk working in Handsworth, West Midlands.

A report in the Leeds Mercury of the divorce proceedings stated that Taylor went home to find that his wife had gone away and she was subsequently found living with Barnes at an address in Manchester.

"I have lost all love for my husband," she said when traced. "I love Sydney Barnes and he loves me. It is the only thing I could do to join him."

Barnes remarked at the divorce hearing:

"I hope you will move it as short and as light for me as you can or you will spoil my professional career as a cricketer."

A decree nisi was granted with £300 damages against Barnes. The damages were awarded to George Taylor for reasons of adultery by his wife.

Her marriage to Taylor had taken place at St Paul's Church, Aston, Birmingham in 1893 and it was stated that together they were introduced to Barnes in early 1902 at a dinner-dance. It was not long afterwards they eloped to Manchester where they lived together as man and wife in the Stretford area. She gave the excuse to one witness that she had never really loved her husband. She loved Barnes and he loved her. Barnes was at the time cricketing coach to a club at Smethwick. It was in April of that year that Taylor, who was a commercial clerk earning £150 a year, went home and found that his wife had left him. He and a solicitor's clerk made inquiries and traced them living together at Rycroft Road, Stretford as man and wife. It was the solicitor's clerk who was present at the time when he and Taylor served the divorce papers on her and asked if at any time had she accompanied Barnes to the cricket fields. At the time he was engaged in a match for Lancashire against Somerset. She replied that she didn't and that she did not intend doing so until they were properly married. She said she lived alone at the Rycroft address with the exception of a servant coming in occasionally.

The divorce settlement had some bearing on his earnings as a professional cricketer. Barnes had told her that his accident in Australia had deprived him of a good deal of money, as he expected to make £400 out of the Test Matches. It was believed for this reason, it did have some effect on the actual amount claimed for damages.

The jury, after the judge had completed his summing-up, returned the amount of damages at £350 but as only £300 was claimed the judge advised them to reduce the amount to £300. The damages were ordered to be paid within a fortnight.

Alice Maud Barnes died of heart failure on 6th November, 1944 at the family home at Coppice House, Teddesley, Penkridge.

CERTIFIED COPY OF AN ENTRY OF DEATH

GIVEN AT THE **GENERAL REGISTER OFFICE**

Application Number 8116097-1

REGISTRATION DISTRICT	CANNOCK
1944 DEATH in the Sub-district of Brewood	in the County of Stafford

Columns:—	1	2	3	4	5	6	7	8	9
No.	When and where died	Name and surname	Sex	Age	Occupation	Cause of death	Signature, description and residence of informant	When registered	Signature of registrar

CERTIFIED to be a true copy of an entry in the certified copy of a Register of Deaths in the District above mentioned.

Given at the GENERAL REGISTER OFFICE, under the Seal of the said Office, the 13th day of March 2017

DYE 142950

See note overleaf

CAUTION: THERE ARE OFFENCES RELATING TO FALSIFYING OR ALTERING A CERTIFICATE AND USING OR POSSESSING A FALSE CERTIFICATE ©CROWN COPYRIGHT
WARNING: A CERTIFICATE IS NOT EVIDENCE OF IDENTITY.

PMS

23

The Royal Hotel, Colwyn Bay

Barnes in trouble with the Police

During the time Barnes was residing in North Wales he was summoned to appear at the Colwyn Bay Magistrates Court on 2nd April, 1924. It was at a time he decided to retire from cricket and become the licensee of the Royal Hotel, a well-established local pub and restaurant situated in the centre of the town. After only 11 months in the job there was an incident which involved the police and which resulted in him being charged with permitting drunkenness on the premises.

The circumstances which led to Barnes finding himself in, for what was an unenviable situation for him, was recorded in the court papers. It read that on 18th March, 1924 a man who was very drunk was seen to enter the restaurant portion of the Royal Hotel. A police sergeant and two constables followed the man into the premises and drew Barnes' attention to the man's condition. The police left but an hour later returned and spotted the man, who was now in the company of three other men, sitting at a table in the restaurant. The table was full of empty and half-full glasses. The police sergeant stated that he could see the man was still very drunk and felt it necessary to produce a witness at the magistrates' court, who was a customer in the bar at the time, to swear on oath in front of the bench that he agreed with the police that the man was indeed very drunk. The police sergeant said that he did not suggest to Barnes at the time that the man be ejected because he held that that was his duty. It was not until the man left the premises and was outside on the street that he was arrested for being drunk and disorderly.

In court Barnes was asked how long he had been in the licensing trade. He replied just nine months since July the previous year. He was then asked did he know it was an offence to allow men who are intoxicated to remain on the premises for any purpose whatsoever? Barnes replied:

"Yes, I do."

The Chairman of the bench, after some deliberation, said he was sorry that the justices could not agree with the outcome, therefore the case would have to be adjourned for another hearing. The Magistrates' Clerk let it be known later that day that two of the magistrates were in favour of dismissing the charge and two were in favour of convicting Barnes.

At an earlier hearing on 14th March, the man in a letter to the court pleaded guilty to drunkenness and was fined 15s including costs.

On 8th May, 1924 at the Colwyn Bay Sessions, Barnes was again charged with permitting drunkenness on the premises of the Royal Hotel. At the commencement of the hearing Barnes' solicitor informed the bench:

"My client is no longer the licensee of the premises. He has given up the position and is going back to playing professional cricket."

In reply, the solicitor representing the police said that if it was the wish of the bench the case should not go on. Under the circumstances, the police would not press charges. Ultimately, in view of an expression from the bench, the solicitor consented on behalf of the Superintendent of Police, to the case being withdrawn only on payment of costs by the defendant, in view of the fact that when the case was previously heard the bench was equally divided. This was agreed. Barnes, in a letter to the court, had stated that it was his intention to leave Colwyn Bay. However, very soon afterwards he did move but continued to reside in the borough just a mile away at a property in Colwyn Crescent, Rhos on Sea.

The Royal Hotel (situated in the centre of town, Colwyn Bay)

It was the after-lunch session and the batsman had been drinking too heavily during the break. He staggered up to the captain and confessed that he could see three of everything.

"Well," said the captain, "when you get out there and the three balls come towards you, just hit the middle one."

The batsman weaved his way to the crease and was bowled first ball. He made his way back.

"What happened?" demanded the captain. "Didn't you hit the middle ball?"

"Yesh," replied the batsman, "but I used the outside bat!"

Court Cafe, Allestree, Derby

It was in 1932 when Barnes became the owner of a new purposely-built cafe just outside Allestree village, near Derby situated at the junction of Devonshire Avenue and Duffield Road. At the time he was playing for Castleton Moor in the Central Lancashire League and for Staffordshire in Minor Counties. It was said that because there was a tennis court at the back of the premises, hence the name – Court Cafe. It was an attractive place, with steps at the front and plenty of flowers in the garden, as is shown in the picture which was taken in the 1930s.

"COURT CAFE, ALLESTREE, DERBY"

To celebrate the opening of the cafe he invited family and friends to the premises for a special commemorative meal on Monday, February 15th, 1932.

PHONE No. 2575.   THE COURT CAFE,
                                ALLESTREE,
                                    Nr. Derby.

Mr & Mrs S. F. Barnes
would esteem it a favour to have the
pleasure of the Company of

M _____

to celebrate the opening of the above premises
on Monday, Feb. 15th. 1932

A Small Dance will be held at 8 o'clock.

Cars at 10-30 p.m.   R.S.V.P.

BREAD & BUTTER, Etc.
Bread & Butter, white or brown
Buttered Scone, Tea Cake, Girdle Pancake
Roll & Butter
Buns (various)

TOAST
Buttered Toast
Muffin, Tea Cake or Scone
Pyclet or Girdle
Dry Toast

CONFECTIONERY
Plain Cakes and Pastries
Fancy Cakes
Eclairs, Meringues, Cream Puffs
Slice Cake
Genoa, Cherry, Plain or Seed
Vanilla, Coffee or Chocolate
Dundee or Sultana
Cheltenham

SAVOURIES
ON TOAST
Poached Egg, Anchovies, Baked Beans or Spaghetti
Sardines or Tomatoes
Scrambled Egg
Kidneys

SUNDRIES
Boiled Egg or Poached Egg
Fried Egg and Chips
Welsh Rarebit
Buck Rarebit

GRILL
Chop or Steak
Mixed Grill
Sausages
Chips

COLD
Chicken   Ham
Roast Beef
Ham or Tongue
Pork Pie

BEVERAGES

Tea ... ... per cup
Tea one person ... per pot
Tea two persons ... "
Tea Russian ... ... "
Coffee with Cream ... per cup
Cafe au Lait ... "
Cocoa made with Milk "
Chocolate with Whipped Cream "
Milk hot or cold ... "
Soda and Milk ... "
Horlicks Malted Milk ... "
Bovril or Oxo ... "
Cydrax ... "
Soda Minerals ... "
Minerals ... "
Soda Water and Still Lemonade "
Lemon Squash ... "

The Court Cafe
(G. F. BARNES)
ALLESTREE
TELEPHONE DERBY 2575

It's not known how long Barnes ran this business but it became the Court Barbecue Restaurant, owned by a chap named Joe Waldren, which opened in the late 1950s. Behind the building was a timber built convenience store also owned by Joe Waldren from which provisions were delivered in his Morris Minor estate car to local residents.

Court Barbecue played host to a 1970s World Beauty Queen, Eva Rueber-Staier, while on a promotional visit to Derby. It was about the time she was very friendly with George Best, the Northern Ireland and Manchester United footballer renowned for his attraction to beauty queens. A local Allestree resident recalls:

"My son had his wedding reception at the same place nearly 30 years later in the late 1970s when it was called The Palm Court Restaurant and was almost unrecognisable from the old Court Cafe."

29

The Palm Court Restaurant, in Allestree – how it looked in the last few decades of its existence

What follows is a copy of the back cover of the menu card for a luncheon at the Palm Court held on 3rd April 1979. The menu card had been signed by approximately 28 guests; the majority were former Derbyshire cricketers. Signatures include Hendrick, Miller, Russell, Barnett, Taylor, Anderson, Lister, Mellor, Pope, Elliott, Borrington, Swarbrook, Walters, Steele, Wincer etc.

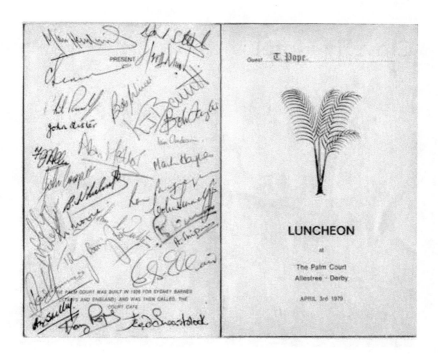

On the night of Saturday, 7th July 2007 the Palm Court restaurant was destroyed by fire. Firefighters took three hours to extinguish the flames. It was reported that no one was hurt in the incident. Fire investigators spent the following day using a specialist sniffer dog to look for evidence of accelerates. It was confirmed that the fire was being treated as arson and they appealed for witnesses to come forward. No one has ever been charged. The restaurant had ceased business in 2005 and the empty building had been disused for more than two years.

The site the restaurant occupied has now been redeveloped and is now a small cluster of 13 three-and-four-bedroomed residential properties.

Worth mentioning, just over a mile away, stood the late-Victorian Clovelly Hotel. Prior to demolition, the Clovelly was run by the late Roger Pearman, a former Middlesex cricketer and Derbyshire Cricket Club chief executive.

31

Clovelly Hotel

Integral to the Clovelly was an L-shaped public bar, called Sobers, which alluded to the great West Indian cricketer and was a clever play on words. Befitting of Pearman's cricketing background, there was some wonderful sporting memorabilia displayed in the bar, including a scorecard from the famous 1956 Ashes Test match in which England spinner Jim Laker beat Barnes' record of 17 wickets when he took 19 Australian wickets.

The Gisborne family, who at one time owned Allestree Hall, donated land as a war memorial which is now the home of various sports clubs including Allestree Cricket Club. One of the all time 'cricketing greats' who had connections with the village was S. F. Barnes – he set up the Court Café; later it became known as the Palm Court before closing in 2005.

1873-1900

The Early Years

Sydney Francis Barnes was born on 19th April, 1873. He was the second son of five children (three boys and two girls). His father, Richard Barnes, was from Shropshire and at a very young age he moved with his parents to Staffordshire where he worked for more than 63 years for a Birmingham firm, Messrs. Muntz Metal Co. based in the Selly Oak district. As a youngster he did play a little cricket but only locally. Neither of Barnes' brothers "touched a bat or ball" so he was the only member of the family to take an active part in the game, his genius for which cannot be traced to heredity or family tradition.

His first experience of matches was gained at about fifteen years of age with a very small club that had its ground at the back of the Galton Hotel, Smethwick and his association with the town club began shortly afterwards. It was a great day for him when he was chosen to play in the third team and he soon won his way into the 2nd XI for whom he also got runs and wickets of some note. It was about this time that he first learned that a ball could be made to turn after pitching. At the commencement of the 1893 season he got his place in the 1st team playing in the Birmingham League. He was 20 years of age.

Smethwick's first eleven professional was Billy Bird of Warwickshire, who came one evening a week to the ground to coach the players. Bird bowled medium-paced off-breaks and it was from him that Barnes learned how to spin the ball from the off. Like with most youngsters today it was no different then. Barnes' chief ambition was to bowl fast like his hero Tom Richardson and to get batsmen out *"by sending the wickets flying!"* Barnes said that all the coaching he ever received did not amount to more than three hours all told. If when batting he was beaten and the bails flew off, he would on many occasions ask the bowler for his opinion – if he had incorrectly played straight, or across the flight of the ball, or were his feet in the wrong position. When bowling he always had in mind the length to which a batsman would play forward when he should have played back and he would ask a batsman if his arm had been straight up when he delivered the ball. That is the way Barnes practised and he tried to think things out for himself. Whether it was the result of Bird's coaching or his own ability to apply what he thought out for himself, he was given a trial with Smethwick's first team. In his first match he didn't exactly cover himself with glory. He was not asked to bowl and when he went in to bat one ball from the fast bowler was enough. As he returned to the pavilion he heard someone say:

"You're no bloody good!"

This remark had a profound effect on Barnes' development and determination to succeed against the odds, which was such a marked feature of his later years. He was dropped for the next game, but the following week he was back in the team. That day was the beginning of his career as a cricketer. The captain sent him in to open the innings. He made only 20, but he stayed in for an hour and was afterwards told that he had got his runs well. In the next match he played against Pallett, a right hand slow bowler who was doing great things for Warwickshire. The wicket was "sticky" but Barnes managed to stay there for an hour and a half and scored over 30. The Smethwick captain, who at the time played for Staffordshire, was very impressed and was heard to say that a new county man had arrived – Sydney F. Barnes.

It was after this that Barnes first came into the limelight as a bowler. Smethwick were playing Handsworth Wood and lost the toss. Barnes was keeping wicket and their opponents had made only eight runs when he was told by the skipper, Dick Thomas, to take off his pads and bowl. In those days he was bowling fast-medium off-breaks. He knew nothing of the leg-break and he was so successful that when the last man came in he had taken six wickets for seven runs. The last man had a go and hit three fours off him before Barnes had his revenge. He finished with seven wickets for 19 runs. The following week he played against the Warwickshire Club and again kept wicket. He did not bowl and one cannot think why after his previous performance, but he did score 49 runs. His performances for Smethwick eventually brought him to the notice of the Warwickshire County Club and he was asked to play in the last match of the 1893 season against Gloucestershire at Bristol. He was not, of course, qualified for Warwickshire, but in those days, it seems, it was enough to play if the club you played for was near Birmingham. As it happened, however, rain completely spoiled play and Barnes did not get a chance to bat or bowl.

The following season in 1894, while still playing with Smethwick, he played for Warwickshire against Cheshire and the match again was seriously interfered with by rain. He did bowl but claimed no wickets and only scored 11 runs. In 1895 he played in the first two matches of the season for Warwickshire against Derbyshire and Surrey and because he was only able to take two wickets for 145 runs they evidently did not consider his performance justified him playing for the county again that season. Barnes played just one more match for them in 1896 against Essex and failed to take a wicket. He did not play for Warwickshire again. One wonders what the Warwickshire authorities of that time would have said if they had been told that Barnes would, in a few years, develop into the greatest bowler ever.

That he had faith in his ability and was able to inspire confidence in others with his progress in becoming a fine bowler, in spite of his discouraging debut in county cricket, he was able to enter the professional ranks in 1895. He commenced with the Rishton club in the Lancashire League at a salary of £3 10s a week, his duties including those of groundsman. The contract further added that 7s 6d be paid if he scored 50 and also 10s 6d per match for bowling when he captured six wickets or more. It was considered £3 10s was quite a decent sum in those days when beer was three half pence a pint and you could buy five cigarettes for a penny. Certainly Barnes would have been much better off financially had he been playing today. As it was, he soon set about earning his money for Rishton and beginning that phenomenal career in league cricket that was to continue for another 40 years and more.

In his first season he took 71 wickets at a cost of slightly under 10 runs a wicket, as well as averaging nearly 20 with the bat. The following summer he did even better with 85 wickets, followed by 87 and in 1898 he was only three short of his 100 wickets at an average cost of 8.46 runs. In his five seasons with the club, with whom he first learned to bowl the leg-break, he took 411 wickets for an average of 9.10. A successful start to his professional career by any standards, so much so that he was asked to join the ground staff at Old Trafford, which he turned down. He said:

"I could not see that it would benefit me, so I declined."

He did play for the Lancashire second eleven in 1899 in a match against Staffordshire and took 10 wickets including a match-winning analysis of 8 wickets for 38 runs in the second innings. His last season for Rishton was also 1899 and later in that year he did play twice for the county side, again without being qualified, against Sussex and at the Oval against Surrey. Barnes did not do too badly against Surrey, sending down no fewer than 44 overs, of which 15 were maidens, 3 wickets for 99 runs. Once again he was approached by Lancashire to join them but they could not meet his terms. The Lancashire authorities claimed that they could secure three men for what Barnes was demanding. At the same time Barnes was not satisfied with the terms Rishton had offered him, so he went to the Burnley club which also played in the Lancashire League. There he was even more successful than at Rishton. In the two seasons he played for them he took more than 100 wickets. In 1900 he captured 111 wickets and in 1901, 114 wickets.

An expectant father rang the hospital to see how his wife was getting on. By mistake he dialled the number for Lord's.

"How's it going?" he asked.

"Fine," was the answer. "We've got two out already and hope to have the rest out before lunch. The last one was a duck."

1901-1914

Test Match Glory

Barnes played for England in 27 matches from 1901 to 1914, taking 189 wickets at 16.43, one of the lowest Test bowling averages ever achieved. In 1911-12, he helped England to win the Ashes when he took 34 wickets in the series against Australia. In 1913-14, his final Test series, he took a world record 49 wickets against South Africa.

In 1901 when he was playing for Burnley he again turned out for Lancashire and this time against Leicestershire, which was to have surprise consequences for him. Lancashire batted first and made 328 for 8 declared and Leicestershire only making 140 in their first innings had to follow-on. In their second innings Barnes took 6 wickets for 70 in 29 overs, seven of them maidens.

Barnes had well and truly arrived!

Australia v England 1901-02

Internationally renowned batsman Archie MacLaren, the
England and Lancashire captain, was invited by the Melbourne
Cricket Club to take a team to Australia during the English
winter of 1901-02. This was the last privately organised team
to represent England at Test level before permanently playing
under the colours of the MCC. Both Yorkshire's Wilfred
Rhodes and George Hirst were expected to be in the team
but the county was not willing to release them. This meant
the team, when announced, was judged to be weak, but it did
contain several players at the beginning of their careers who
went on to succeed at Test level. MacLaren, aware of Barnes'
success in only his one appearance for Lancashire in 1901, in
addition to his skill with the ball playing in the Lancashire
league, invited him to the nets at Old Trafford. Completely
kitted up in his pads, gloves and with his sacred bat in hand,
MacLaren faced up to Barnes and during the session was
painfully thumped on the left thigh and hit hard on his gloves
from a length. Barnes was reported to have said:

"Sorry, sir!"

only for MacLaren to reply:

"Don't be sorry, Barnes, you're coming to Australia with me."

Actually the story of his selection is not complete
without mentioning that on the day when Lancashire beat
Leicestershire, MacLaren approached Barnes at the end of the
match and asked him if he would try to get Burnley to release
him so that he could play full-time for Lancashire. Barnes said
he would ask the committee. Australia was not mentioned
on that occasion but a couple of days later after Barnes had
written to Burnley he received a letter from MacLaren asking
him if he would join his Australian touring side.

Barnes hadn't replied and in fact did not mention it to
anyone until a week later and only to the Burnley captain on

match day. His captain advised him in strong language to reply at once and accept.

"*Perhaps I don't want to go,*" said Barnes jokingly.

But, of course, he did reply, thanking MacLaren for considering him, and accepting his offer. Barnes was later to write on being selected for the tour:

"*Such a thought a month ago it would have been ridiculous, but here I was about to take part in the greatest of all matches against Australia, in Australia.*"

Barnes had realised how fortunate he was in getting such an opportunity. On the boat, on the way to Australia, he confronted MacLaren and asked him why he had been chosen when it was a fast bowler he wanted. MacLaren asked him what kind of bowler he considered himself to be. Barnes replied that in the cricket he played he had to get results on any kind of wicket and he had to adapt himself to circumstances. If the wicket took spin he explained he did not bowl his heart out with fast stuff, but if the wicket was good and firm he did bowl faster.

"*You are fast enough for what I want,*" replied MacLaren and added, " *I think we shall get on well together. I would much rather a man says what he thinks on the field than be a "yes" man.*"

In reply Barnes told him bluntly:

"*I shall never be a 'yes' man. If I don't agree with you I shall say so.*"

His tour selection was a big surprise. To the cricket-loving fraternity generally, it appeared to have been the most daring experiment in the history of the game to have chosen 'the unknown' Barnes. Between 1895 and 1899, he had only played at county level three times for Warwickshire taking just 3 wickets and twice for Lancashire taking 4 wickets. In 1901 he had only played the once for Lancashire against Leicestershire. One can imagine the sensation that the choice of a player for a Test tour with so undistinguished a record would cause today. Plucked from the Lancashire League and only a few games at county level. There would be television and radio appearances and innumerable articles by the cricket correspondents. In fact, even in those days, there was a great to-do in the newspapers, with the headlines:

"Who is this fellow, Barnes?"

MacLaren was heavily criticised for choosing a team which was woefully deficient in good bowlers and was particularly criticised for including Barnes who had accomplished little or nothing to justify the choice.

MacLaren and Barnes had their differences, but maintained a grudging respect for each other which probably did not extend beyond the cricket field. On the trip to Australia the ship carrying the England touring party ran into severe storms rocking the boat fiercely. Trying to comfort his less experienced colleagues, MacLaren said:

"If we do go down, at least that bugger Barnes will go down with us."

To the surprise of the cricketing public, Barnes was a sensation. He took Australia by storm. The first match of the tour was against South Australia at Adelaide and he took five wickets, four in one innings. Next came Victoria at Melbourne on a wicket spoiled by rain. Barnes took 5 for 61 in the first innings and then followed this up by bowling unchanged throughout taking 7 for 38 in the second innings. The win by England over Victoria gave general satisfaction and congratulations all round in the visitor's camp. There was an enthusiastic scene at the finish and the victorious England team received a great ovation from the home supporters. Barnes especially. On any wicket this, it was said, was a noteworthy performance. MacLaren was heartedly congratulated on the Lancashire bowler's success. The team had risen in public estimation because Victoria was considered the strongest colonial eleven fielded that season. It was agreed that Barnes, the Burnley professional, was doing exceedingly well. Barnes had bowled magnificently throughout and had already taken 17 wickets at a cost of 9.77 runs in two matches, which for an "unknown" man was regarded a remarkable performance. The feat of taking 7 wickets on a sodden Victoria wicket was considered a marvellous display for a fast/medium-paced bowler and that it was just a bit incredible that he made the ball rise a lot on a sodden wicket.

In the first Test match at Sydney he bowled 35 overs in the first innings and captured 5 wickets for 65 runs and the profound impression he made by the quality of his bowling was fully confirmed when he took 13 wickets in the next Test match at Melbourne delivering 64 overs in the second innings. It was considered in the press reports that followed, that his bowling in both games was far and away the best feature of the game.

Barnes recalled some years later that he was somewhat 'green' – a youth just out of local cricket and had never seen a Test match. He went on to say:

"The players we opposed I knew only by what I had read in the newspapers. To me they seemed more or less supermen. Nevertheless, I was not in the least nervous, perhaps because I did not realise the importance of the occasion. I have not been worried by "big occasions" because I have played so much competitive cricket at which the crowds always show great keenness and express themselves rather more forcibly than politely. If a crowd is getting at me I take that as a compliment. If I were no good they would ignore me. I have known outbursts by spectators at league matches in England much worse than those for which the Australian barracker's are notorious. Well, in that first Test we won the toss and batted first scoring a mammoth 464 runs. MacLaren scored 116. When Australia batted I opened the bowling against the great Victor Trumper, who was then at his marvellous best. Off the second ball I sent down I caught him! I remember as though it was yesterday the ball coming back to me, a bit wide on the right side. I caught it in a casual way with one hand. As Trumper was walking back to the pavilion Jessop and MacLaren came up to me and the skipper exclaimed that next time I get a catch like that get both hands to it. I was amazed, and showed it, only for him to reply that I might have missed it and he might have gone on to score 200. I was not pleased.

In the first innings I did take 5 for 65. This might sound strange but I didn't think at the time it was a great performance, because I had been used to getting much better analyses in league cricket. I obviously didn't realise the difference in the standard of play. In the second innings I only got one wicket for 74 but bowled well enough to be kept on for most of the time because MacLaren thought I was bowling well even if I wasn't getting wickets. He said that I was making the bowler at the other end better. From that I learned that day one of the strategies of captaincy."

England won that Test match by an innings and 124 runs and at the end Barnes was very proud when he read that MacLaren had said he bowled as well as Tom Richardson, his ideal fast bowler.

The second Test at Melbourne was a different story. It had been raining a few days before the start of the game so MacLaren, after winning the toss, put Australia in to bat first. According to Barnes, the wicket was fairly easy to make the ball turn but only slowly. England did exceptionally well to dismiss them for 112. Barnes' figures were 6 for 42.

Barnes is quoted as saying:

"When we went in to bat, the order was to get runs or get out so that we could have Australia batting again later the same day on what would be a really sticky wicket. Well, we got out only too well for 61 in an hour and a half and Australia went in again. When play ended for the day they had lost 5 wickets and I had taken them all. Naturally we were very satisfied, but imagine our surprise when we arrived at the ground next morning and found that the wicket was absolutely perfect again. I had heard many stories of how Australian wickets recover quickly, but I could not believe it happened so quickly as that. It was achieved hardly in accordance with the rules then, by placing blankets and rolling and rolling until all the moisture was absorbed. I remember Tom Hayward remarking that not only were we playing the Australian cricketers and the Australian umpires but we were playing against the Australian groundsmen. There was also during the game some differences of opinion with the scoring, too. During that day only three more wickets fell. I remember this day particularly well

because apart from the luncheon and tea intervals I bowled without a rest sending down 47 overs. In all, in that innings, I bowled 64 overs for 121 runs but was well rewarded with 7 wickets. That afternoon I asked MacLaren about a rest, but he said he couldn't take me off as I was bowling so well. It was the longest spell I ever bowled in Australia without a rest."

Australia were all out for 353 in the second innings, leaving England to get 404 runs to win but failed scoring only 173. Australia won by 229 runs. Some consolation for Barnes. The ball was presented by the Melbourne Cricket Club to Barnes. The inscription reads 'Presented by the Melbourne Cricket Club to S.F. Barnes, 2nd Test Match, 13 wickets for 164 runs. Australia won by 229 runs.'

The third Test followed immediately at Adelaide and lasted into the sixth day. England won the toss and made 388. When Australia went in, Barnes opened the bowling, but in the seventh over his knee gave way. He had had new spikes put into his boots before the match and they gripped the ground only too well, holding his foot, with the result he had twisted his knee. He limped off the field, thinking he would have the knee bandaged and return in a few minutes, but despite treatment he was unable to do so. The match was won by Australia who, in Barnes' absence, made 315 with four wickets to spare. In fact he bowled no more on the tour. His inability seriously depleted England's strength and it was also suggested that his inactivity with the ball had a detrimental effect on morale in the England team for the rest of the tour.

The fourth Test at Sydney was lost by seven wickets to spare. In the fifth Test at Melbourne, England went down again losing by 32 runs even though Australia were all out for 144 in the first innings. It was thought by many that because of the narrowness of the Australian victories a fit Barnes may well have swung the Ashes England's way.

A record of 19 wickets for just over 19 runs apiece in 131 overs in his first two Test matches and on Australian wickets, was adjudged to be a brilliant start to a great career in international cricket. Despite a shortened number of games on the tour because of his injury, he was hailed as the best English bowler seen in Australia up to then, easily heading the Test averages and taking 41 wickets in total in the first-class games he played in.

England v Australia 1902

The party returned to England in April accompanied by the Australian touring team, for what promised, and proved to be, a titanic struggle in the English summer of 1902.

The Test series that summer was one of the most enthralling ever played between the two countries. Edgbaston was the venue for the first match in May. England fielded a side which was considered to be the best ever to represent the country, and this was without the injured Barnes. MacLaren was captain and with him was C.B.Fry, K.S.Ranjitsinhji, F.S.Jackson, G.L.Jessop, Tyldesley, Lilly (wicket-keeper), Hirst, Bround, Lockwood, and Rhodes. A team with no obvious weaknesses. England declared on 376 for 9, thanks to a brilliant century from Tyldesley. Rhodes with 7 for 17 and Hirst 3 for 15 demolished the Australian batting. Their total of 36 all out is still the lowest by either side in an Ashes series. Unfortunately, the weather took a turn for the worse and robbed England of a great victory. The match was officially drawn.

The next confrontation was at Lord's and completely ruined by the weather only allowing two hours of play possible. Abandoned because of rain when England were 102 for 2 in their first innings.

It was at Sheffield for the third Test on 3rd July before some good weather allowed the series proper to get underway without any interruptions. Barnes was a last-minute choice. He had been living in Manchester and at nine o'clock on the morning the game was to start he received a message from MacLaren wanting him to go to Sheffield at once as he was needed to play. When Barnes arrived at the ground the match had begun. Because of such short notice he was unable to get to Sheffield in time to go out on the field with the other players at the start of play. Haigh, the twelfth man in the team as originally chosen was out on the field as substitute and everybody had jumped to the conclusion he was first choice. But when he retired to the pavilion and Barnes (a Lancashire bowler) appeared, some keenly enthusiastic Yorkshire men called out their disapproval. These same Yorkshire men, to give them justice, when Barnes magnificently justified his selection, were loudest in their acclaim.

"I followed," Barnes wrote afterwards, *"And for the life of me couldn't understand why the spectators booed when I appeared. It proved to be because Haigh was coming off the field after substituting for me until I arrived. When he had gone out on the field with the others at the start of the match it had been assumed that he was playing and his disappearance was a big disappointment to the Yorkshire crowd having to give way especially to a Lancashire player. Never in the whole of my career have I met with such a hostile reception, but I contented myself with the thought that it was no affair of mine if I was played instead of Haigh. I was not responsible for picking the team. When Braud had bowled Trumper it was with the last ball of the over and after an over from the other end MacLaren tossed the ball to me. Talk about booing – my earlier reception was a conversational murmur compared to the row that ensued now and I may say that the attitude of the crowd did not change during the whole of the match, but was to become directed against the captain instead of me. Well I had the ball and I had to bowl and it was hard lines on Braund in one way, but MacLaren knew that Braund was not so effective against a left-hander. So I started off with the crowd still booing. However, by the end of the first over they were applauding me for I quickly got the wickets of Duff and Darling and when the innings ended for 194 I had taken 6 for 49 in 20 overs which included nine maidens. Not too bad a start in my first Test in England. In the second innings my knee caused me some anxiety and I dare not put everything into my bowling. I took only one wicket for 50, but strange to relate it was that of Joe Darling, out first ball in each innings and in the same way, caught by Braund in the slips."*

This was after Saunders and Noble had got England out for 145, only four batsmen getting double figures, and then Australia making 289, Clem Hill this time getting 119. Noble again wrecked the England innings. They were all out for 195 and lost the match by 143 runs. Barnes' seven wickets in the match were taken for fewer runs than any of the other England bowlers. Today such figures would ensure any man being selected again. The selectors came under some heavy criticism with England 1-0 down with two to play, deciding to drop Barnes as well as Fry and Jessam – beggars belief. However, there was at the time an enormous wealth of talent to choose from. Barnes was disappointed but felt later that it probably was for the best as his knee was not really strong enough.

He did not go to Australia with the 1903-04 team under the captaincy of P.F.Warner, and did not play in any of the five Test matches during the visit of the Australians in 1905. Neither did he visit South Africa under the auspices of the MCC in 1904, nor play in any of the Test matches when the South Africans came to England in 1907.

Australia v England 1907-08

When the next England team sailed for Australia in 1907 he was included and took part in all the Tests. There had been three trial matches to help the selectors to choose the team but because of his commitments with Staffordshire and Porthill he was not available for any of them. It was said that it was his splendid form for Staffordshire which led to his return to first-class cricket.

The tour began well for Barnes. Against New South Wales in their first innings, he bowled 20.2 overs and captured 6 wickets for 24 runs on a perfect batting wicket. It was reported that he bowled at varying pace with great skill, not bowling a single ball of bad length. The first Test was at Sydney and Australia won narrowly by two wickets. In Australia's first innings Barnes opened the bowling and did break the opening stand by getting McAllister out, but that was his only wicket in the innings at a cost of 74 runs. England had scored 273 but Australia had a first innings lead of 27. England scored exactly 300 in the second innings leaving Australia to get 274 to win which they did with 2 wickets to spare. Barnes only managed 2 for 63.

The second Test at Melbourne produced an exciting finish and this time an England victory by just one wicket. Barnes this time was the hero with his batting but had also done damage to Australia's batting in the second innings. England led after the first innings by 116. Australia scored really well in their second innings and at one stage they were 250 ahead with only 5 wickets down. England were in trouble and struggling. At this point of the innings Barnes confronted his captain and suggested that he should try bowling round the wicket to a leg-side field, which he commenced doing. The result was that he took the last 5 wickets for 20 runs and Australia were all out for 397, which gave England a fighting chance. Barnes finished with 5 for 72. England began batting soundly but there was something of a middle order collapse. Barnes went in at number 9 to join Crawford with 84 still needed to grab a win. The thrilling finish to follow was described many years later by Barnes himself as follows:

"J.N.Crawford was batting, but he left at 209. Humphries joined me and by steady scoring we took the total to 243 when Humphries was given out lbw to Armstrong. In my opinion it was the wrong decision, as I am convinced he played the ball and I told the umpire so. I got a little annoyed and as Fielder, the last man, came out from the pavilion I went to meet him, told him what had happened and said, "Come on, Pip ,we'll knock 'em off now." I advised him to push his bat straight down the wicket at everything. We then wanted 39 runs. Things went smoothly and we scored whenever possible until only two more runs were needed. He was facing Armstrong and played one to mid-on. It was a very risky run, but as we were both of one mind we got home safely. Then I faced Armstrong. As was usual with him, all the fielders with the exception of two were on the leg side. The ball came at my legs and I drew away from the wicket and pushed the ball to the off. It was an easy run and as I played the ball I was off down the pitch expecting Fielder to do the same, but to my amazement I saw he hadn't moved.

"For God's sake, Pip, get going!" I shouted. By this time Hazlitt at cover point had gathered the ball, but instead of throwing it to the wicket-keeper he aimed for the stumps – and missed. So Fielder got safely home and the match was won. While all this was happening, the excitement among the spectators had been terrific, but so far as the players taking part were concerned there might not have been a spectator on the ground. All they could think about was watching the ball. Some of the England players had been sitting in the enclosure for two hours, not daring to move for fear of breaking the spell, so to speak. They told me that tears were running down the cheeks of Fane and the manager of the team, Major Philip Trevor."

That winning run was just sheer joy and especially for Fielder as he ran on and on, clinging onto his bat high up in the air, and didn't slow down until he was half way to the pavilion. What a reception awaited him and Barnes from the sporting Melbourne crowd – especially Barnes.

This was the only match in the series that England were victorious. The third Test at Adelaide, Australia won by the handsome margin of 235 runs. They had scored a mammoth 506 runs in their second innings and Barnes was fairly fortunate with his figures of 3 for 83 which followed 3 for 60 in their first innings.

It was a couple of days after the third Test that Barnes wrote to the Staffordshire County Club:

"The England team was an extra-ordinary one socially. Every member being very friendly and Arthur Jones, captain, whose illness was the real cause of them losing the Test matches, was a good skipper (he missed the first three matches). *They had been unfortunate with the weather and the umpiring was very bad. We have had a very good tour but Test cricket is too serious for me."*

In the next match on the tour against Victoria he was very successful taking 5 for 32 and 6 for 25.

But in the fourth Test at Melbourne he had a poor match, taking only one wicket in an England collapse losing by 308 runs, even worse than they had performed in Adelaide.

Barnes did a lot better in the final Test at Sydney, but not enough to win the match for England. However, some consolation that Australia won by a much narrower margin of 49 runs. He bowled magnificently for his 7 for 60 in the first innings. The Australians won the match with their score of 422 in the second innings. Trumper scored a superb 166 which included 18 fours. Barnes bowled 27 overs in that innings for 1 wicket and 78 runs.

Because his knee was troubling him he only bowled in the second innings against Western Australia in the last match of the tour. Worth mentioning is that with the bat he scored 93, which was his highest score in first-class cricket.

England v Australia 1909

In 1909 the Australians set foot on English soil once again and the first Test was played at Edgbaston. Barnes, who was again in fine form for Porthill and Staffordshire, was not available, the reason being that he had caught whooping cough from his son, Leslie. It was commented in the press that he should have been picked for all five Tests because 'he was clearly the best bowler England had'.

England won the first Test by 10 wickets but Australia got revenge in the second Test at Lord's, winning by 9 wickets. Barnes did play in the third Test at Leeds but still not really fit. He was coughing a lot while on the field but acknowledged by everyone that he bowled really well in the Australian first innings for his 1 wicket for 37 runs. England's batting failed in their second innings and Australia led by six runs. Barnes was at his best in their second innings taking 6 wickets for 63, bowling 35 overs, 18 of which were maidens, an astonishing performance for a Test match. England had to get 214 to win but failed. Australia won by 126 runs.

In the fourth Test at Manchester the match was drawn. Barnes took 5 for 56, sharing the wickets with Blythe who got 5 for 63. In their first innings Australia were all out for 147. England fell short, only scoring 119. Australia did better in their second innings declaring at 279, Barnes taking only 1 wicket. The game ended when England had scored 108 for 3 with no more time available.

The Oval was the venue for the fifth and final Test. Barnes had to be content with 2 for 57 and 2 for 61. It was a hard and fast wicket which resulted in high scores from both sides. Australia won the toss and batted first scoring 325. England followed and led by 27 runs. In Australia's second innings they declared at 339 for 5. The Australian Bardsley was in magnificent batting form and in so doing made history by being the first person to score a century in each innings of a Test match. England were left with needing 312 to win. They made 104 for 3 when stumps were drawn – match was drawn.

Australia v England 1911-12

In the autumn of 1911, the 16 selected England players, including 38 year old Barnes, set off for Australia and it would be, on this successful tour, always remembered historically for the great bowling combination of Barnes and Frank Foster. The facts are remembered with pride by every man with an enthusiasm for English cricket, and the part these two played was long talked about. Barnes was by now universally adjudged the finest bowler England had ever sent out to Australia. The team was considered to be a strong England side capable of bringing the Ashes home. There was some splendid batting and fielding, which did contribute to the success of the team effort. Nevertheless the Australian players who played against them were unanimous in their praise that the main reason for England's success was the fact that they had two bowlers of the very best, right at the top of their form. This one factor that they were both in form at the same time was in itself a big factor in the team's success. Adjudged as an exceptional bowler (Barnes) at one end and an ordinary bowler (Foster) at the other, the batsman had some sort of chance. He can at the worst keep up his end against the good man and be confident to score runs off the other. The fact that he is able to get runs at all, lends him confidence to face the man who is bowling exceptionally well. But when you get two bowlers of exceptional ability, bowling like demons, then the batsman is indeed in for a rough time. There can be no respite; almost every ball is the one which may take his wicket if he does not treat it with the utmost care and respect, and he has no sooner gone through an over with one man than he is called upon to face another just as deadly. The Australians were really up against it. In actual fact the only game England did lose on the tour was the first Test. Before then the first match was against South Australia and considering they only had four days' net practice after a long journey they won easily. After spending 10 days in Queensland, they played at Brisbane, before the first Test at Sydney, and beat the home side. Barnes and Foster bowled with deadly effect. Barnes took 3 for 62 and 4 for 49 and Foster's total in the match was 8 for 98.

For the first Test Johnny Douglas took over the captaincy of the England side because Pelham Warner was sick. It was adjudged by some that but for one controversial decision he made, it is doubtful whether England would have lost this only match on the tour. The criticism by many was that he did not open the bowling with Barnes but instead opened the bowling himself. It was likely that Douglas' mistake was not knowing Barnes well enough to realise how temperamental he could be. Barnes was of a different nature. He always opened the bowling and if he was not put on first he thought he had been slighted. His masterful bowling at all levels of cricket was with the new ball and with the determined effort he was renowned for, he was recognised by many as the best bowler in the world very capable of winning matches with the new ball. His absence at the opening end gave confidence to the Australian batsmen who, in reply, piled on the runs. He had not got over this 'overlooked' feeling when he was asked eventually to go on, and the opinion was that he did not give his best. Clem Hill had scored 46 before being run out, and Warwick Armstrong 60. Victor Trumper, batting at number five, scored an aggressive 113 runs, including 12 fours, before being caught in the covers by Jack Hobbs. R.B.Minnett was caught by Foster off Barnes for 90. The Australian innings closed just before lunch on the second day for 447. Barnes was the most successful England bowler, but his 3 wickets cost 107 runs. It might well have been different if he had opened with Foster. England replied with 318, and Australia ended their second innings with 308 (Foster taking 5 for 92), leaving England with the almost impossible task of scoring 438 to win. They were all out for 291.

The second Test match at Melbourne which commenced on 30th December 1911 is deservedly remembered as Barnes' match. It was regarded as one of the best ever prepared Australian batting wickets and the vast crowd had confidently expected that the home batsmen would pile up a huge score. Barnes showed that he would not be having any of that. Australia won the toss and understandably on a good, firm, hard wicket elected to bat. Before lunch he had taken out the first 4 of Australia's finest batsmen for 1 run. He had bowled for an hour and 10 minutes with figures of 9 overs, 6 maidens, 4 wickets for only 3 runs. Somehow, Australia had managed to acquire 34 for 4 before lunch. The astounding fact of this renowned piece of bowling is that Barnes was suffering from some dizziness, actually telling his captain:

"I'll have to 'chuck it – I can hardly see the other end."

He was taken off and did not bowl again until after lunch.

Barnes' own description at what happened:

"A few days before the second Test I felt very ill. I woke up one night and found myself soaked in perspiration. Next day I saw a doctor, who expressed doubts in getting me fit in time for the game. However, although I felt weak I was able to play and when I got the ball in my hands I had a curious feeling that I could do anything with it. I very nearly did. Australia won the toss and batted on a perfect wicket. Charlie Kelleway and Warren 'Curly' Bardsley opened the innings and Foster sent down the first over to Kelleway. A maiden. Now my turn I bowled to the left-handed Bardsley. The first ball swung in to him and hit him on his toe and went on to the wicket and the bails came off. Kelleway came next. For three parts of the way up the wicket the ball was going outside his legs. He stepped in front and did not attempt to play it. It dipped into him and he was lbw. Clem Hill, another left-hander, followed. I was bowling fast out there. I gave him one that was an off-break to him, and then an in-swinger. The atmosphere happened to be very humid so I was able to get some swing on the ball. Then I sent him one going away and he let it go. The last ball of the over pitched to his leg and hit the off stump. Yes, that was a finger spin. It would have been an off-break to a right- hander. Clem said afterwards he had never had to face such a tough over before. Warwick Armstrong was next in, and a leg-spinner went across nicely and very quick off the ground. He played back, snicked it and was caught in the slips. It was one of the most sensational starts in the history of Test matches. And only a few days before I had been feeling like anything but cricket. After lunch Foster bowled Trumper with a beautiful ball and a few runs later I had Minnett caught at cover, making my analysis five for six. Six wickets were down for 38. The remaining Australian batsmen did better, however, and the total reached 184 when it had looked as if they would be lucky to make 50. Herbert Horden showed that he could bat as well as bowl by scoring 49 not out."

There was an incident worth mentioning in which Barnes played a characteristic part when some unwarranted barracking by a section of the Melbourne crowd was directed at him. A mass of spectators, not happy with the situation they were witnessing, stood up and tried to yell Barnes down.

Barnes went down all right – he threw the ball down, then sat down and refused to resume until decent order was resumed.

Pelham Warner, who should have skippered the side but because of illness did not take part in any of the Test matches, was able to watch the match from the pavilion that day and wrote afterwards of Barnes' performance in that innings:

"The present generation of Australian cricketers admitted that they had seen no finer bowling and the older men were equally enthusiastic. It was certainly one of the greatest feats. If not the very greatest ever accomplished in a Test match and no Spofforth, or Palmer, or Richardson, or Lockwood, or Lohmann or Turner, could possibly have surpassed it. The Australians have long held that Barnes is the finest bowler we have ever sent them and in England many critics are of the opinion that in the whole world there is no greater bowler. His wonderful bowling was all the more remarkable as for two days previously he had been far from well."

In reply, England scored 265 (Hearne 114) and were 81 runs ahead. Australia in their second innings began badly, losing 4 wickets for 38 runs. However, they did fight back and the innings closed for 299, leaving England to get 219 to win. Barnes 3 for 96 and Foster 6 for 91 shared the wickets. England won by 8 wickets with Jack Hobbs scoring 126 not out, the final total being 219 with the loss of only 2 wickets. The Australian players publicly stated after the match that it was the best bowling they had ever faced.

England's victory, which made it 'one all' in the series made the next encounter more interesting amongst the cricketing public between the two teams at the start of the third Test at Adelaide. No English team had won a Test match there for 20 years. Australia won the toss for the third time and batted first. Barnes took the first wicket but it was Foster who did most of the damage. He finished with 5 for 36 and Barnes had 3 for 71, Australia being all out for 133. England had a great second day in reply with a magnificent total of 501 (Jack Hobbs 187), and led by 368. Australia fought back well and at the end of their second innings totalled 476 (Hill 98, Bardsley 63), only eight runs behind. Barnes, whose bowling was described as 'wonderfully steady', had bowled 46 overs in the innings and had taken half the Australian wickets for just 105 runs. England won the match by 7 wickets and were now 2-1 up in the series.

In the next Test match at Melbourne, England won the toss and, because the wicket was slightly soft after recent rain, Australia were made to bat first. Barnes and Foster were bowling well and it was not long after lunch that they captured 5 Australian wickets for 83 runs. Due to some missed catches, Australia did manage to eventually reach 191. Barnes had taken 5 for 74 and Foster 4 for 77. England's innings included a record breaking feat by Hobbs (178) and Rhodes (179) in an opening partnership of 323. Hobbs' wicket went first, Rhodes the next day. England's total reached a mammoth 589 runs, three runs more than the previous best.

The world record for a first wicket partnership of 415 was set on 29th February, 2008 by Neil McKenzie and Graeme Smith of South Africa against Bangladesh.

Australia were all out for 173. Douglas got most of the wickets, 5 for 46, Foster 3 for 38, Barnes 2 for 47. England won easily by an innings and 225 runs. England 3, Australia 1. The Australian newspapers described the defeat as 'a great shock to our sporting pride' and 'a cricket misadventure of the first order'.

Not surprisingly, Australia made four changes for the fifth and final Test at Sydney, which England won by 70 runs. England won the toss and elected to bat with the innings reaching 324. Australia replied on a rain affected wicket, which helped the bowlers. They were all out for 176, the wickets being well shared, with Barnes having slightly the best figures of 3 for 56. England were all out for 214 in their second innings which meant

Australia had to get 363 to win. They failed, only scoring 292. Barnes 3 for 56 and 4 for 106, Foster 1 for 55 and 4 for 43. England had achieved something no other team visiting Australia had ever done before and that was victory in four of the five Tests.

Barnes' final tally in the Test series was a magnificent 34 wickets. This was a record to last until the 1924-5 tour when Maurice Tate took 38 wickets though at greater cost. This, in turn, was beaten by Jim Laker in 1956.

The "barracking" on Australian soil that Barnes experienced on the Melbourne ground was nothing compared to the "barracking" the England side had to endure on the Sydney ground in 1904. It was during the second day of the fourth Test. As an example, bottles were thrown on the cycle track running round the ground and soon the fringe of the playing area was littered with broken glass. The ground staff were sent to clear this up and then there were more bottles thrown with yelling and insulting remarks from a section of the crowd. The trouble arose when the umpires, thinking that the rain had not sufficiently stopped, would not let the game proceed. Then when play did start they yelled and shouted at every ball and there were 35,000 people looking on. They chanted *"crock, crock, crock"* and advised the umpires to get their coffins ready and inquired, *"How much did you pay them, Warner?"* Then they tried to baulk the English bowler Rhodes by shouting *"One, two, three"* in time with his run up to the wicket. Though this probably disconcerted the batsman more than the bowler. Yes, they were a lovely crowd at Sydney in those days!

England XI v The Rest XI 1911

It was in 1911 that the England selectors commenced Test Trials in preparation for forthcoming Test matches against

Australia or South Africa by organising probables v possibles in the form of England v The Rest. Lord Hawke, President of the MCC, wrote to Barnes inviting him to play in this 3-day match at Lord's commencing 29th May, 1911. Because of his commitments with Staffordshire and Porthill, The North Staffordshire League side, he declined the invitation, but he did appear in a number of other first-class games in which he reminded the selectors how good he was. One of the matches was a Players v Gentlemen 3-day match held at Lord's on 10/11/12 July, 1911. He took 9 wickets in the match and his performance may well have had a good deal to do with his selection for the Australian tour, quite apart from his very good season with Staffordshire.

The original Lord Hawke letter to Barnes is for sale. Dated 20th June on letterhead from 107 Jermyn Street, S.W. it reads:

"Dear Barnes – Selection committee will be pleased if you will play for England v The Rest at Lords 29th – Yours faithfully (signed) Hawke."

Available from – AntiQuarian Bookseller, Dr Richard Ford, 70 Chaucer Road, London, W3 6DP.

England XI v The Rest XI 1912

This was a Test Trial 3-day match that Barnes did play in on 6/7/8 May, 1912 at the Kennington Oval. There were eight of the England side just back from the triumphant tour of Australia. Barnes again distinguished himself this time by doing the 'hat-trick' for the first and only time in first-class cricket. This was in The Rest's first innings with an analysis of 4 for 27. In the second innings he took 3 for 59. England won the toss and batted first, scoring 352. The Rest could only manage 119 and had to follow on. England won by an innings and 13 runs.

The Triangular Tournament 1912

This was a Test cricket competition hosted in England between Australia, England and South Africa, who were the only Test-playing nations at the time. The ultimate winners of the tournament were England with four wins in their six matches. The other two were drawn. Barnes found himself taking part in the only Triangular Tournament that has ever been played.

England's first match was against the South Africans at Lord's on 10th June. The South Africans decided to bat first and were skittled out for 58. Barnes and Foster did the damage, both bowling in great form and being rewarded by sharing the wickets. Foster got his 5 wickets for 16 runs while Barnes got his 5 for 25. Foster's victims were all clean bowled. However, it was considered Barnes was the better bowler because he was turning the ball both ways and had kept a perfect length. In reply to England's 337, South Africa played better in their second innings and scored 217. This time Barnes at his very best captured 6 wickets for 85 runs, Foster 3 for 54. England won the match.

England's next match was against Australia at Lord's on 24th June and was ruined by the weather. England declared at 310 for 7. Because of the rain there was only enough time for Australia to reach 282 for 7. Barnes' bowling presented no difficulties and he finished with 0 for 74. Match drawn.

Barnes was among the South African wickets again in their second match against them at Headingley, Leeds commencing on 8th July. England batted first and made 242. South Africa were dismissed for 147. Barnes was almost unplayable, taking 6 for 52, and in their second innings 4 for 63. A total of 10 wickets in the match. England won by 174 runs.

England's second match against Australia at Old Trafford, Manchester on 29th July was a washout. Rain completely spoilt this game. After England completed their innings for 203 only 13 overs were possible of the South African innings. No wickets had fallen and only 13 overs were bowled. This was the only Test match Barnes did not bowl a ball. Match drawn.

South Africa got another thrashing against England at The Oval on 12th August. Barnes bowled brilliantly in even deadlier form than in any of the previous Test matches. The South African batsmen failed miserably against the deadly bowling of Barnes, only scoring 95 all out in the first innings and 93 all out in the second. In the first innings on a sodden slow wicket both Barnes and Frank Woolley together 'exterminated' them, but the second innings Barnes virtually dismissing them unaided by taking 8 wickets for 29 runs. His 13 wickets in the match cost him only 57 runs. England won by 10 wickets. In the three matches against the South Africans he had taken 34 wickets.

The final match of the tournament was played again at The Oval on 19th August, England triumphing over Australia by 244 runs. Barnes and Woolley were rewarded with 5 wickets each, Australia all out for 111. One remarkable ball from Barnes worth mentioning was against Bardsley. It pitched well outside his leg stump. He left it alone, but he failed to cover the whole of the wicket. Amazingly, the ball turned sharply, hit the leg stump causing the bails to go flying. Goodbye, Mr Bardsley! England scored 245 in their only innings which was enough to win the match. Barnes only bowled 4 overs in Australia's second innings. The wickets were shared by Frank Woolley (5 for 20) and Harry Dean (4 for 19).

This was a remarkable series for Barnes. He had taken 39 wickets for 404 runs at an average of 10.35. A fantastic average for a Test series, comparing almost with some of his astonishing figures in league cricket, which are mentioned later in this book.

The Triangular Tournament table at the end of the series read as follows:

	M	W	L	D	Points
England	6	4	0	2	4
Australia	6	2	1	3	2
South Africa	6	0	5	1	0

The England team that won the Ashes in the Triangular Test series in 1912

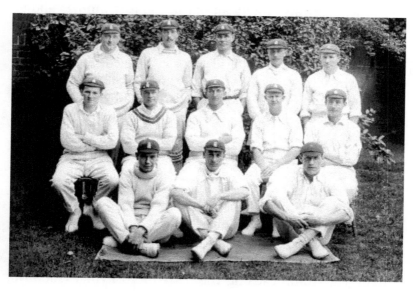

Back row (left to right): W.Brierley, F.Woolley, S.F.Barnes, W.Rhodes, E.Humphreys. Middle row: F.R.Foster, G.Jessop, C.B.Fry, Pelham Warner, R.H.Spooner. Seated on ground: E.J.Smith, Jack Hobbs, H.Dean.

South Africa 1913-14

Once again Barnes was selected to play for England to tour South Africa based on his bowling performances in Minor Counties and league cricket. He was regarded as first choice in an English team that was said to be the most powerful side sent to South Africa up to that time. On the matting wickets of South Africa he was a sensation, performing record feats, destroying the South African batsmen similar to what he'd done to them in the Triangular Tournament on English wickets just a few months before. In the eight innings of the four Test matches he played in, he averaged over 12 wickets per match, totalling 49 wickets averaging 10.93. In the first of the two Tests at Johannesburg he set up a new record. He took 9 wickets in an innings and a total of 17 wickets in the match. In the fourth Test at Durban he took 14 wickets. What is most surprising is his age. He was 41 when he created these records. On arrival in South Africa, Barnes missed the first two matches England played, because he was not feeling well. His presence set the wheels in motion when he played his first game against South Western Districts. His tour began with the brilliance against South Western Districts that was to continue until the end. After taking just 1 for 28 in the first innings he ran riot in the second innings. In 10 overs he took 7 for 25. Barnes had arrived! In the next match his total figures were 13 for 48 against Grahamstown Colleges.

The first Test followed at Durban on 13th December. According to Herbert Starstruck (England wicket-keeper) Barnes made all the batsmen who faced him look quite ordinary, beating each one of them at least four times every over. Herbie Taylor, he said, was the only batsmen who could tame him and go on to make 109 runs in South Africa's first innings total of 182. Barnes took 5 for 57. In reply England scored 450 which included a century (119) from Douglas and some fine batting from Hobbs (82). In their second innings South Africa were all out for 111 and England had won by an innings and 157 runs. Barnes again took half the wickets, 5 for 58. It was after this game the South Africans said:

"Oh! Wait till he gets to Johannesburg. We'll break his heart."

Presumably because the wicket at Johannesburg was considered to be a good batting wicket to play on. Barnes' answer came swiftly and deadly just before the second Test in a match at Johannesburg against Transvaal, whose side included the best of the South African players. Barnes took seven wickets for 109 in the match and in so doing gave a strong warning to his South African critics.

It was in the second Test in Johannesburg on 26th December that England (with Barnes) trounced South Africa by an innings and 12 runs. Barnes was definitely the 'Man of the Match'. He took 7 for 109 in the first innings followed by 9 for 103 in the second innings. He set up a record of 17 wickets for 159 runs which stood for nearly 50 years. Jim Laker broke it at Old Trafford, Manchester in a Test match in 1956 with 19 wickets for 90.

In the third Test, again at Johannesburg, on 2nd January 1914 England won by 91 runs. England batted first and scored 238 (Hobbs 92). South Africa struggled with 151 all out. Hearne had the best of the bowling figures, 5 for 49, Barnes 3 for 26. England followed their first innings with 308. South Africa then made 304. Barnes bowled with determination again and was well rewarded with 5 for 102.

In the fourth Test at Durban on 4th February the match was drawn. Play was cut short on the fourth day because of rain and bad light. However, not before it was another great triumph for Barnes. He took 7 for 56 in the first innings and 7 for 88 in the second innings. However, if the game had not been affected by the weather England would have probably lost. South Africa had batted first and scored 170. England replied with 163. South Africa batted really well in their second innings, notching up 305 runs. England then struggled after 80 overs, when at 154 for 5 the rain and bad light halted play with England still needing a further 159 to win.

Barnes didn't play in the fifth Test at Port Elizabeth. England won by 10 wickets. It had been reported at the time that he was not well with some throat infection and was confined to his bed. The real reason was actually further from the truth. His wife and son had joined him on the trip and before setting out the South African authorities had agreed to help with his expenses if he did anything outstanding. He felt that he had done enough to deserve some help but they didn't do anything about it. In the circumstances he refused to play and was very upset because he felt let down. Barnes wished he had played in the fifth Test. He would have liked to have taken his total of wickets in the series to 50.

"I didn't," he said years later, "because I got at loggerheads with the management. I had taken my wife and son on that trip for health reasons and had been promised they would take the hat round to help with my expenses if I did anything outstanding. Well, I didn't do badly. But they didn't do anything about it. So I got mad. I was an obstinate cuss when I liked in those days. It struck me that if I had been doing something to lengthen the matches instead of shortening them, I would have been more popular. So, as we had won the rubber, I put my head down and refused to play in the last Test. Maybe it would have been different now. Age mellows. But in those days I was intense. I spun the skin off my fingers and bowled with blood smearing the ball."

Barnes was called the cricket hero of the hour in January1914 after his wonderful bowling with the English team in South Africa. His contribution had already made the Test matches a "procession" of England victories and they were not due to return to the country until the spring. When considering the great part he has played in other international contests in maintaining the prestige of English cricket the London Evening News had said Barnes should be paid a marked tribute of gratitude. The suggestion was backed up by a county cricketer who said:

"There is no need to organise an elaborate testimonial. I suggest that a sum should be raised for purchasing a gift, say of a silver cup or other suitable trophy, to be presented to the great cricketer when he steps off the boat on his return to this country in a few weeks."

Herbert Strudwick, the English wicket keeper on the tour, was quoted as saying:

"Barnes' bowling was really wonderful. I have not had a great deal of experience on matting wickets, but he is the best bowler by a long way that I have seen under those conditions."

Opening batsman for England, Sir Jack Hobbs, on the tour said:

"Barnes was practically unplayable on matting. His command of length and flight was superb and he made the ball turn so much that three or four times in one over he would beat the bat and miss the stumps."

Later, Wisden gave its verdict:

"Barnes dwarfed all other bowlers. It would be hard indeed to praise beyond his deserts. Everyone felt before he left England that, with his remarkable finger spin, he would do well on matting wickets, but his success exceeded all expectations. He was simply irresistible. Moreover, according to common report, he beat the bat about twice an over without hitting the wicket."

Barnes never played for England again.

During the First World War years, 1914-1918, Test cricket closed down until 1919.

In 1920, despite being 48 at the time, he was invited to tour Australia again but he declined the offer. He was happy to go, and content with the remuneration offered, but he believed that he would be able to give of his best only if he were joined on tour by his wife and child. The selectors refused what at the time must have been considered a preposterous request and, inevitably, Barnes in turn dug his heels in. What was an issue was the old question of expenses cropping up again because he wanted his wife and son to go. Because the MCC refused to grant him anything towards his expenses, he declined the invitation.

There is a popular misconception that Barnes took most of his wickets against South Africa. This is not true. While he did demolish South Africa in the seven games he played against them, his performance against Australia was far greater. There was also the factor of easy wickets against South Africa during this period but he was not included in all the matches. It is worth mentioning that without Barnes in the 1905-06 Tests in South Africa, England lost 4-1. In 1907, on home soil, England won 1-0 (2 games drawn) and in 1909-10, in South Africa, England lost 3-2. It was clear from these results South Africa was no pushover.

Then they took him to South Africa at the ripe old age of 40 and in the four Tests he played he took a record 49 wickets at 10.9 each, England winning the series 4-0. It was Barnes who made the South Africans look like they couldn't tell which end of the bat to hold, struggling to keep him out. This was entirely due to the improving genius of Barnes rather than South Africa being no-hopers.

In the 20 England v Australia games Barnes took 102 wickets at 21.6 each, getting a 5 wicket haul 12 times. England played Australia 43 times between 1901 and 1914 and of these Barnes played less than half. This, in spite of the fact that he was by far the most devastating bowler in Test matches during this period with 189 wickets in 27 Tests. A total of 87 wickets against South Africa in 7 games and he was also easily the most successful bowler against Australia.

England during this period were not considered a very strong side. They could ill afford to keep a bowler like Barnes out, yet they did. It is anybody's guess what his tally would have been had he played those additional 20 games against Australia and the 15 against the South Africans.

Barnes was a fascinating man. Living proof that talent will overcome social circumstances. Professionals, at least the established ones, were not generally badly treated in his day but they were expected to know their place. Barnes simply refused to play the game even to the extent of refusing to play the fifth Test in the South African 1913/14 series because neither the MCC nor South Africa would pay for his wife and son to stay with him.

This ball was presented to Barnes by the South African Cricket Association. The inscription on the ball reads "MCC v South Africa, 2nd Test Match, Wanderer's Ground Johannesburg, December 26, 27, 29, 30, 1913. 1st Innings 26.5 overs, 7 maidens, 56 runs, 8 wickets. 2nd Innings 38.4 overs, 7 maidens, 103 runs, 9 wickets. Two Test Match Records – most wickets in one innings and most wickets in a match.'

A 'letter to the Editor' which appeared in a UK newspaper in 1924.

"I read a suggestion the other day that Sydney Barnes who is to play for Staffordshire this year, may be "resurrected" for the Test matches in South Africa. I may be wrong but I fancy the writer was either hard-pressed for a subject or he knows nothing of the position. Barnes, it is said, showed hardly any falling-off in form last year, possibly not. I think it is extremely likely that were he to re-appear in first-class cricket next Summer he would surely match the best of them on the field of play. Yet there is a variety of reasons why he is not likely to be included in a Test team. The selectors are looking out for the young ones; they have the Australians in view, and until they have proved themselves the South Africans will be regarded as providing the opportunity for experiments. Yet another argument against the inclusion of Barnes is that he is not in favour with the selectors who have fairly long memories. One way or another, it may be said, that it will be a miracle indeed if Sydney Barnes appears for England in the coming Test Matches."

Summing up 5-wicket hauls in Test match cricket

He actually claimed for England in 27 Tests twenty-four 5-wicket hauls (five or more wickets in an innings) between 1901 and 1914. A 5-wicket haul is a notable achievement and as of 2014, fewer than 50 bowlers have taken more than 15 five-wicket hauls at international level in their cricketing careers. Barnes had only played seven first-class matches when he was chosen to tour Australia, and played only 47 County Championship matches throughout his entire career, opting to play Minor Counties and Lancashire League cricket instead. He based his decision upon two main reasons. Playing club cricket was more financially rewarding, and he was worried about having to bowl too much in first-class county cricket, and suffering from fatigue. He was considered by many in the game that he was a bit of a "prima donna" who would only put in the effort when he was in the right mood, and being suitably paid. He did not play any Test cricket between July 1902 and December 1907. After his recall to the England side, he played regularly until the outbreak of the First World War in 1914.

Barnes made his Test debut in December 1901 against Australia at the Sydney Cricket Ground and it was in this match that he took his first international five-wicket haul. He claimed five wickets and conceded 65 runs (noted as five for 65), in the first innings of the match. On his second Test appearance, during the same tour, Barnes collected six wickets in the first innings and seven wickets in the second innings, to complete the first of seven occasions in which he took ten or more wickets in a match. Barnes' best bowling performances were against the South African cricket team in their 1913-14 series in South Africa. Barnes took five-wicket hauls in four of the five Test matches on the tour, and claimed ten or more wickets in three of them. During the second Test, he recorded the best figures of his career, collecting eight for 56 in the first innings and nine for 103 in the second. His match figures of 17 for 159 were the best in Test cricket at the time, and though since surpassed by Jim Laker's 19 wickets in 1956, remain second among all bowlers in Tests. The series marked Barnes' final appearances in Test cricket.

Test Match Bowling

Australia

venue	overs	maidens	runs	wickets
1901-2				
Sydney	35.1	9	65	5

venue	overs	maidens	runs	wickets
	16	2	74	1
Melbourne	16.1	5	42	6
	64	17	121	7
Adelaide	7	0	21	0
1902				
Sheffield	20	9	49	6
	12	4	50	1
1907-8				
Sydney	22	3	74	1
	30	7	63	2
Melbourne	17	7	30	0
	27.4	4	72	5
Adelaide	27	8	60	3
	42	9	83	3
Melbourne	23	11	37	1
	35	16	69	1
Sydney	22.4	6	60	7
	27	6	78	1
1909				
Leeds	25	12	37	1
	35	18	63	6
Manchester	27	9	56	5
	22.3	5	66	1
Oval	19	3	57	2
	27	7	61	2
1911-12				
Sydney	35	5	107	3
	30	8	72	1
Melbourne	23	9	44	5

venue	overs	maidens	runs	wickets
	32.1	7	96	3
Adelaide	23	4	71	3
	46.4	7	105	5
Melbourne	29.1	4	74	5
	20	6	47	2
Sydney	19	2	56	3
	39	12	106	4

South Africa

venue	overs	maidens	runs	wickets
1912				
Lord's	13	3	25	5
	34	9	85	6
Leeds	22	7	52	6
	21.2	5	63	4
Oval	21	10	28	5
	16.04	4	29	8
1913				
Durban	19.4	1	57	5
	25	11	48	5
Johannesburg	26.5	9	56	8
	38.4	7	103	9
Johannesburg	16	3	26	3
	38	8	102	5
Durban	29.5	7	56	7
	32	10	88	7

"It would be far easier to agree that Barnes was the most difficult bowler to face — of his times and beyond. Every opponent, however partisan or lacking in grace, agreed to his absolute supremacy with the ball. No bowler in history has had such universal repute as the greatest. Even in 1930 (56 years of age) the batsmen who faced him came away shaking their heads in disbelief."

Arunabha Sengupta (Indian novelist and cricket historian)

The England cricket team that regained the Ashes in the triangular Test series.

Frank Foster (1889-1958)

Frank Foster is the man forgotten and Barnes is the man who will always be remembered for his bowling which resulted in bringing home the Ashes for England. However, the 1911/12 tour will be in the minds of many Australians who look back praising both England's front-line bowlers – the well-known Barnes and the little-known Frank Foster. The amateur all-rounder, a left-arm fast-medium pace bowler, and who proved to be a very aggressive batsman who could score many runs quickly, was playing that summer for his home county, Warwickshire. His on-form bowling helped the county, after losing the first match that season to Surrey, unexpectedly win the county championship for the first time in its history. He was an obvious choice for the Ashes tour that winter and with Barnes also showing top-form it was inevitable England would be strong competition against the Aussies in their own 'back yard'. Although England lost the first Test match they won the next four and the series. Barnes and Foster bowled brilliantly throughout and had made it extremely difficult for the batsmen at both ends. Irrepressible Barnes, irrepressible Foster, the statistics show them both to have been outstanding. Barnes did take 34 wickets but Foster's 32 wickets were for fewer runs. It's a fact their bowling won the series but Foster did contribute more by scoring 226 with the bat. Catches 7 each. He was 22 years of age.

Bowling	Matches	overs	maidens	runs	wickets	ave.
F.Foster	5	275.4	58	692	32	21.63
S.Barnes	5	287	64	778	34	22.88
J.Douglas	5	139.5	30	355	15	23.66
F.Woolley	5	68.1	12	209	8	26.12
J.Hitch	3	50	2	183	5	36.60
J.Hearne	4	46	2	196	1	196.00
W.Rhodes	5	18	3	57	0	-

Batting	Matches	innings	not-out	h/score	runs	ave.
J.Hobbs	5	9	1	187	662	82.75
W.Rhodes	5	9	1	179	463	57.87
F.Woolley	5	7	1	133*	289	48.16
G.Gunn	5	9	0	75	381	42.33
J.Hearne	4	9	1	114	281	35.12
F.Foster	5	7	0	71	226	32.28
C.Mead	5	6	1	46	105	21.00
J.Douglas	5	7	0	35	102	14.57
E.Smith	4	5	0	22	47	9.40
S.Barnes	5	7	1	14	35	5.83
J.Hitch	3	4	1	4	8	2.66

During the tour he top-scored with 158 against S. Australia and 101 against Victoria.

Who was Frank Foster and what happened to him?

Born 31st January 1889 at Deritend, Birmingham, in the county of Warwickshire. He was educated at the Solihull School in the West Midlands. He first played for Warwickshire in 1908, and in 1911 he accepted the captaincy and led his team to win the county championship, heading both the batting and bowling averages. It was no surprise when he was chosen to join the England team to tour Australia in 1911/12.

In his international career he played eleven times for England. In 1914 for Warwickshire he did the double – 1,000 runs and 100 wickets. In one innings he made a triple century scoring 305 against Worcestershire. This stood as a county record until Brian Lara's 501 for Warwickshire in 1994. At another time other big batting scores worth mentioning were 200 against Surrey and 105 in less than one hour against Yorkshire.

It was in 1915 tragedy struck. Injuries from a serious motorbike accident changed his life. It was only because of his fitness that prevented his foot being amputated, but it meant that his first-class cricket career was over.

Thereafter, Foster sadly commenced his life on a downhill path. At the start he was given a healthy salary in the family business, but because he was no good at his job he was sacked. Soon afterwards he moved to London and in 1931 was named in the investigation of the brutal murder of a young prostitute whose body was found in an empty shop. She had been strangled and during a police search of her seedy flat a cheque for £10 was found which had been signed by Foster. His version of events was accepted at the inquest though eyebrows were raised.

There was to be no redemption. Foster was now on a truly slippery slope. He disowned his young family, ran up huge gambling debts and was eventually formally declared bankrupt.

He returned to Birmingham during the Second World War and in 1946 at the age of 52 was involved in cricket in some way, at the Edgbaston ground. Until it was reported that he had been banned from the ground. The reason given:

"For his disgraceful conduct in the past season, notably towards amateur players and the catering staff."

Four years later he was in trouble with the police on charges of larceny and fraud. He was escorted from the dock to the establishment that had begun its life as the Northamptonshire County General Lunatic Asylum, later known in Foster's day as a psychiatric hospital. Four years later he died alone there – penniless. Such a sad story of a cricketer born in a wealthy family whose life was shattered physically and mentally. The complete opposite to Barnes as a youngster who was brought up in stricken poverty and in the Victorian slums of the North, to die in a peaceful, green country environment in his beloved county of Staffordshire, and with his loving family close by his bedside.

"No, I don't feel Barnes was the greatest cricket bowler ever, just like I don't feel Bradman was the greatest cricket batsman ever. Though both these guys possess impressive stats, both at the Test and the First-Class level. The thing that militates against them is the limited number of Tests they played. And these too, against limited opponents, in favourable conditions. For example, Barnes played 20 out of his 27 tests against Australia. He never bowled outside England, Australia or South Africa. Same is the case with Bradman. It's like Virat Kohli playing only against Sri Lanka, or Anil Kumble bowling only in India. So the point I am trying to make is that these guys never went outside their comfort zone. Barnes didn't have to toil on sub-continental pitches like Glenn McGrath or Wasim Akram did, or Dale Steyn is doing right now. Or bowl in front of hostile crowds, on pitches made especially to nullify the threat, as was the case with Murlidharan in Australia. The thing is, we love to romanticize the past so much, that we forget that the best players of all time could be among the ones we have actually grown up watching. We like to cling to the myth that there was someone, in the distant past, who could conjure up runs (or wickets) at will, and we try to make him the yardstick to which all others, who came after him, must be gauged. But sadly, that is not the right thing to do."

Shashank Sinha (Sri Lanka)

Gentlemen v Players

This was a first-class cricket match generally held in England twice or more a year for well over a century. It was held between teams consisting of amateurs (the Gentlemen) and professionals (the Players). The difference between the two was defined by the English class structure of the time, with the players deemed to be working-class wage-earners and the Gentlemen members of the middle and upper classes, usually products of the English public school system. Whereas the Players were paid wages by their county clubs or fees by match organisers, the Gentlemen nominally claimed expenses. The whole subject of expenses was controversial and it was said that some leading amateurs were paid more for playing cricket than any professional.

Barnes bowled for the Players against the Gentlemen at Lord's in 1903, 1909, 1911, 1912, 1913 and 1914, at The Oval in 1902 and at Scarborough in 1911. He did bowl for them in a match in 1903 but his knee injury gave him a problem after delivering just one over. At Lord's in 1909 he got a hat-trick in the first innings and took 5 for 22, and 8 for 55 in the match. In the 1911 match he secured 9 wickets for 105 runs. In the match at The Oval in 1912 it was reported that Barnes proved almost unplayable on a drying wicket. He took only 4 wickets for 48 runs but it was said:

"He was terribly difficult to play, the ball turning sharply from the leg and kicking straight up in a bewildering fashion."

He enjoyed another triumph at the expense of the Gentlemen in 1913. He had to be content with just 2 wickets for 67 runs in the first innings. In the second innings his bowling again was described as almost unplayable:

"Barnes has seldom looked harder to play, his quick break from leg being combined with extreme accuracy and length.

The way in which the wicket keeper kept wicket to this wonderful bowling was beyond praise."

His bowling consisted of 19 overs, 8 maidens, 38 runs and 7 wickets.

In his last match for the Players at Lord's in 1914, in only the second time in 8 years the Gentlemen won. In the first innings he collected 4 wickets for 71 runs. In the second innings, bowling with his usual remarkable consistency, he captured another 4 wickets this time for 74 runs. He also did very well with the bat scoring 25 not out and 35.

His record against the Gentlemen was 45 wickets for 687 runs, giving an average per wicket of 16.62.

In years long since gone by I believe I was quite an adequate batsman, especially on sticky wickets, and two of the innings I am proud of, though numerically only moderate, were against Barnes. The first was 24 runs for Gentlemen v Players, at Lord's, in 1913, and the second, 58 runs, in the same match four years earlier. On both occasions the wicket was a 'gluepot' and Barnes spun the ball so fiercely that he tore lumps out of the turf. He was the greatest bowler I ever played and there surely has been no greater bowler in the history of the game.

It was said of Barnes that he was grim and unresponsive. I did not find him so. He was reserved and taciturn and did not often smile, but when he did his whole face lit up. I felt I knew him fairly well. He was one of those men who respond to kindness and to the little courtesies of life and he served myself with well-becoming loyalty. I trusted him and he knew that, and never for a moment did he betray that trust. And how superbly he bowled, not only with tremendous skill but with concentrated determination. Never for a moment did he give in or relax his efforts.

Sir Pelham Francis Warner MBE (1873-1963)

Middlesex and England

November, 1948

The World's Greatest Bowler 1914

An article appeared in a New Zealand magazine in 1914 with the heading:

'The World's Greatest Bowler'.

On the tour of South Africa that year for England he was a sensation, performing record feats, destroying the South African batsmen similar to what he'd done to them in the Triangular Tournament on English wickets just a few months before. It read:

'The world's greatest bowler, Sydney F. Barnes, is the secret hero of the hour. His wonderful bowling with the English team in South Africa has already made the Test matches a "procession" of English victories, and taken along with the great part he has played in other international contests in maintaining the prestige of English cricket.'

He has shown himself on his day, the most difficult right-armed bowler in England, with his deadly quick break from the leg – the feature of his bowling. After leaving Lancashire he dropped out of first-class cricket for a time, but playing with Staffordshire, his native county, which was in the Minor Counties League, he kept before the public from 1904, and has of course, been the strength of the team, which thanks to him has on two occasions in 1906 and 1908 won the Second Division Championship.

In 1906 he took 119 wickets in ten county matches for less than eight runs each, and in the three seasons immediately following his averages have been 6 (79 wickets), 9 (92 wickets) and 7 (76 wickets). He also for some years played with the Porthill Park club in the North Staffordshire League carrying all before him.

Barnes' style is thus described:

He has every attribute of a great bowler. He brings the ball down from a great height, i.e. breaks both ways, he keeps good

81

length, and finally, his flight is most deceptive. His leg-break is not only accurate, but very quick off the pitch. On first going in, one is apt to think, judging by the flight of the ball, that it will pitch off the leg stump, while as a matter of fact eight times out of ten it pitches on the wicket. This is probably due to the fact that he bowls from the extreme end of the crease.'

1888-1940

A career in Minor Counties, League and County Cricket

Smethwick 1893-1894 Rishton 1895-1899 Burnley 1900-1901
Church 1904-1905 Porthill 1906-1914 Saltaire 1915-1923
Castleton Moor 1924-1928 Rochdale 1929-1930
Rawtenstall 1931-1933 Keighley 1934 Smethwick 1935-1936
Lytham St. Anne's 1937 Bridgnorth 1938-1939 Stone 1940

Warwickshire 1893-1896 Lancashire 1899-1903
Staffordshire 1904-1935

Smethwick

Barnes' career began in 1888 when he was fifteen and played
for a small club which had a ground behind the Galton Hotel
in Smethwick. Soon afterwards, he joined Smethwick Cricket
Club and played for the third team. He was taught to bowl
off-spin by Billy Bird, the Smethwick professional who had
played for Warwickshire. He then taught himself later to

bowl leg-spin. In due course, he was selected for the second team and then earned a place in the first team, playing in the Birmingham and District Premier League, at the start of the 1893 season. In his first match he was not asked to bowl and when it was his turn to bat, one ball from a fast bowler was enough. On his return to the pavilion he heard someone say: *"You're no bloody good!"* He was not picked for the next game but was back in the team the following week. It was then he began to show promise and gain some adulation from his captain. He actually opened the batting (in those days he was a wicket-keeper) and scored 20, staying in for an hour and was told he got his runs well. In the next match he began to attract attention with the bat on a 'terribly sticky' wicket facing a right-hand slow bowler, Henry Pallett, who was doing great things for Warwickshire. He batted cautiously and steadily for over an hour and scored 30 in difficult circumstances. It was after this that he began to be noticed as a very useful bowler. In a match against Handsworth Wood the Smethwick captain put Barnes on to bowl and he was so successful by the time the innings ended he had taken 7 wickets for 19 runs. He didn't bowl the next week, which was a bit of a surprise after his success the week before, but he did score 49 with the bat. **Warwickshire** were impressed with his performances for Smethwick, so invited him to play against Gloucestershire at Bristol in the last match of the 1893 season.

The following season, while still playing for Smethwick, he played again for Warwickshire, this time in their first season in the County Championship proper, against Cheshire. He managed to score 11 runs, did not bowl in the first innings and in the second innings bowled 8 overs, no wickets for 27 runs. In the 1895 season he played the first two matches for Warwickshire against Derbyshire at Edgbaston and Surrey at The Oval. He managed to get one wicket in the first match and two at The Oval. It would appear that his 3 wickets for 145 runs did not justify picking him again that year but in 1896 he did play for them against Essex. He had the displeasure of batting and getting a duck and bowling in both innings without getting a wicket. Not surprising that Warwickshire did not to want to play him again.

Rishton

In the meantime, in 1894, Barnes, as a 21-year-old fast bowler, was asked to join the ground staff of Staffordshire County Cricket Club but found the terms unattractive. Instead, he joined Rishton Cricket Club in the Lancashire League where the pay was better than in any form of county cricket, largely because of match bonuses and collections. He soon set about earning his money for Rishton and beginning that phenomenal career in league cricket which was to continue for more than 40 years. In his five happy and successful years as a professional at Rishton he learned to develop the leg-break, so devastatingly, taking 411 wickets for an average of just over 9 runs. In 1898 he was only 4 short of 100 in that season. **Lancashire** were impressed and asked him to join the ground staff at Old Trafford. He declined because he could not see that it would benefit him financially. He did actually play for the Lancashire second eleven in 1898 and in his last season with Rishton in 1899 he played twice for the county side against Sussex and in a special benefit match for his hero, Tom Richardson, against Surrey. He didn't do too badly on a perfect Oval batting wicket, sending down 44 overs, 3 wickets for 99 runs. Once again he was approached by Lancashire to join them but they could not come to the terms he had requested. At the same time he was not satisfied with the terms Rishton had offered him. The club president was heard to say that they would want three men for Barnes' price. So Barnes decided to accept Burnley's offer, who also played in the Lancashire League.

Rishton Bowling				
overs	maidens	runs	wickets	average
1895-347	97	705	71	9.92
1896-406	95	959	85	11.28
1897-382	115	753	87	8.65
1898-373	113	813	96	8.46
1899-314	81	760	72	10.55

Rishton Batting				
inns	not-out	runs	h/score	average
1895-23	0	422	87	18.34
1896-23	0	366	72	15.91
1897-17	1	255	49	15.93
1898-23	2	414	106	19.71
1899-19	2	441	100	25.94

The Lancashire League

The member clubs of the Lancashire League, financed by the economic powerhouse of the cotton industry, had pre-League contact with the very best of the English and Australian Test match cricketers. Formed in 1892, the League went on to attract a multitude of Commonwealth stars, many of them 'Ashes professionals' whose League experience benefited themselves, their clubs and their communities. For some professionals, the league provided their bread and butter, for others an end-of-career payday, recuperation from injury or part of their cricket education. Some came at the height of their powers. Others appeared as substitute professionals. No other organization has provided its amateurs with the thrill, privilege and memories of sharing the stage with such a rich gallery of international sporting talent. The legendary tales of genius, competitiveness, charisma and showmanship have helped bond 14 clubs from north-east Lancashire together, their membership remaining unchanged since 1897. In its first season the league consisted of only 13 clubs (the 14 current members minus Todmorden) before Bury played in 1893 and 1894 to give the league 14 clubs. Bury left for the 1895 season before Todmorden joined in 1897. The membership of the league has not changed since. In addition, Edenfield have entered the 20/20 Cup since 2007 but have not entered any other Lancashire League competition. From the 2017 season three new clubs, Clitheroe CC, Darwen CC and Great Harwood CC, entered the League. The Lancashire League crowds were exceptionally knowledgeable, the cricket extremely well organised and of a high standard, the amateurs comparing with many county players and the professionals among the best in the world. The games were hard fought, competitive, and the crowds expected the teams to provide top-class cricket. It was unlikely that a professional like Barnes would have involved himself in anything resembling a circus. Playing just one or two days a week, the teams were fresh and able to give their best in every game. There was none of the drudgery that one endured in county matches which Barnes resented during his few seasons with Lancashire. As a result there was a bubbling enthusiasm to get on with the game. Cricket was played in all but the most inclement weather. Unlike in county cricket, the players were not always looking around the horizon for a drop of rain or a small cloud to obscure the light, and then running thankfully into the pavilion like gingerbread men afraid of melting.

Burnley

He played for Burnley in 1900 and 1901, and was even more successful than at Rishton. They won the league in 1901 with Barnes. He achieved more than 100 wickets in both seasons.

Burnley bowling				
overs	maidens	runs	wickets	average
1900-436.2	120	1024	111	9.22
1901-362	86	925	114	8.11

Burnley batting				
inns	not-out	runs	h/score	average
1900-29	3	685	81*	26.34
1901-23	1	495	71*	22.50

Lancashire bowling (in his two full seasons):				
overs	maidens	runs	wickets	average
1902-719.2	211	1,758	82	21.43
1903-1,023	363	2,339	131	17.85

Church

It was in the winter of 1901 that he played in Australia. On his return and after the next two seasons of regular service with Lancashire at county level, he returned to league cricket as professional in the Lancashire league in 1904 for the Church club. His wage was £6 a week plus a job at William Blythe Ltd, manufacturer of inorganic speciality chemicals. He signed for two seasons, but although they did not win the league championship (which they expected to with Barnes) they did not have the occasion to complain. In his first season with them he established a new professional aggregate record with the bat of 31.7 scoring a total of 666 runs. He also participated in a record stand for the club of 209 runs for the second wicket – Barnes 113 not out and Duckworth 74 not out. He took 64 wickets at 10.2, overshadowed somewhat by Thomas Flowers who took 7 wickets at 9.51, establishing a new amateur record. The following season, Barnes captured 82 wickets at 9.34 but scored only 264 runs. Church finished third place in the league. During the latter part of the second season he was informed by the Church committee they would offer him new terms for another season, but the club could only be able to manage on reduced terms. His reply, as might have been expected, was very much to the point:

"As much more as you like, but not a penny less and you will pay me more if I play for you again."

Not surprisingly, they could not meet his terms so he left at the end of the 1905 season.

Seventeen years later on June 17th, 1922, Church spent 1s 10p on a telegram which brought about a reunion with Barnes. Up to the weekend of June 21st they were relying upon substitute professionals that season whilst waiting for the arrival of Frank O'Keefe from Australia. Barnes agreed to play for them in their big match against Nelson in the Lancashire League. He was now 49 but by his own standards, was still in full flight. He was paid £25 for just that one afternoon's service, a princely sum at the time but he did not disappoint. Nelson's professional was the Australian Ted MacDonald who blasted Church, all out for 58. The magnificent Barnes' spiteful reply was 6-19 and the powerful Nelson were routed for 44. Game won. Frank O'Keefe was the big signing from Australia who took over for the rest of the 1922 season, but it is likely that the abiding memory of those ten Church amateurs was of the chance to walk out onto the West End cricket ground in the company of Barnes, and all agreeing that the 1s 10p cable to him was money well spent.

Church bowling				
overs	maidens	runs	wickets	average
1904-260.3	57	636	64	9.93
1905-330.3	79	815	90	9.05

Church batting:				
inns	not-out	runs	h/score	average
1904-25	4	666	113*	31.71
1905-20	4	264	50*	16.50

Staffordshire bowling:				
overs	maidens	runs	wickets	average
1904-269.4	62	679	66	10.28
1905-193.2	44	508	44	11.54

Staffordshire batting:				
inns	not-out	runs	h/score	average
1904-15	2	456	76*	35.07
1905-10	0	190	53	19.00

Porthill

In 1905 the Porthill committee were called together to consider proposals to engage a professional for the 1906 season. That committee considered it advisable to engage Barnes and he was given a two year contract. That contract was to pay Barnes £12 a week (in today's money about £1,200). Porthill's committee at the time was made up of very astute businessmen and with guarantees from the local businesses to cover at least a third of Barnes' wages this was truly a great piece of business. The signing of Barnes saw membership increase and gate sizes swell. In fact gates of 2,000 to 5,000 would flock to see the great man and Porthill were taking £70 a game on admission fees. In some cases when Porthill played away they asked for a share of the gate as to secure Barnes appearing in the game and often sent their own gate men to make sure the opposition did not understate the gate money.

It was in the 1906 season he achieved an amazing record by topping both the batting and bowling averages and he did the same in every one of the nine years he was with Porthill. He was in good company too because at that time the Porthill side included other county players, both batsmen and bowlers. The 1906 season saw Barnes take 103 wickets at 5.14 and his batting average was 43.46 after scoring 652 runs. Against Leek Highfield, Barnes carried his bat for 76 then took all 10 wickets for 12 runs. And to rub 'salt in the wound' against the same team the following season he took all 10 wickets again.

Also in 1907 against Silverdale in the same innings he did the "hat-trick" twice. That year the game everybody wanted to see was Porthill against Burslem and reports state that a crowd of more than 5,000 turned up at the 'Hill' to watch the encounter, returning a gate league record and amassing around £8,500. Porthill set Burslem 107 but Barnes took Burslem apart, taking 8 for 19, eventually bowling them out for 51.

In 1908 he took all 10 wickets against Leek. A very interesting story to tell about those 10 wickets. Barnes opened the bowling to the Leek captain. The first ball went for a single. He then proceeded to take the first 9 wickets without another run scored against him. The story goes that while waiting for the number 11 batsmen one of the Porthill fielders shouted to Barnes in a state of nervous tension:

"For God's sake, Syd, please bowl him out. If he hits a ball to me I'm bound to drop it."

91

And sure enough he did. The next ball was a "sitter" which went to this very fielder. In his anxiety he fumbled it and dropped it. Leek added another 30 runs for the last wicket before Barnes found the stumps. If the fielder had caught the ball his figures would have been an astonishing 10 for 1. Also in 1908 with the bat he scored 142 not out against Tunstall and 120 not out against Norton. In 1909 he achieved another 10 wickets haul, this time against Crewe Alexandra.

He had nine years of phenomenal success prior to the War for Porthill. They won the Championship in 1906-7-8 which set up a new record for the league. They were runners-up in 1909 and 1910, champions in 1911, second again in 1912 and champions again in 1913 and 1914. In those nine years they headed the league tables six times. During that time Barnes scored a total of 5,625 runs and took 893 wickets. What was also remarkable is the following:

1907 – 112 wickets for an average of 3.91, a league record.
1908 – 122 wickets was a record for the league.
1910 – a batting average of 68.90 was a league record.

His time at Porthill ended in 1914.

During his time at Porthill, Barnes was also playing regularly for **Staffordshire** in the Minor Counties competition and had been since 1904. The county had not had a great deal of success until Barnes became associated with it. His performances with the ball meant Staffordshire started to become a very good side. It was in 1906, during the first season with Porthill, that he took 119 wickets (a Minor Counties record) for fewer than 8 runs each. There were some other remarkable performances that year:

Suffolk – 5 for 6 in an innings that lasted 70 minutes.
Bedfordshire – 8 for 10.
Yorkshire 2nd II – 12 for 88.

Lancashire 2nd II – scored 99 (with the bat) followed by 7 for 50.
Cambridgeshire – scored a century and then 8 for 43.
Suffolk (again) – 6 for 21 including an innings of 55 then 8 for 51.

It was the same story, very nearly, in 1907. Staffordshire finished second in the championship. With the ball, Barnes took 79 wickets at an average of 6.36 a wicket. There was a game against Durham at Stoke which was considered the most remarkable match ever played in any class of cricket. The game was all over in less than four hours and was due to Barnes' exceptional bowling. Durham batted first and with the first 4 balls of his second over, he took the first 4 wickets. In doing so he completed a hat-trick and had taken his 300th wicket in the Minor Counties Championship. Barnes finished with 6 for 23. Durham managed to score 47. Staffordshire didn't do much better with 66 but then Durham in their second innings only scored 20. This time Barnes took 4 wickets in 7 balls finishing with 6 for 7 and for the match, 12 for 30. Staffordshire only needed 3 runs to win which they did by 10 wickets.

Durham first innings		Staffordshire first innings	
H.Brooks b Mee	16	W.Brown b Morris	6
G.Turnbull b Barnes	5	A.Hollowood c Brooks b Brydon	19
A.H.Stoner lbw b Barnes	0	C.L.Winser b Morris	7
A.L.Scott Owen b Barnes	0	S.F.Barnes b Brydon	14
T.Coulson b Barnes	0	H.D.Stratton b Stoner	0
R.C.Harrison b Barnes	3	E.H.Bourne b Morris	2
J.Thackeray c Barnes b Mee	9	S.Pike c Coulson b Morris	0
J.Kirtley c Barnes b Mee	0	J.W.Johnson b Morris	8
C.H.Parkin b Mee	5	P.Briggs not out	1
R.Y.Brydon not out	1	R.J.Mee b Morris	1
A.Morris c Hollowood b Barnes	5	D.Houseman b Morris	2
Extras (3nb)	3	Extras (6 b)	6
Total (all out, 14.5 overs)	47	Total (all out 35.4 overs)	66

Staffordshire bowling	Durham bowling
Barnes 6/23, Mee 4/21	Turnbull 0/12, Morris 7/22, Brydon 2/15 Stoner 1/11

Durham second innings		Staffordshire second innings	
H.Brooks c Houseman b Barnes	1	J.W.Johnson not out	3
G.Turnbull c Johnson b Mee	1	D.Houseman not out	0
A.H.Stoner b Barnes	1	W.Brown did not bat	
A.L.Scott Owen b Mee	5	A.Hollowood did not bat	
T.Coulson b Barnes	0	C.L.Winser did not bat	
R.C.Harrison b Barnes	0	S.F.Barnes did not bat	
J.Thackeray b Barnes	2	H.D.Stratton did not bat	
J.Kirtley b Mee	0	E.H.Bourne did not bat	
C.H.Parkin c Houseman b Mee	4	S.Pike did not bat	
R.Y.Brydon lbw b Barnes	2	P.Briggs did not bat	
A.Morris not out	1	R.J.Mee did not bat	
Extras (1 b, 2n	3	Extras	0
Total (all out, 11 overs)	20	Total (no wicket, 4 overs)	3

Staffordshire bowling	Durham bowling
Barnes 6/7, Mee 4/10	Coulson 0/3

In 1908 Staffordshire won the championship. It was said that perhaps it would be more accurate to say that Barnes had won the championship for them. The Minor Counties was now divided into four groups and after heading their group Staffordshire played Hertfordshire in the semi-final and then Glamorgan in the final, both matches being played at Stoke. Amazingly, against these two sides he took 24 wickets for an average of 3.5. He bowled 60 overs for only 78 runs. It's doubtful these figures have ever been equalled in the whole history of cricket:

Hertfordshire – 4 for 14 and 5 for 11.
Glamorgan – 7 for 18 and 8 for 35.

There was an extraordinary incident in the Glamorgan match. Glamorgan had to follow on and the last man in was Harry Creber. When he arrived at the wicket to face Barnes the umpire remarked:

"I wonder how he is going to bat today?"

"What do you mean?" said Barnes.

"Well," said the umpire, *"sometimes he bats right-handed and sometimes left-handed."* Then he asked the batsman, *"How are you going to bat today, Harry?"*

Creber indicated he would bat left-handed. The sight screens were moved, the field changed over and Creber took guard. Then he looked up and said:

"No, I think I'll bat right-handed."

So the screens were moved again, the field changed over and he took a right-handed guard. Barnes bowled him one just outside the off-stump, Creber hit it backhanded and it went through the slips for four.

"By jove," Creber said, "I'm batting well left-handed, I'm going to bat left-handed."

While the screens were being moved yet again and the field changed, Barnes had made up his mind to put a stop to all this. So, with his next ball he bowled an underhand and it hit Creber hard on the pad. Barnes appealed and the umpire put his hand up to give him out. Immediately, the Glamorgan captain protested that Creber was not out and, indeed could not be out but instead Barnes should have been no-balled. Barnes told him:

"You ask the umpire."

But the umpire had been laughing so much he could not call no-ball to Barnes. Glamorgan later did protest to the MCC but nothing more was heard of the matter. The next season when Staffordshire played Glamorgan at Swansea, Creber asked Barnes if he would agree to having a photograph taken together, as, he said, people seemed to think there was some ill-feeling between them as a result of what had happened the year before. Barnes was glad to do so and that was the end of that.

Some interesting comments from Barnes in 1914 about the tough competition he was experiencing in the Minor Counties:

"The other day a gentleman came up to me politely wanting some answers to several questions which he fired at me, one after the other. Who are the Minor Counties? What are they? What do they do and who plays for them?

It was a tall order all at once and it took me quite a long time to tell him all he wanted to know. After all, the Minor Counties take part in what proves, year after year, to be a very fine competition and whether the newspapers take very much interest in the doings, or not, the public may take it from me that the men who partake in these games treat them very seriously indeed and are proud they are chosen to represent their county.

In fact it is quite a demanding game of cricket as any I have ever played. It is sheer hard going at the time.

The games in the Minor Counties are played at top pressure especially so because they only last two days and in the course of those two days there are two innings to be completed on each side just as in the first-class county games which occupy three days.

In my opinion the class of cricket played by the Minor Counties is as good as first-class cricket. There are plenty of good individual players. Many men who have left the Minor Counties competition and gone to first-class cricket have done almost as well and occasionally better.

Again, I am convinced that the best of the Minor Counties clubs – say Glamorgan or Norfolk – would at least hold more than their own against clubs who usually figure in the lower half of the first-class table. Norfolk especially are particularly strong in the batting line up. The question of whether or not a system of automatic promotion of the Minor Counties to the first-class division would work has often been discussed. There are many things which might be said in favour of a scheme whereby the weakest clubs in the first-class arena could vacate their places to the strongest combination in the second-class. Probably such a system would have the effect of making the championship more of a pulse-stirring competition and would provide more of that wild excitement which is so much in demand.

But in my opinion so far as the Minor Counties is concerned such a system of automatic promotion simply could not be worked. There is more than one reason against it. In the first place there is the question of finance. Just as many of the first-class clubs find themselves in need of funds at the end of every season and so do the Minor Counties find it extremely difficult – nay, one might almost say impossible – to make ends meet without aid outside their gate money.

There is another difficulty which stands in the way and this has to do with the players now appearing in Minor Counties cricket. Almost without exception the professional appearing with the Minor Counties teams have Saturday afternoon engagements. I know such is the case with my own county Staffordshire and a longer programme which would necessitate playing some of the games over the weekend would mean that some of the best players would be unable to take part.

On the whole, therefore, I do not think that the system of automatic relegation and promotion applied to first-class cricket is a workable idea at the present moment."

Staffordshire won the minor counties championship three years in succession. With Barnes instrumental, he took 1,441 wickets for Staffordshire at 8.1 and also scored quite a few centuries, he is quoted as saying:

"If I was out for records I could have made a lot more runs."

Porthill bowling:				
overs	maidens	runs	wickets	average
1906-256.3	79	530	103	5.14
1907-216.5	63	439	112	3.91
1908-352.1	133	693	122	5.68
1909-224.5	76	428	100	4.28
1910-252.3	93	476	82	5.80
1911-306	77	792	109	7.26
1912-213	70	395	66	6.98
1913-240.5	73	532	114	4.66
1914-209	71	434	85	5.10

Porthill batting:				
inns	not-out	runs	h/score	average
1906-19	4	652	104*	43.46
1907-20	5	473	116*	31.53
1908-18	5	544	142*	41.84
1909-16	2	481	90	34.35
1910-18	7	758	129*	68.90
1911-22	2	813	87*	40.65
1912-17	3	470	51*	33.57
1913-20	6	903	86*	64.50
1914-19	3	531	120*	33.18

Staffordshire bowling:				
overs	maidens	runs	wickets	average
1906-373.1	100	932	119	7.83
1907-246	82	505	79	6.39
1908-397.4	139	817	92	8.18
1909-285	85	676	93	7.26
1910-363.5	99	879	90	9.76
1911-337.2	113	750	104	7.21
1912-191	75	376	70	5.37
1913-196.3	48	397	65	6.10
1914-159.3	57	297	48	6.18

Staffordshire batting:				
inns	not-out	runs	h/score	average
1906-15	1	431	100	30.78
1907-13	1	226	53	17.38
1908-16	0	336	79	21.00
1909-12	2	176	65	17.60
1910-16	1	310	59	20.66
1911-15	2	563	150	43.30
1912-8	0	168	49	21.00
1913-11	2	366	83	40.66
1914-7	0	230	67	32.85

Saltaire

He had spent nine seasons playing for Porthill in the North Staffordshire League when Saltaire made their approach ahead of the 1915 season. During the war years a great many of the first class professionals had engagements with Bradford League clubs whilst doing war work. It might well have been there was no rule limiting the number of professionals a club might play. They were all earning decent money by travelling round the Bradford circuit. Barnes had a glint in his eye as he spoke to the deputation who had travelled from Saltaire to chat with him. If the truth be known another report slightly contradicts the approach Saltaire, it was said, had made to him. Barnes saw an advert in the Athletic News in April 1915 stating that Saltaire were looking for a left-arm bowler. He immediately contacted the club and asked:

"Will I do?"

The same day he had a reply saying:

"Come tomorrow. Will arrange terms."

Whatever the circumstances, terms were eventually agreed guaranteeing Barnes £3.50 per match plus travel expenses. He was quoted later saying:

"But not what I would have liked. But then it was that or nothing as no other cricket was being played in England."

Grand Cricket Match
Sydney Barnes Benefit

Saltaire v Bankfoot
in
Saltaire Park
on Saturday Next
4th September, 1915

Wickets pitched at 2.30

Admission 3d Ladies Free
Refreshments Provided

When Barnes moved to Saltaire they gave him £10 to cover removal expenses. Such was his success, he negotiated a doubling of his match fee for the 1916 season. People were starved of county games because of the war; 8,000 watched the Saltaire v Keithley match that season. The stars and big crowds at the Bradford League games was certainly providing a welcome distraction to the raging war.

Saltaire could afford to pay him well because of the crowds he attracted to Roberts Park and to the grounds Saltaire visited just to go and see him play. Saltaire's visit to Bowling Old Lane in 1923 attracted 6,400 spectators which was a league record attendance. The 1918 Priestley Cup Final between Saltaire and Bankfoot drew an attendance of 13,320. A bigger crowd than Bradford City FC got on the same day. The game was tied, each scoring 99 runs after Barnes had done the hat-trick and taken 8 for 50. The replay was watched by 10,069 and was won by Saltaire by 7 wickets. In the same season Barnes made his highest score ever, 168 against Basildon Green. In 1921 his earnings rose to £9 a match. In addition he had been given a benefit every season up to 1921 and also enjoyed talent money, as well as collections from the crowd for taking 5 wickets or scoring a half-century. He was for a while coaching school boys at Bradford Grammar and also gave private tuition to young cricketers. Even more impressive was the gate of 14,179 to watch the 1921 final between Saltaire and Keighley at Park Avenue, a figure which was claimed a world record for a one-day match in club cricket.

Barnes was employed as a cashier and accountant at Messrs J. Robsons, Gas Engine Makers, Shipley in 1920. At the time, the idol of the Saltaire crowd had the distinction of being the first man invited to play for England in the team which would tour Australia at the end of the season. It was reported at the time that Barnes had not yet decided to accept and had stated that if he does he would take his wife and boy with him on the tour. He was hoping the MCC would allow him something towards the expense of taking his family. However, negotiations fell through and in the end Lancashire county player Cecil Parkin was chosen instead.

With an abundance of Test players and numerous others from the first-class counties it was not surprising that match attendances in the Bradford League were high. Because of the war the League was practically the only competitive cricket being played. Barnes' years with Saltaire outshone the previous years with Porthill as his performances show. Barnes was bowling every week against some of the best batsmen in England and against teams with scarcely any weakness in their batting order. He started off with 92 wickets in his first season at an average below 5. He took 832 wickets in League matches at an average of 5.9, passing the century of wickets three times in a season. He also did a certain amount of bowling in the Priestley Cup and in 1922 his total of wickets in 20 league and 4 Cup Ties for Saltaire was 150 for only 618 runs.

Barnes was at times unplayable. Amongst his great feats was taking 10 wickets on three occasions. In a match against Basildon Green at Basildon on 15th May, 1915 Barnes achieved 10 wickets conceding only 14 runs. That something was greatly expected by the spectators from Barnes's bowling goes without saying. Six times he hit the wickets, in addition to which he got a couple of lbw decisions and another couple stumped. He took the last 5 wickets with successive balls, thus establishing a new record for the Bradford League. In the same year he did the same against Bowling Old Lane, 10 wickets for 33 runs, and in 1918 against Keighley 10 wickets for 36 runs.

Keighley	
D.Roebuck c and b Barnes	23
E.Robinson b Barnes	5
J.W.Hearne lbw Barnes	12
H.C.Robson c Eastwood b Barnes	2
S.Haigh b Barnes	19

A.Kellett st Whitley b Barnes	7
F.Horner b Barnes	17
J.Roberts c b Barnes	0
J.J.Williams st Whitley b Barnes	7
J.H.Crawford c Swithinbank b Barnes	0
W.Hanson not out	1
Extras	7
Total	100

Barnes' bowling				
overs	maidens	runs	wickets	average
15.5	3	36	10	3.6

The previous year on 28th May in a Bradford League match against Keighley, Barnes figured strongly in this contest, taking 9 wickets for 41 runs. This game attracted 8,000 spectators, no doubt mainly to watch Barnes in action and he succeeded to please. The Keighley side included J.W.Hearne (Middlesex) and Schofield Haigh (Yorkshire). Their regular opening pair then held the league record for an opening partnership.

His achievement at Basildon Green included 5 wickets in 5 balls. In 1918 against Windhill he took 4 in 4 balls and 5 in 7, and in 1922 he had 4 in 5 balls against Idle and 6 in 8 balls against Laisterdyke. In a Priestley Cup-tie in the latter year he actually took the first 9 wickets for no runs. In 1917 he had 9 for 19 against Low Mor, 9 for 41 against Keighley, and 8 for 20 against Basildon. In the same years his batting average was above 30 runs, scoring in all 3,018 runs and averaging 24.33 per innings for the whole period with Saltaire.

Barnes' name will figure in the records of the Bradford League for as long as it lasts. In each of the nine seasons he was with Saltaire he headed the league bowling averages. His best figures being in 1922 when he bowled 247 overs, 63 maidens, 122 wickets for 501 runs with an average under 5 an over.

Some time after he had left Saltaire, Barnes was stopped by a man who, after asking after his health, told him:

"I won pounds on you when you played for Saltaire. I used to back you to take 5 wickets, but I won so often that I had to bet on 6 wickets as this was the season when you took 150 wickets and averaged more than 6 a match. I won a pot of money. Let's have a drink for the sake of old times."

Saltaire bowling				
overs	maidens	runs	wickets	average
1915-108	40	407	92	4.42
1916-251	53	603	93	6.48
1917-233.3	57	527	107	4.92
1918-236	60	583	112	5.20
1919-212	62	576	68	8.47
1920-265	90	536	100	5.36
1921-292.4	71	638	112	5.69
1922-311	80	618	150	4.11
1923-150.1	49	269	70	3.84

Saltaire batting				
inns	not-out	runs	h/score	average
1915-16	3	441	69*	33.92
1916-22	2	239	69	16.45
1917-17	3	273	60	19.50
1918-18	5	338	64*	26.00
1919-15	5	192	44	19.20
1920-17	2	203	38	13.53
1921-21	5	564	77	35.25
1922-20	4	447	73	27.93
1923-11	4	231	64	33.00

Castleton Moor

In 1924 Barnes joined Castleton Moor in the Central Lancashire League and in the same year he resumed playing for **Staffordshire** in the Minor Counties League. During the war years Barnes had only been playing league cricket. It was not until 1919 that the first-class county competition was resumed, followed by the Minor Counties in 1920 when it was Staffordshire that won the championship without Barnes. Castleton Moor was one of only three clubs in the Central Lancashire League that had not won the championship. They were known as the 'babies' of the league but made no secret of the fact that they intended to make a big bid for championship honours. Barnes was being paid a much higher fee than any other professional in the league but his time with the club proved very much a paying proposition as well as for other league clubs who also benefited financially because he was a big attraction wherever he played. It was the Saltaire story all over again. In 1922 before Barnes joined them they were 10th out of 12 clubs in the second division and in 1923 they were 10th again. In his first season (1924), they finished 5th, and his contribution was capturing 90 wickets for the season.

In 1925 Castleton Moor re-engaged Barnes for a further three years. Up to then Barnes had only been a Saturday professional and had very largely carried the team on his shoulders. It was in the 1925 season Castleton Moor topped the second division, which gained them promotion to the first division. Barnes was mainly responsible for this, taking 136 wickets for just over 6 runs each. There was a strong desire by the club officials to remove the stigma of Castleton Moor being regarded as a one-man team. For that reason the club had arranged that from the beginning of the next season Barnes would donate some attention to coaching the players. The club let it be known that they had good material at its disposal and under Barnes' tuition both the batting and bowling strength of the team improved.

With practically the same team, including Barnes considered to be at his best form, they proved to be a formidable side in 1926 by winning the first division championship in their first year. Again, Barnes had earned his money exceeding one hundred wickets (113) for the season. His wonderful display of bowling had again brought him into the limelight and all the critics were agreed that he was bowling as well as ever. It was even reported that Pelham (Plum) Warner (Chairman of Selectors mid 1920s) was regretting that England lacked another bowler.

In 1927 they were runners-up with Barnes increasing his wickets haul to 119 and as expected, there was never a dull moment when he was playing. A story which amused many in those days was when he was caught napping in a Central Lancashire League game against Werneth in August of that year. He was batting and because it was his own fault paid the penalty by losing his wicket. He had played a ball back to the bowler, F. Brown (Werneth professional) and then casually stepped out of his crease to pat down a patch. Brown immediately threw the ball to the wicket keeper who put down the wicket and Barnes was given out. The umpire could not give any other decision. Sharp words were spoken from Barnes. There was no doubt from spectators and players alike, including the umpire, Barnes was seen to be angry (his anger directed at Brown) on his long walk back to the pavilion.

In his last season (1928) with the club, Castleton Moor achieved the double by winning the championship for the second time and the league Cup (Wood Cup). During his time with Castleton Moor, altogether in five seasons, he had taken 583 wickets for under 6 runs apiece and with the bat he had scored 1,324 runs for an average of 16.4.

Alas, the time had come at the end of the 1928 season when the club decided it could no longer afford his services.

It was at a time when league clubs were known to be having financial problems, including Castleton Moor. The decision to part with Barnes was reached on purely financial grounds and it was with reluctance that the resolution to let him go was passed. The Mayor was present at the general meeting of members when it was decided to release him. In a speech he gave to the meeting he paid tribute to Barnes:

"Not only is he a great bowler but is a thorough gentleman in every meaning of the word. No professional has ever enthused such loyalty into his players as Barnes has done during the last two years. I wish to kill once and for all the notion which seems to have been broadcast during the last few years that Barnes is a bad man to get on with. He is a very reticent man, and like all geniuses he has his own way of doing things, but he is certainly not difficult to get on with; the boys adore him and will be very sorry indeed if he goes elsewhere."

During his time at Castleton Moor in 1924, his return to play for **Staffordshire** in the Minor Counties league took off in the same year when he took 73 wickets. His 1925 season was least successful for the county. He missed 3 of the 10 matches and only took 31 wickets. His bowling average was only the third time since 1904 that had gone into double figures. It was in 1926 he was his successful self again. Cheshire found themselves at his mercy when he returned match winning figures of 11 for 37. This was followed by 7 for 32 against Norfolk and even better figures of 8 for 17 and 6 for 14 against Lincolnshire.

The Staffordshire Cricket Club committee in their report of the 1926 season stated that the most outstanding feature was the continued excellence of the bowling of Barnes who, at the age of 50, took 76 wickets at an average of 8.21 runs. Barnes captured his 1,000th wicket for Staffordshire during that season. In 14 seasons he had taken 1,050 wickets. The report added that it was the intention of the committee to recognise his achievement during the coming season. It was stated that a testimonial fund would be opened. Lord Lichfield, presiding, said that Barnes' record was extraordinary seeing that Staffordshire never played more than ten matches in a season.

'Plum' Warner paid a warm tribute to Barnes in December, 1927, when he was honoured by his native county in recognition of his having taken his 1,000[th] wicket for the county:

"I say deliberately having played against him and with him on the same side, and this is my considered opinion, I believe Barnes to be the greatest bowler the world has seen so far, and I have this support behind me that the Australians have no doubt on that point."

The Staffordshire team was described by Warner as the Yorkshire of the Minor Counties cricket.

Staffordshire won the Minor Counties championship for the seventh time in 1927. And it was in that year Barnes continued his successful bowling for the county by taking 81 wickets with an average of 6.08 runs, and largely through the deadliness of his bowling Staffordshire had finished top and once again he headed the bowling league averages.

Sir Francis Joseph, in the absence of Lord Dartmouth, President of the Staffordshire club, handed a cheque for £156 to Barnes being the amount subscribed to the testimonial. Mr Russell, captain, presented Barnes with a silver cigarette case on behalf of the team.

In 1928, the last season with Castleton Moor, he once again headed the Minor Counties League with a bowling average of 55 wickets for 7.34 runs each. Bowling as well as ever he took 6 for 13 against Middleton, 7 for 26 against Crompton and 7 for 13 against Hayward. Playing for East Lancashire the following week against Todmorden in the Worsley Cup, he took 7 for 9 in 21 overs and still finished on the losing side.

Castleton Moor bowling				
overs	maidens	runs	wickets	average
1924-268.2	67	581	90	6.45
1925-432.1	132	820	136	6.02
1926-348.3	108	677	113	5.99
1927-303	92	608	119	5.10
1928-344	97	804	125	6.43

Castleton Moor batting				
inns	not-out	runs	h/score	average
1924-17	1	234	47	14.62
1925-24	6	491	50	27.27
1926-19	3	216	33	13.50
1927-18	4	195	28	13.92
1928-19	1	188	26	10.04

Staffordshire bowling				
overs	maidens	runs	wickets	average
1924-256.5	79	525	73	7.19
1925-184.5	57	417	31	13.45
1926-312.2	98	624	76	8.21
1927-253.2	81	493	81	6.08
1928-215.4	70	404	55	7.34

Staffordshire batting				
inns	not-out	runs	h/score	average
1924-16	0	269	41	16.81
1925-10	0	277	74	27.70
1926-13	1	190	69	15.88
1927-12	0	255	70	21.25
1928-10	2	87	28*	10.87

Minor Counties v South Africa 1929

In a 3-day match a Minor Counties representative team played the South African touring side at the County Ground, Stoke-on-Trent on 12/13/14 June, 1929. Minor Counties won the toss, chose to bat first and were 201 all out. Barnes went in at number 7 and scored 17. The South Africans replied, 139 all out. Barnes bowled superbly and took 8 wickets for 41 runs. In their second innings the Minor Counties innings was interrupted by rain, which forced them to declare at 182 for 6. However, there was not enough time to finish the game to the end so it was declared a draw. Only 15 overs were possible for the South African second innings and it had to finish when they had only scored 40. Barnes had taken the only wicket.

Minor Counties first innings		South Africa first innings	
W.T.Cook b Owen-Smith	45	H.W.Taylor c Hodgson b Barnes	28
P.F.Remnant b Owen-Smith	62	B.Mitchell b Barnes	7
E.D.Dynes c Mitchell b McMillan	7	Q.McMillan hit wkt b Barnes	21
H.W.Hodgson b Quinn	25	D.P.B.Morkel st Farrimond b Barnes	0
T.K.Dobson b Owen-Smith	1	R.H.Catterall c Dobson b Barnes	11
A.Lockett b Owen-Smith	8	H.B.Cameron c Meyer b Barnes	2
S.F.Barnes b McMillan	17	I.J.Siedle retired ill	2
W.Farrimond c Cameron b Owen-Smith	3	H.G.Deane c Meyer b Barnes	20
R.J.O.Meyer c sub b McMillan	11	H.G.O.Owen-Smith b Barnes	26
E.W.Hazelton not out	5	N.A.Quinn b Meyer	4

F.Edwards c McMillan b Owen-Smith	2	A.J.Bell not out	0
Extras (12b, 2lb, 1w)	15	Extras (8b, 7lb, 3nb)	18
Total	**201**	**Total**	**139**

South Africa bowling	**Minor Counties bowling**
Owen-Smith 6/38, McMillan 3/66, Quinn 1/26	Barnes 8/41, Meyer 1/30.

Minor Counties second innings		**South Africa second innings**	
W.T.Cook c and b Bell	92	H.W.Taylor not out	13
P.F.Remnant run out	0	H.B.Cameron b Barnes	11
E.D.Dynes b Bell	20	Q.McMillan not out	11
H.W.Hodgson b Bell	8		
T.K.Dobson c Cameron b Quinn	35		
A, Lockett not out	13		
R.J.O.Meyer st Cameron b Bell	0		
E.W.Hazelton not out	2		
Extras (10b, 3b)	13	Extras (4b, 1nb)	5
Total (6 wickets declared, 58 overs)	**183**	**Total (1 wicket, 15.2 overs)**	**40**

South Africa bowling	**Minor Counties bowling**
Bell 4/47, Quinn 165.	Barnes 1/19

Rochdale

At 56 years of age he continued his professional career at Rochdale. His two seasons (1929 and 1930) with the Central Lancashire League club brought him 203 wickets at an average of 7.32.

Rochdale bowling				
overs	maidens	runs	wickets	average
1929-367.5	100	755	114	6.62
1930-331.4	80	732	89	8.22

Rochdale batting:				
inns	not-out	runs	h/score	average
1929-16	4	265	56	22.08
1930-18	4	237	41	16.92

Staffordshire bowling:				
overs	maidens	runs	wickets	average
1929-291.4	83	565	68	8.30
1930-165.1	56	293	51	5.74

Staffordshire batting:				
inns	not-out	runs	h/score	average
1929-10	0	81	28	8.10
1930-10	2	252	63*	31.50

Rawtenstall

Barnes was on the move again in 1931 when he signed professional for Rawtenstall for three seasons at 58 years of age. Just the week before the signing he had taken 7 wickets for 20 runs for **Staffordshire** against Lancashire seconds.

In a match for Rawtenstall in June, 1931 he accomplished a splendid all-round feat which enabled his side to inflict on Haslingdon their first defeat of the season. The two clubs are less than two miles apart so the match was in the nature of a local derby. Barnes took 5 wickets for 20 runs and brought his season's total to 51 wickets for less than 5 runs each. Then he made 50 runs with the bat and gave Rawtenstall a 4 wicket victory.

In the same season Nelson's professional was the West Indian, Learie Constantine. A massive crowd was therefore guaranteed in the match against Nelson for the confrontation between Constantine and Barnes. The West Indian began with 96 not out in Nelson's 175 and he followed this with 4 for 34 as Rawtenstall were bowled out for 103. Barnes received a stern reprimand from the Committee for not getting his 7 wickets:

Pro, what exactly are we paying you for?"

Barnes was 57 years of age; Constantine was very much his junior at a mere 31 years of age!

Barnes did not otherwise disappoint, ending the season with 115 wickets at an average of 6.3, but Rawtenstall could only finish fourth in the League, ten points behind Nelson.

He had another great season in 1932 capturing more than 100 wickets (113).

Known as 'The Cricketing Marxist', Cyril Lionel Robert James (1901-1989) was one of the leading black intellectuals of the 20th century, a Marxist theorist of the first rank, and also one of the finest writers on cricket, with his legendary book 'Beyond a Boundary'. In 1932 he wrote an article about Barnes and the match between Rawtenstall and Nelson that year, including just one of the many encounters Barnes had with the dynamic all-round West Indian cricketer Learie Constantine, which attracted crowds in large numbers to watch:

"Sydney Barnes is generally admitted to be the greatest bowler cricket has yet seen. I had a glimpse of him the other day in action. He is 59 years-of-age, yet the man is still a fine bowler. It was an experience to watch him. To begin with, Barnes, not only is he fifty-nine, but looks it. Some cricketers at fifty-nine look and move like men in their fifties. Not so Barnes. You can almost hear the old bones creaking. He is tall and thin, well over six feet, with strong features. It is rather a

113

remarkable face in its way, and could belong to a great lawyer or a statesman without incongruity. He holds his head well back, with the rather long chin lifted. He looks like a man who has seen as much of the world as he wants to see.

I saw him first before the match began, bowling to one of his own side without wickets. He carried his arm over as straight as a post, spinning a leg-break in the orthodox way. Then he had a knock himself. But although the distance was only a dozen yards and the ball was being bowled at a very slow pace, Barnes put a glove on. He was not going to run the risk of those precious fingers being struck by the ball. When the preliminary practice stopped he walked in by himself, with his head in the air of a man intent on his own affairs.

His own side, Rawtenstall, took the field to get Nelson out. League sides will sometimes treat the new ball with Saturday afternoon carelessness. Not so Rawtenstall. Ten of them played about with an old ball. Barnes held the new. He fixed the field, two slips and the old fashioned point, close in. Mid-off was rather wide. When every man was placed to the nearest centimetre, Barnes walked back and set the old machinery in motion. As he forced himself to the crease you could see every year of the fifty-nine, but the arm swung over gallantly, high and straight. The wicket was slow, but a ball whipped hot from the pitch in the first over, and the second slip took a neat catch. When the over was finished he walked a certain number of steps and took up his position in the slips. He stood as straight as his right arm, with his hands behind his back. The bowler began his run – a long run – Barnes still immobile. Just as the ball was about to be delivered Barnes bent forward slightly with his hands ready in front of him. To go right down as a normal slip fieldsman goes, was for him, obviously, a physical impossibility. But he looked alert, but I got the impression that whatever went into his hands would stay there. As the ball reached the wicketkeeper's hands or was played by the batsman, Barnes straightened himself and again put his hands behind his back. That was his procedure in the field right through the afternoon. Now and then by way of variety, he would move a leg an inch or two, and point it on the toe for a second or two. Apart from that, he husbanded his strength.

He took 7 wickets for about 10 runs, and it is impossible to imagine better bowling of its kind. The batsmen opposed to him were not of high rank, most of them, but good bowling is good bowling, whoever plays it. Armistead, a sound batsman, was obviously on his mettle. Barnes kept him playing; then he bowled one of his most dangerous balls – a flighted one, dropping a foot shorter without any change of action and, what is much more dangerous, pitching on the middle wicket and missing the off. Armistead, magnetized into playing forward, had the good sense to keep his right toe firm. The wicketkeeper observed Armistead's toe regretfully, and threw the ball back to Barnes. Up to this time Armistead had relied almost entirely on the back stroke. It had carried him to where he was without mishap. A forward stroke had imperilled his innings. Behold, there the elements of a tragedy, obvious, no doubt, but as Mr. Desmond MacCarthy says, the obvious is the crowning glory of art. Armistead played back to the next ball but he couldn't get his bat to it in time. Barnes hit him hard on the pads with a straight ball, and the pads were in front of the wicket.

He went from triumph to triumph, aided no doubt, by the terror of his name. When Constantine came in I looked for a duel. Constantine was not going to be drawn into playing forward. Barnes was not going to bowl short to be hooked over the pavilion, or over-pitch to be hit into the football field. Constantine also was not going to chance it. For on that turning wicket, to such accurate bowling, who chanced it was lost.

Constantine jumped to him once, and a long fielder picked the ball up from the ground, where it had been from the time it left the bat. Barnes bowled a slow one, that might also be called short. It pitched on the leg stump. Constantine shaped for the forcing back stroke. The field was open. But even as he raised himself for the stroke he held his hand, and wisely. The ball popped up and turned many inches. Another ball or two, and again Barnes dropped another on the same spot. It was a sore temptation. Constantine shaped again for his stroke, his own stroke, and again he held his hand; wisely, for the ball broke and popped up again. So the pair watched one another, like two fencers sparring for an opening. The crowd sat tense. Was this recitative suddenly to burst into the melody of fours and sixes to all parts of the field? The Nelson crowd at least hoped so. But it was not to be. Some insignificant bowler at the other end who bowled mediocre balls, bowled Constantine with one of them.

After that it was a case of the boa constrictor and the rabbits, the only matter of interest being how long he would take to dispose of them. But, nevertheless, old campaigner as he is, Barnes took no chances. Slip would stand on the exact spot where the bowler wanted him, there and nowhere else. When a batsman who had once hit him for two or three fours came in, Barnes put two men out immediately. As soon as a single was made, the outfieldsmen were drawn in again and carefully fixed in their original positions, although the score might be about 50 for 8 or something of the kind. Barnes had lived long enough in the world of cricket to know that there at any rate it does not pay to give anything away. Nelson failed to reach 70. As the Rawtenstall team came in, the crowd applauded his fine bowling mightily. Barnes walked through it intent on his own affairs. He had had much of that all his life.

Constantine, running seventeen yards and hurling the ball violently through the air, began sending back the Rawtenstall batsmen. One, two, three wickets and bails flying every time. Forth from the pavilion came Barnes. He faced the West Indian fast bowler. He was older than Constantine's father and the wicket was faster now. Barnes got behind the ball, the ball pitched-up, and played it back along the pitch to the bowler. He judged the ball quickly and so got there in time. He kept his left shoulder forward and that kept the bat straight. He played the slower bowlers with equal skill, and whenever there was a single to be taken he took it. He never lost one, and he was in difficulties to get into his crease once only. "Yes" and "No" he said decisively in a deep voice which could be heard all over the ground. His bones were too stiff to force the ball away. But his bat swung true to the drive and he got over the short ball to cut. He stayed there for some 40 minutes for 10, and as long as he was there his side was winning. But Constantine bowled him behind his back. Barnes satisfied himself that he was out and then he left the crease. He came in slowly amidst the plaudits of the Nelson crowd, applauding his innings and their satisfaction at his having being dismissed. Courtesy acknowledged the applause. For the rest he continued as he had begun, a man unconsciously scornful of his milieu. After he left, Rawtenstall collapsed.

Since then, Barnes has taken 5 for a few and startled Lancashire a few days ago by taking 9 for 20. In the years to come, it will be something to say that we have seen him."

Sir Learie Constantine (1901-1971)

He played 18 Test matches for the West Indies before the First World War. A lawyer and politician, he served as Trinidad's High Commissioner to the United Kingdom and became the first black peer. He was Wisden's Cricketer of the Year in 1939. He became a life peer in 1969. He played for the Lancashire league club Nelson. In his final years he served on the Race Relations Board of the Sports Council and was on the Board of Governers at the BBC. He died suddenly of a heart attack on 1st July 1971.

Playing for **Staffordshire** in 1932 there was little or no falling off in Barnes' form. He had achieved another single figure average in a season on mostly hard wickets. He finished the season by taking 32 wickets for 196 runs in the last three matches. His overall total for the season was 56. The 1933 season was beginning to show a decline in his bowling but there were still some notable performances. From the middle of July onwards he did not play again that season because of his knee injury. The games he did play, his overall figures were 108 overs, 222 runs, 7 wickets. Though he failed to take many wickets, compliments were voiced on how the batsmen, who had to face him, were always struggling for runs. He actually bowled 32 maidens in his 108 overs. Sir Len Hutton faced him when he played for Yorkshire Colts against Staffordshire. He recalled that early in his innings he padded off a good length ball from Barnes pitching just outside the off-stump. Barnes, he said, shouted down the wicket in a stern voice:

"If you do that again I shall appeal."

Hutton referred to Barnes as 'perhaps the greatest bowler of all time'.

His last season with Rawtenstall in 1933 was a little disappointing because he had only taken 54 wickets, well below his best. Some thought that because there was very little rain during the season the ground was 'rock hard' and perfect for the batsmen but no help for the bowler. Some thought his form was declining and that he was no longer able to defy the hard true wickets as he once could. There was some truth in this but also a known fact that Barnes was now well into his 60s and also nursing a knee injury which kept him out of the game for almost half the season.

Rawtenstall bowling				
overs	maidens	runs	wickets	average
1931-333.4	94	725	115	6.30

1932-440.3	159	819	113	7.25
1933-275.2	62	741	54	13.72

Rawtenstall batting				
inns	not-out	runs	h/score	average
1931-20	4	338	52*	21.12
1932-22	3	229	30	12.05
1933-15	0	204	35	13.06

Staffordshire bowling				
overs	maidens	runs	wickets	average
1931-241.5	77	523	61	8.57
1932-268.3	76	505	56	9.01
1933-108	31	222	7	31.71

Staffordshire batting				
inns	not-out	runs	h/score	average
1931-13	1	145	26	12.08
1932-10	0	133	43	13.30
1933-7	2	112	46	22.40

The Manchester Cricket Club engaged Barnes to act as bowling Instructor (coach) for the first six weeks of the 1933 season

Keighley

Barnes returned to the Bradford League in 1934 as professional to the Keighley club. He bowled with his usual accuracy but not quite his old effectiveness. However, when there was a break in the long spell of dry weather he proved himself again by finishing the season with a fine haul of wickets. In one particular match against a very strong Bingley side, winners of the League and the Priestley Cup, he took 8 wickets for 9 runs. From other matches worth mentioning was his 6 for 13 against Keighley, and the 7 for 29 in the return, whilst at a Cup-tie at Bingley his analysis showed 5 for 38. A total of 86 wickets for the season was his answer to those who thought he had lost his effectiveness as a bowler.

So far as **Staffordshire** was concerned, the sad story of 1933 was repeated in 1934 and for the first time in his professional career Barnes was dropped because of lack of form.

Keighley bowling:				
overs	maidens	runs	wickets	average
1934-413.4	122	891	8	10.36

Keighley batting:				
inns	not-out	runs	h/score	average
1934-15	6	208	33*	23.11

Staffordshire bowling:				
overs	maidens	runs	wickets	average
1934-56	17	113	3	37.66

Staffordshire batting:				
inns	not-out	runs	h/score	average
1934-4	0	1	1	00.25

Smethwick

After an absence of 40 years he returned for the 1935 season to his first club, Smethwick, who engaged him as professional to play in the Birmingham League. When fees were being negotiated he felt, even at 62 years of age, he was worth more than Smethwick said they could afford to pay him. Barnes was confident that his reappearance for his old club would bring in the crowds to watch him play. They eventually agreed that after all expenses had been deducted from the club's share of the gate money, the remainder should be shared equally between the club and Barnes. This was in addition to what he would receive as a fee. His popularity did increase gate receipts to such an extent it covered the extra amount paid in wages demanded by him, and also gave the club a fair share of the income.

It was half-way through the 1935 season and in a match against Walsall, the Birmingham League leaders, his bowling, capturing 6 Walsall wickets for 30 runs, took his total for the season to 52 at a low average of 5.25 runs. This was the best average of any bowler at any time then in the Birmingham League. It was said that the wickets during that season had been entirely in favour of the batsmen. When the circumstances are considered together with the fact that Barnes was now aged 62, his achievements in 1935 constituted one of the wonders of the game. The season ended with him being top of the bowling league averages with 75 wickets for 8.65 runs.

The Stafford Cricket Club, at the start of the 1935 season, had also secured the services of Barnes. Over his latter years he now had a reputation as an excellent coach in which capacity he had been engaged at the Old Trafford ground and at the Denston and Marlborough Colleges.

The 1935 season was finally his last for **Staffordshire**. He had reached that age where he now realised that playing for his beloved county it was time for him to call it a day. But not before adding a further 9 wickets to his impressive career total. In 22 seasons with Staffordshire he had taken 1,441 wickets at a cost of 8.15 runs a wicket.

In 1936 he did play one more season with Smethwick. It was very wet and this could have been the reason for him taking fewer wickets. Just 38 wickets for 438 runs at an average of 11.52. Smethwick only won three matches and finished a poor eighth in the league.

Smethwick bowling:				
overs	maidens	runs	wickets	average
1935-298	86	649	75	8.65
1936-174	37	438	38	11.52

Lytham St Annes

In 1937, and at 64 years of age, it was remarkable that he was still able to earn his professional status, this time for the St Annes club playing in the Ribblesdale League. Barnes had proved to be a Box Office draw where the gates were £15 a match in comparison to gates of less than £5 for many seasons past. He served them well too and at his age showing no sign of weakness.

Lytham St Annes bowling:				
overs	maidens	runs	wickets	average
1937-516.2	69	761	61	12.47

Bridgnorth

At 66 years of age Barnes was still taking wickets in 1938. In 18 games playing for the Shropshire club Bridgnorth, he took 126 wickets at an average of 6.94 runs. His stamina was considered remarkable. He had played every day in one week and on two of the days bowled unchanged. Barnes was in good shape physically. It is a fact nobody in advancing years in any action-packed sport can go on playing forever and Barnes was aware of this, especially as a professional, and took the greatest possible care of himself. He was no longer committed to county cricket bowling day after day, six days a week and was now able to rest during the winter months. However, he was playing regularly enough to avoid stiffening up which he thought might cause a strain, putting paid to his professional career for good.

An interesting story playing for Bridgnorth against Ludlow. Bridgnorth batted first. At the tea interval Bridgnorth declared and Barnes had made 55 not out. The captain said to Barnes:

"Syd, you won't be fit to open the bowling."

Barnes replied:

"Well if you don't put me on straight away it will be no use putting me on later, I'll be too stiff."

Unbelievably, the magic of Barnes, he opened the bowling, bowled unchanged throughout the innings, and took 7 wickets.

He was now going through a ritual before a match, rubbing himself down with a strong smelling embrocation much to the annoyance of some of the players in the dressing room who didn't like the smell. After a game, the first thing he did after bowling was to have a rub-down and put on a clean dry shirt. There were times when he had various forms of support at his disposal for joints and muscles. Some fellow players commented that before a match he would tie a string across two corners of the dressing room and hang his various bandages, like washing on the line, some for bowling and some for batting.

Bridgnorth bowling:				
overs	maidens	runs	wickets	average
1938-336	77	875	126	6.94

Stone

The year 1939 was the outbreak of the Second World War and the first season since 1895 that Barnes did not have a professional contract. It was in 1940 that the Stone Cricket Club, playing in the North Staffordshire and South Cheshire League, persuaded him to coach at the club and to play a few games. As well as coaching at the club he was in a similar capacity coaching the boys at the Alleyness Grammar School, Stone. The fee must have been attractive and worth the effort and pain for a 67 year old Barnes. He turned out for Stone in 17 matches and was called on to bowl in 12. He took 28 wickets in the season at 8.28 each, which included his final wicket in league cricket taking his grand total to 6,229 wickets as a professional cricketer.

Stone batting:				
overs	maidens	runs	wickets	average
1940-76.4	10	232	28	8.28

His last professional engagement was at 69 when he was cricket coach at the Harrison Colliery, Little Wyrley, Staffordshire.

"Staffordshire had not really had a great deal of success in minor county cricket until the name of Sydney Barnes was associated. And that changed Staffordshire's importance as well. His performances with the ball meant that Staffordshire started to become quite a good side. And very, very early on he was actually the main instigator in them winning the Minor Counties Championship three years in succession."

Tim Fielding, Secretary, Sydney Barnes Society.

1913-1947

The Welsh Pretender

From 1923 to 1930 Wales played 16 first-class matches, and had some success against touring teams, drawing with the New Zealanders in 1927 and beating the West Indies a year later. In 1929 they played the South Africans and only lost by 10 runs. Barnes, by this time well into his fifties, took 49 first-class wickets for Wales, including 7–51 in the victory over the West Indies.

Sydney Francis Barnes' worldwide fame had been won by his successful bowling in Test matches for England. His last match for England was against South Africa in the fourth Test at Durban in 1914 at the age of 41. But his wonderful international record did not end there! The genius ended up playing in first-class matches for Wales.

It was 13 years later, in September 1927 at the age of 54, did he play his first full international match for Wales against New Zealand at The Oval, Llandudno. Other games for Wales followed against the West Indies (1928), MCC (1927, 1929, 1930), Lancashire (1928), Sussex (1929) and Minor Counties (1930). He also played representative matches for North Wales against South Wales (1923, 1927), South Africa (1924, 1929),

Lancashire (1924, 1925, 1926, 1928), and a specially selected Empire XI (1942). He did play for Denbighshire against Staffordshire in August 1930 and again in 1931.

It was on the 20th August 1930 at the famous Lord's ground at St John's Wood, London that Barnes made his last appearance in first-class cricket, and it was for Wales against the MCC at the grand old age of 57.

There had been speculation in those days how it was that he qualified to play for Wales. The answer was simple. He had a residential qualification as he had been living in Colwyn Bay for more than two years. The 1911 Census Records shows that he was living at Wolstanton, Staffordshire at the time with wife Alice and son Leslie. In the 1914 Trade and Street Directory, seen at the Colwyn Bay library, 'S.Barnes' and family is listed as living at Cayton House, Pendorlan Avenue, Colwyn Bay. Further records show that in 1923 he moved to a newly built property at Glanfryn, Colwyn Crescent, Rhos-on-Sea.

Glanfryn, 19 Colwyn Avenue, Rhos on Sea

THE LEGENDARY CRICKET GENIUS SYDNEY F. BARNES

While living in Colwyn Bay he travelled each weekend to play in the Lancashire League and up to 1929 in Minor Counties matches for Staffordshire. It was in early 1930 that he moved back to live in Staffordshire.

The earliest recollection of Barnes and his involvement in a cricket match in North Wales, and especially in the Colwyn Bay area, was discovered by research undergone by Dave Parry (Colwyn Bay CC) and Dr Andrew Hignell (Glamorgan). It was Andrew who had discovered and obtained an old 1913 postcard with a photograph of a cricket team and had recognised one of the players to be Sydney Barnes and a suspicion the photo had been taken somewhere in the Colwyn Bay area. He immediately got in touch with Dave and between them they were able to confirm the date of the image and also to clarify that the picture had been taken in Colwyn Bay. In fact the high wall in the background and the distinctive roof in the distance was soon recognised by Dave that the picture was taken in the grounds of the Rydal Penrhos Public School, known in those days as Rydal Mount. Following this, Dave visited the Conwy County Local Authority Archives Department in Llandudno to check the records of the local newspaper (The North Wales Weekly News). If there was a reference to Barnes the cricketer it would be there. Sure enough he found that on 25th September, 1913 he did play in a fundraising match at Rydal Mount. The game had been organised to raise money for a local hospital charity and was thought his involvement might well have been that his move to North Wales was to do with his wife's well-being, although no mention has been found that she was in ill-health.

This charity match was well reported because Barnes was taking part and it was known everywhere then that he was a world famous cricketer:

128

Colwyn Bay Pierrots v Colwyn Bay CC
World famous cricketer playing at Colwyn Bay

Great excitement was aroused in cricket circles in Colwyn Bay when it became known that Sydney Barnes, the well-known Staffordshire cricketer, had been engaged to play in the match organised on behalf of the local Cottage Hospital between Colwyn Bay Pierrots and the Colwyn Bay Cricket Club which took place on Wednesday 21st September, 1927.

Barnes was now generally acknowledged to be the world's most formidable bowler and his performances with the English XI stamped him as one of the greatest with the ball ever seen in first-class cricket.

The match took place on the Rydal Mount School ground, by kind permission of the Headmaster Mr G.F.A.Osborn, together with Councillor W.E.Purdy, who had taken an active part in organising the match. They both acted as umpires. Barnes played with Pierrots, who won the toss and batted first.

The recent rain had rendered the wicket heavy and difficult to play on, but the champion bowler knocked up a fine score of 84 not out, followed by a bowling display reported as being 'wonderful' with all the wickets falling to him.

There was a good attendance present and a substantial sum was raised for the Cottage Hospital fund. The final result was Pierrots 124, Colwyn Bay 83.

Pierrots		Colwyn Bay	
Jackson Browne b Large	9	T.W.Ashcroft b Barnes	11
E.Frere lbw b Large	7	Codling c Frere b Barnes	4
Greenwood lbw b Large	0	J.Hammersley c Sutton b Barnes	0
Sydney Barnes not out	84	Rev J.Williams b Barnes	17
Cordingley run out	6	R.C.Wrinch b Barnes	6
Percy Graham st. Anderson b Ashcroft	1	J.Large b Barnes	0
S.Frere b Ashcroft	2	A.S.Bradburn b Barnes	19
Bert Dicken b Hammersley	3	W.P.Lucas b Barnes	0
Gulliver b Ashcroft	2	A..Fleet b Barnes	4
Sutton c Fleet b Hammersley	1	W.Clutton b Barnes	16
Norman lbw b Hammersley	0	L.A.R.Riley c Browne b Barnes	0
H.S.H.Anderson not out	0		
Extras	9	Extras	6
Total (10 wickets all out)	**123**	**Total (11 wickets all out)**	**83**

Colwyn Bay Bowling	Pierrots Bowling
Large 3 wickets, Ashcroft 3 wickets, Hammersley 3 wickets.	Barnes 11 wickets

Pierrots won by 41 runs

Dave Parry further researched if Barnes had ever played for the Colwyn Bay Cricket Club. When he was living at 'Glanfryn' it was only a three-minute walk to the cricket ground. Sadly only one score-book from before the Second World War survives in the archives at the Colwyn Bay club. A report of a match in 1924 against Ruthin shows S. Barnes batting at number 6 scoring 3 runs. As was the practice at that time, the newspaper did not report bowling figures but if he did bowl it is assumed he failed to take a wicket. Co-incidentally, the report of this match happened to be on the same page as the detail of the transfer of the licensee of the Royal Hotel, which had been held by Barnes. Dave asks the question did Barnes play in the match as an amateur, "warming up" before taking up his position as Castleton Moor's professional? More than likely. Two weeks later, though, on 17th May, the Colwyn Bay team that played at home against Denbigh included F.(L).Barnes who batted at number 9 and scored 4 runs. This was the day before his son Leslie's 20th birthday. It is possible that the newspaper had printed an incorrect initial for Barnes. In Andrew's book "The Skipper: a Biography of Wilf Wooller" he wrote that Barnes spent many long hours at the nets at the Colwyn Bay club but there is no record of him ever being an official member of the club. Dave was able to confirm that the only reference to him in any of the surviving club archives is in the minutes of the committee meeting of 27th April, 1925 as follows:

"Letter read from S.Barnes asking for hire of the Billiard Room for the celebration of his son's 21st birthday. Proposed by Mr Lowe and seconded by Mr Pilsbury."

The committee decided that it was not considered to be in the best interest of the members to allow any portion of the club to be used for private functions. The secretary was instructed to inform Barnes of the decision.

Colwyn Bay Cricket Club

The club was founded in 1923 and started playing at its new Penrhyn Avenue ground at Rhos-on-Sea in 1924. For many years it has been recognised and assessed as the best ground in North Wales. It has staged a series of very lucrative cricket weeks for more than eighty years. Since the 1920s, the club has hosted annual festival matches, involving the MCC and touring teams, as well as Denbighshire's games in the Minor County Championship during the 1930s, plus other exhibition games against invitation sides drawn from the highly successful Lancashire Leagues.

The chance of seeing some of the top names in the cricket world greatly appealed to the rapidly expanding population living in the resort towns dotted along the North Wales coast, and between 1940 and 1944, the Colwyn Bay club staged a number of fundraising games for the War Effort.

Wilf Wooller, the highly influential captain of Glamorgan, knew only too well about the fervent support for cricket on the North Wales coast having lived close to the ground and happily playing there since his early teens when he was a pupil at Rydal School. His father had also helped to lay out the ground, so it was no surprise that Wilf, after taking over the Glamorgan captaincy in 1947, brought the county side to Colwyn Bay to play in the annual festivals held there. Ever since the mid-1960s, Glamorgan have staged an annual match in North Wales at the well-appointed Colwyn Bay ground, attracting thousands of spectators. History was made there in 2000, when Steve James scored Glamorgan's first-ever triple hundred, 309 not out against Sussex. History was made again in 2016, when Aneurin Donald equalled the world record for the fastest double-century in first-class cricket. The teenager's efforts from just 123 balls matched Ravi Shastri's record, besides becoming the youngest double-centurion in Glamorgan's history.

Colwyn Bay is a town, community and seaside resort in the Conwy County Borough on the north coast of Wales overlooking the Irish Sea.

Another very interesting connection with the Colwyn Bay club at the time was how disappointed Barnes must have been that his only son, Leslie, failed to take the game seriously. He and Harold Edge, the Colwyn Bay professional, often took Barnes Junior to the nets for practice and coaching, during the playing season, usually before breakfast. How both father and son were able to use the facilities at the club and not be members, which in those days was strictly for members only, beggars belief. Also there is evidence to suggest that they both played at least one game for a club team. All the effort Dad put into encouraging his son to become a serious cricketer made no difference. It failed. The youth's ambition was to become an engineer.

Dave Parry has been scorer and historian for the Colwyn Bay CC for 41 years. Retired school teacher at both Eirias High School, Colwyn Bay and the Penrhos Rydal Public School. A Member of the Association of Cricket Statisticians and Historians.

Dr Andrew Hignell is scorer and historian of Glamorgan County Cricket Club. He has supported Glamorgan Cricket since the early 1970s and was appointed the Club's Statistician in 1982 and since 2004 has been their 1st XI scorer. Andrew has a doctorate in geography and taught for eighteen years before becoming Glamorgan's scorer. He has written more than a dozen books on cricket. He is the Secretary of the Association of Cricket Statisticians and Historians.

North Wales XI v South Wales (Glamorgan)

It was in 1922 that the movement to establish a North Wales Cricket Association had been successful and to celebrate the occasion, the Association arranged a match between a North Wales XI and South Wales (Glamorgan) during a special cricket week at The Oval, Llandudno on 23/24 May, 1923. Upon hearing that Barnes was legitimately available for selection he was chosen to play in this match for North Wales, which was his very first representative game for Wales.

North Wales won the toss and decided to bat. The South Wales side won the match by 6 wickets. Barnes took 8 wickets for 83 runs.

North Wales first innings		North Wales second innings	
C.A.Rowland c Bates b Rowland	13	lbw b Mercer	6
E.N.Ray lbw b Mercer	12	b Mercer	0
I.Pell b Harrison	4	lbw b Bates	9
S.F.Barnes c Davies b Bates	17	b Abel	5
C.P.Woods b Harrison	0	b Bates	52
G.A.Erlebach c Whittington b Mercer	4	b Davies	1
C.D.Yonge c Morgan b Bates	14	c Mercer b Davies	5
D.C.Rosser b Bates	0	c Mercer b Bates	7
C.D.Hutchinson c Bates b Mercer	3	c and b Mercer	0
Orton not out	0	b Abel	6
Clutton st Sullivan b Mercer	0	not out	1
Extras (2 lb, 1nb)	3	(1 lb, 1 w)	2
Total (all out, 47 overs)	70		94

South Wales bowling
first innings
Mercer 5/20, Abel 0/8, Harrison 2/25, Davies 0/2, Bates 3/12
second innings
Mercer 3/28, Abel 2/27, Bates 3/18, Davies 2/19

South Wales first innings		South Wales second innings	
T.R.Morgan lbw b Barnes	9	not out	5
T.B.Williams lbw b Clutton	4	lbw b Clutton w	13
W.E.Bates c Rosser b Barnes	10	lbw b Clutton	0
T.E.Abel b Barnes	39	lbw b Barnes	0
E.C.Francis b Barnes	1	did not bat	
G.B.Harrison c Hutchinson b Clutton	1	did not bat	
T.A.L.Whittington lbw b Barnes	1	did not bat	
G.E.Cording b Orton	3	did not bat	
D.Sullivan not out	2	did not bat	

W.H.Davies b Barnes	12	b Barnes	18
Extras (22 b, 1 lb)	23	Extras (2 b)	2
Total (all out, 51.2 overs)	127	(4 wickets , 14. overs)	38

North Wales bowling
first innings
Barnes 6/57, Clutton 2/23, Pell 0/5, Orton 1/19
second innings
Barnes 2/26, Clutton 2/10

The Oval, Llandudno

There was no doubt, in 1924, the Oval at Llandudno was rightly chosen to play the North versus South game because it was the most attractive, well-kept ground in North Wales and therefore more than adequate for staging first-class matches. A well-prepared hallowed turf that was and still is in pristine condition, with the blessing of a natural drainage system due to a light sandy based soil. An idyllic spot in pleasant surroundings with a panoramic view of a rural setting in the background, situated next to the Great Orme mountainside and just a stone's throw away from the centre of the sea-side town (in Victorian times it was called the Queen of the Welsh resorts), the Irish Sea and the beautiful Conwy Estuary. An ideal spot at a time when determined efforts were being made, soon after the war years, to revive cricket in North Wales and to introduce first-class cricket to the area.

North Wales Select XI v South Africa

This was scheduled as a two-day match (8/9 September 1924) played at The Oval, Llandudno. Barnes was given the opportunity to play against this South African touring side when it was considered by many that he should have been included in the England side to meet the South Africans during the summer months that year. An interesting 'Letter to the Editor' appeared in a local newspaper which summed up the feelings and probable reasons for him not to have been included in the England side:

"I read a suggestion the other day that Sydney Barnes who is to play for Staffordshire this year, may be "resurrected" for the Test matches in South Africa. I may be wrong but I fancy the writer was either hard-pressed for a subject or he knows nothing of the position. Barnes, it is said, showed hardly any falling-off in form last year, possibly not. I think it is extremely likely that were he to re-appear in first-class cricket next summer he would surely match the best of them on the field of play. Yet there is a variety of reasons why he is not likely to be included in a Test team. The selectors are looking out for the young ones; they have the Australians in view, and until they have proved themselves the South Africans will be regarded as providing the opportunity for experiments. Yet another argument against the inclusion of Barnes is that he is not in favour with the selectors who have fairly long memories. One way or another, it may be said, that it

THE LEGENDARY CRICKET GENIUS SYDNEY F. BARNES

will be a miracle indeed if Sydney Barnes appears for England in the coming Test Matches."

The outcome of the five Test matches (without Barnes) between England and South Africa were:

1st Test won England, Edgbaston, Birmingham 14/17 June
2nd Test won England, Lords, London 28/30 June
3rd Test won England, Headingley, Leeds 10/15 July
4th Test drawn Old Trafford, Manchester 26/29 July
5th Test drawn The Oval, London 16/18 August

However, the 51 year-old 'youngster' was available to meet the South Africans at the end of their tour when they arrived in Llandudno a few days before the game to play against a North Wales XI. At 51 years of age it was said this was the heyday of his career and he was still a long way from retiring. It was true that his appearances in first-class matches were few and far between, but as time went by, occasionally some innocent touring side and especially on the 'Green, Green Grass of Home' (tell that to Tom Jones!) would still feel the great strength of his bowling arm. The South Africans made their headquarters at the Imperial Hotel, five minutes from the ground. The Llandudno Cricket Club was very proud to host this match as it coincided with the opening of a new pavilion. There was a Civic Reception when the Chairman of the Council formally welcomed the 17-strong party to Llandudno. The following day both teams (including Barnes), and invited guests, were entertained to a luncheon by the President of the North Wales Cricket Association at the Imperial Hotel, Llandudno. The North Wales team also included Albert Thomas (Northants and Wales) and E.Bateson (Eaton College cricket captain).

The match was spoilt by the weather. Scheduled as a two-day game there was no play on the second day. The rain, which had fallen in torrents the night before, had soaked the pitch so badly that play was out of the question until mid-afternoon and even then sawdust had to be used to enable the bowlers to obtain a foothold. Unfortunately, rain fell heavily the next day and saturated the wicket completely which made play quite out of the question. At first the preparation of a new wicket would permit play after lunch but a further heavy downpour at noon dispelled the hope of any play and the match was abandoned. The large crowd that had come to see the match, when it did eventually start, were well entertained by both sides. North Wales completed their innings and the South Africans with 7 wickets down were 62 runs ahead before the rain stopped play. The Welsh supporters were delighted to have witnessed the genius bowling of Barnes, in such wet conditions, who had taken 5 of the South African's 7 wickets.

North Wales		South Africa	
D.Boumphrey c Meintjes b Carter	9	M.M.Commaille b Barnes	2
F.Moston b Pegler	0	T.A.Ward c W.H.Rowland b Barnes	2
A.E.Mallallieu c Ward b Pegler	4	M.J.Susskind c Clutton b Barnes	0
S.F.Barnes c Hearne b Blackenberg	1	A.W.Nourse c Bounphrey b Barnes	15
C.A.Rowland c and b Blackenbourg	2	R.H.Catterall b Pell	18
A.E.Thomas b Blackenbourg	10	G.A.L.Hearne c Edge b Barnes	13
H.E.Edge b Blackenbourg	2	E.P.Nupen b Edge	5
W.H.Rowland c Nupen b Blackenbourg	0	DJ.Meintjes not out	5
W.Clutton b Pegler	1		
D.M.Bateson not out	2		
Extras (3 b, 2 lb)	5	Extras (18 b, 6lb)	24
Total (all out, 44.3 overs)	49	Total (7 wickets, 42 overs)	111

South Africa Bowling	North Wales Bowling
Blackenbourg 6/12	Barnes 5/32

It was a shame that the weather should have spoilt this match. There was no doubt, given good weather, the match had been anticipated by cricket fans to be a great attraction. With Barnes playing against the tourists it was adding spice to the game. Surprisingly the South Africans had let it be known that they were looking forward to meeting the England bowler and especially if the weather was good. There was no need to remind them that Barnes had taken 7 wickets for 109 in the first innings and 9 for 103 in their second innings in the 1913-14 England tour of South Africa in the second Test at Johannesburg. The groundsman at the Llandudno club was certain that the wicket would suit the tourists better than any they had played on that season, as it was naturally a batsman's wicket. However, even on wet, soggy ground Barnes certainly had the better of them once again. If the match had not been abandoned goodness knows what his final figures might have been.

GRAND CRICKET MATCH

8th and 9th September, 1924

SOUTH AFRICA
V
NORTH WALES

Gloddaeth Avenue Ground,
Llandudno
Wickets pitched at 11am each day

**Messrs Sydney Barnes (All England)
will play for North Wales**

**Admission to ground 2s 4d (including tax)
Enclosure 3s 6d (including tax)
Boys under 14 1/- (incl. Tax)
For Railway facilities see Railway companies
Special Announcement**

Following this match an article appeared in the North Wales Weekly News entitled 'The Method of Barnes'. The writer recollects when Barnes was in the England Test side led by A.C.MacLaren and later went to South Africa with the England team and carried all before him. He goes on to write that he is certainly one of the greatest bowlers the world has known and that only occasionally great stars appear on the cricketing stage and mentions W.G.Grace, " Ranji" and A.C.MacLaren as examples of great players. They dominated the cricketing grounds of England and Australia in the nineties and that Hobbs and Barnes are the cricket celebrities who have soared in the public eye above the rest now. As thousands of Llandudno, Conwy and Colwyn Bay people went to see Barnes at Llandudno perhaps a description of his method may be interesting from the writer, who has had the experience and often faced the music of his attack before thousands of spectators in Lancashire League matches and who on occasion at least managed to score 42 not out off him during an hour and a half's innings, which was a fair test of his bowling.

"The secret of Barnes' successful bowling was in the variety of his attack. He delivers a different ball with each of the six balls of the over. The first ball may be a leg-break, the second an off-break, the third a yorker, the fourth a straight

141

one, the fifth he swerves the ball and the last a half volley. Barnes keeps you on the look-out for all these different balls. Hence, it is through this method he took the wickets in South Africa and at Llandudno of South Africa's greatest batsmen. In my cricketing days I faced great English County players like Ted Peete (England and Yorkshire), Robert Peel (Yorkshire), Frank Shacklock (Nottinghamshire), Doug Wright (Kent), John Crossland (Lancashire) and others, and found that Barnes is the best bowler the world has ever known and that this opinion is also confirmed by the great Australian elevens as well as England's greatest batsmen of the day."

North Wales v Lancashire 1924

This was an end of season two-day match played at The Oval, Llandudno on 17/18 September, 1924. After heavy rain and gale force winds the day before the match, the surprise was that it did commence almost at the advertised time. This was due to the fact there was bright sunshine and a high wind which followed, quickly drying the wicket and outfield. Barnes played for North Wales against a team that had finished fourth in the County Championship in Lancashire's Golden Jubilee season. (In the Roses match Yorkshire were humiliated when requiring only 57 runs to win they were bowled out for 33 runs.) With Barnes in opposition, North Wales were hoping for a good result. The Welsh won the toss and decided to bat. In a low scoring game Lancashire won by 4 wickets. In reply to North Wales' score of 72 (Barnes 3), Lancashire hardly stood up to Barnes' bowling, managed just 82 with his figures being 6 wickets for 51 runs. For Lancashire, Ernest Tyldesley, the All-England Test player, was greeted with applause when going out to bat only to be clean bowled by Barnes when he had only scored 5. In the second innings North Wales totalled

70 (Barnes a duck!). Lancashire batted on after winning the match and scored 125 for 9. Barnes took just 1/29.

Barnes was living in Wales at the time when he added another achievement for the record books in July 1925. He took all 10 wickets for 24 runs for Castleton Moor against Harewood.

North Wales v Lancashire 1925

In the last big cricket match of the season at The Oval, Llandudno, a North Wales XI played Lancashire in a two-day match on 14/15 September, 1925. The North Wales team was specially selected by Mr G.E. Rowland (President of the North Wales Cricket Association), who purposely chose a mixture of youth and experience including Barnes at 52 years of age with the objective to foster the game widely in Wales. The attendances on both days were said to be 'very encouraging'. Lancashire won the toss and elected to bat first and were skittled out for 160 on a good batting wicket. Barnes triumphed taking 7 wickets for 76 runs. He captured another 4 wickets in the second innings. Lancashire scored 129, which was not enough. North Wales won by 2 wickets, scoring 151 for 8.

Wales v MCC 1926

Barnes had been selected to play his first game for Wales in June 1926 after a long absence from first-class cricket. His last appearance had been playing for the Players against the Gentlemen in 1914 when he took 8 for 144. The disappointment was that he was unable to play for Wales in this match owing to dental trouble. In the end the game turned out to be a disappointment because rain had prevented any play on the

1st and 2nd days. The crowds especially were disappointed that Barnes was not playing. The match ended in a draw – Wales 179, MCC 114 for 6.

North Wales v Lancashire 1926

This 3-day match staged on 1/2/3 September, 1926 was a great success for the newly formed Colwyn Bay club. The occasion was a happy one all round as Lancashire had the day before won the County Championship by beating Nottinghamshire after one of the keenest struggles in the history of the competition at the time. This was certainly a proud day for members of the club. The new ground at Penrhyn Avenue, Rhos-on-Sea was staging first-class cricket for the first time. Quite a feat considering the club and ground was only formed two years previously in 1924. Since then and over many years Colwyn Bay have hosted over 30 first-class games and numerous List A matches as well as several matches in the Minor Counties Championship. The ground was first used by Glamorgan in 1966, and since 1990 they have staged a County Championship match annually, attracting big crowds.

Colwyn Bay field three teams in the Liverpool and District Cricket Competition.

Barnes played for North Wales and another attraction was that of A.W.Carr, the England captain at the time, who also played for Lancashire. Despite the dull weather there was a record crowd on the ground after lunch and they witnessed some keen cricket.

Lancs batted first and scored 189. Barnes took 4 for 47. The presence of Carr in the Lancashire side added interest to the game and his batting on the third day afforded pleasure to the spectators. Sydney Barnes, in his long career, had probably never before been hit out of a cricket ground twice in successful balls as he was by Carr. It was noticed though that Carr was most subdued after lunch. Barnes and Jagger had him tide up in a knot on more than one occasion. Rain did delay play on the second day. In the two innings Carr scored 25 and 68 not out. Barnes took 2 for 53 in the second innings. Match was drawn. Lancashire 189 and 157 for 8. North Wales 212 and 52 for 2.

It was in January 1927 that Barnes let it be known, by arrangement, that he would be available during the forthcoming cricket season to tour North Wales clubs with a view to coaching existing talent and to also find new and promising players. In addition he would be able to advise clubs how their grounds could be improved.

MCC v Wales 1927

Barnes made two appearances for Wales in 1927, the first against the MCC at Lord's on 1/2/3 June. The MCC won the toss and chose to bat first. They totalled 450 and Barnes bowled no fewer than 45 overs, 19 of them maidens but took only 2 wickets which cost him 85 runs. It was said he bowled with much skill and was repeatedly unlucky in missing the stumps after beating the bat. It was considered a remarkable performance by him at 54 years of age. He took 1/19 in the second innings. MCC won the match by 7 wickets.

Wales v New Zealand 1927

The New Zealand cricket team toured England in the 1927 season. The team contained many of the players who would later play Test cricket for New Zealand. It was at the time when New Zealand were seeking Test match status and when only England, Australia and South Africa could select representative teams to take part in Test matches. However, they did play 16

145

first-class matches against English counties with five won and four lost. Perhaps the most exciting game was the drawn match against Surrey at The Oval, London. New Zealand scored 313 and Surrey responded with 377 in the first innings. New Zealand in their second innings made a rapid 371. Surrey were within 24 runs of winning this 3-day match before time ran out and the match ended in a draw. Other first-class matches arranged for the New Zealanders included the usual touring side games against university sides and the end-of-season festival cricket up and down the country. There were also first-class matches against the Royal Navy, the Army, the Civil Service and Wales.

It was against Wales that the tourists soon discovered that Barnes was still not past it. They met at The Oval, Llandudno in a 3-day match (2/4/5 September) in a special cricket week festival.

There was a lot of excitement amongst the cricket followers in North Wales and especially in Llandudno when the New Zealand party arrived in the town. It had been decided by the local Town Council they would not only give a civic welcome to the New Zealanders and the Welsh team (including Barnes) but to entertain them to a dinner at the Imperial Hotel. The local dignitaries that were present at the dinner included Lord Llewelyn Lloyd Mostyn (founder of the North Wales Cricket Association in 1922) and G.E. Rowland (President of the Welsh Cricket Union). The tables had been decorated with fern leaves as a reference to the New Zealand National Emblem. The Chairman of the Council, Mr Lincoln Evans J.P., welcomed the guests. He said that on behalf of the local authority and the people of Llandudno it gave him great pleasure to welcome to Llandudno such distinguished players and officials to the town. He hoped that during their stay they would make full use of the excursions that had been arranged for them to see and enjoy a part of Wales renowned for its beautiful rural scenery. Turning directly to the New Zealand players, he said:

"When you arrived in the UK you had no brass bands to meet you. You came in quietly to play cricket and not much was expected of you. It was pleasing to hear that you confounded your critics by beating a number of good English county sides. I forecast that in the near future you will be pitted against other cricketing countries in official Test matches."

He then welcomed the Welsh players and said that everyone in North Wales was very proud of what Glamorgan had done for the game of cricket in Wales. He concluded by saying it was an honour to welcome both teams and officials to the town and hoped the match between the two sides would be a great success.

G.E. Rowland responded to some criticism that had been made concerning Barnes appearing in the Welsh side. He said that he had been resident in the Colwyn Bay/ Llandudno area for over 20 years and under MCC rules was sufficiently qualified to play for either country.

Lord Mostyn followed with a speech which included praise for the hard work G.E.Rowland had done, who had been the leading factor in developing Welsh cricket and to Glamorgan who had also led the way.

Fine weather favoured the match. Wales won the toss and batted first scoring 182. The chief interest lay in the meeting of the tourists and Barnes. When Barnes was taken off before the close of play on the first day he had bowled 10 overs for 7 runs and taken 2 wickets. Each ball was watched in silence and time after time the batsmen were beaten. On one occasion from a ball Barnes sent down, Lowry might have been stumped, but wicket keeper Sullivan was evidently under the impression that the ball would hit the wicket. As he threw up his arms the ball flew past him and went for 4 byes. New Zealand's innings closed at 130 and Barnes had taken 4/47. Wales' score of 182, considering the state of the wicket, was a respectable total. In their second innings the home team scored 183 for 9 declared. New Zealand's second innings commenced on the third day. The spectators were treated to a keen duel between the batsmen and Barnes. In his first 12 overs only 12 runs were scored off his bowling. He was seemingly unplayable before lunch. This was rather surprising as the wicket was much faster than the day before and favoured the batsmen. Barnes bowled for 115 minutes without a rest in the hot sunshine – a rare feat for a man at his age (54). It was an interesting contest and the large crowd enjoyed every ball sent down even though the scoring was painfully slow. New Zealand's innings ended abruptly because bad light stopped play. They had scored 124 for the loss of only 2 wickets. The game ended in a draw.

The New Zealanders

Wales first innings		New Zealand first innings	
W.E.Bates b Alcott	29	C.C.R.Dacre b Thomas	7
J.T.Bell c McGirr b Dare	52	H.M.McGirr c Rowlad b Barnes	0
N.V.H.Riches c Page b Henderson	22	E.H.L.Bernau b Barnes	0
C.F.Walters c and b Allcott	18	T.C.Lowry c Sullivan b Barnes	21
C.A.Rowland run out	2	J.E.Mills c Jagger b Thomas	18

D.Davies c Dempster b Henderson	6	R.C.Blunt c Jagger b Thomas	10
K.C.Raikes c Dempster b Allcott	5	C.S.Dempster lbw b Barnes	14
S.F.Barnes b Henderson	5	M.L.Page c Jagger b Raikes	14
S.T.Jagger Page b Allcott	9	K.C.James b Jagger	23
A.E.Thomas c Blunt b Allcott	16	C.F.W.Allcott c Walters b Raikes	4
D.Sullivan not out	2	M.Henderson not out	1
Extras (8b, 8lb)	16	Extras (14b, 4lb)	18
Total (all out, 67.5 overs	**182**	**Total (all out, 83.3 overs)**	**130**

New Zealand bowling	Wales bowling
Allcott 5/46, Henderson 3/28, Dacre 1/10	Barnes 4/47, Thomas 3/49, Raikes 2/2, Jagger 1/24

Wales second innings		New Zealand second innings	
W.E.Bates b Henderson	18	C.S.Dempster c Raikes b Thomas	70
J.T.Bell b Henderson	10	J.E.Mills b Jagger	27
C.F.Walters c Lowry b Allcott	11	M.L.Page not out	15
C.A.Rowland c and b Page	14	T.C.Lowry not out	6
D.Davies c McGirr b Lowry	42	Extras (5b, 1w)	6
K.C.Raikes b Henderson	33	**Total (2 wickets, 49 overs)**	**124**
S.F.Barnes c Bernau b Henderson	2		
S.T.Jagger c Dempster b Lowry	2		
A.E.Thomas not out	2		
Extras (10b, 15lb)	25		
Total (9 wickets decl, 67 overs)	**183**		

149

Wales bowling
Thomas 1/30, Jagger 1/36, Barnes 0/30

New Zealand bowling
Henderson 4/29, Lowry 3/42, Alcott 1/27, Page 1/52

The following day New Zealand played the Welsh Cygnets. The Welsh batted first and scored 350 for 6 declared. In reply, New Zealand was dismissed for 195.

A few days after the New Zealand match a letter appeared in the local press:

"Dear Sir - I beg to lodge a protest to the shortening of the hours during the cricket match and also to the wasting of time during the game. What justification was there on Monday after the innings of the New Zealanders which terminated at 3.50pm in taking a tea interval and not returning to the field until 4.45pm? In view of the admission charge of 2s I consider that the public should be given, weather permitting, a full day's cricket with the chance of a definite result to the match. If the idea of these first-class matches is to encourage the public to patronise cricket in North Wales the tactics pursued during this match is more likely to discourage support in the future. The advertised hours of play for Monday and Tuesday were 11.30am to 6pm and three quarters of an hour for lunch. On what grounds were the times altered to 12 noon to 6 pm? In conclusion and in fairness to the public, I beg to urge the authority in charge to insist that the motto' play cricket' is adhered. Thank you for your kindness for publishing my complaint, - Tyke."

Staffordshire v North Wales 1927

This was played in June 1927. Because of a violent thunder storm there was only three hours' play on the first day. North Wales had scored 64. Barnes went in at number 6 and was out caught for a duck!

North Wales v MCC 1927

This match was played at The Oval, Llandudno on 21/22 July 1927. Barnes was due to play for North Wales but was unable to do so. Reason not known but probably because of a recurring knee injury which was known he had at the time. The following was notice in a local newspaper advertising the game.

GRAND CRICKET MATCH
21/22 July 1927
at
THE OVAL, LLANDUDNO
NORTH WALES
v
MCC
Wickets pitched each day at
11.30am. Lunch 1pm – 2pm
Admission to ground including tax 1s/4p
Pavilion and Enclosure 2s/4p

North Wales v South Wales 1927

This was the last match of a Cricket Festival Week in Llandudno played at The Oval on 9th September, 1927. North Wales batted first and scored 197. The South Wales team was practically a strong Glamorgan County side but North Wales was also considered to be strong with Barnes included in the side. Barnes scored 13 before he was caught at third slip. He hit three fours in one over. In reply South Wales could only make 92. Barnes finished up with an excellent bowling session.

His wickets costing less than 6 runs apiece – 7 wickets for 40 runs. South Wales were unable to finish their second innings. The match was abandoned because of heavy rain. They had scored 130 and Barnes had taken 4 wickets for 73 runs.

Wales v West Indies 1928

Barnes was in great form for Wales against the West Indies in 1928.

The West Indies team and officials arrived at Llandudno on the evening of the 24th July, travelling from Manchester and Trent Bridge after a crushing defeat in their Test match against England. Both teams were given a civic reception at the North Western Hotel the following day. The Chairman of the Council presided and welcomed both teams on behalf of the people of Llandudno. He said there were two good reasons for the warm welcome. The first was a business reason for the town depending entirely on visitors and the second was that they were always glad to welcome real sportsmen and sportswomen who played the game of cricket in all corners of the world. He was convinced sport played a part in cementing the British Empire together. He sketched the many attractions on offer, winding up with a reference to the Happy Valley, a popular colourful public gardens feature in the resort. G.E. Rowland (President of the Welsh Cricket Union) was present, and in his speech he commented that the West Indies team had brought sunshine with them that day and he hoped it would continue to shine on them in the next Test match against England later that month.

C.K.Nunes, on behalf of the West Indies team, said they had come from a land of ancient mountains and lovely dales to another land of ancient mountains and lovely vales. He thanked everyone for the splendid welcome and great kindness. He felt that it was a great honour to be at the head of a body of men, mostly young men, from the islands which had shown great loyalty to the throne on this visit.

It was said their defeat against England at Trent Bridge had knocked the stuffing out of the West Indians. They had travelled to Llandudno in a gloomy mood and knowing that it was going to be their second encounter that season with Barnes.

Rain fell in the early morning on the first day but play started only a quarter of an hour late. West Indies won the toss and elected to bat first on a wicket which was a bit on the slow side. The attendance before lunch was easily a record for North Wales and after lunch the ground presented a wonderful sight with spectators three and four deep surrounding the whole of the boundary. On a damp wicket and with a moist sea breeze blowing in from the bay, the master bowler was in his element. Scoring was slow and it took the West Indies an hour to reach 50. Barnes bowled a spell of 90 minutes during which he bowled 15 overs, which included seven maidens, for 21 runs and captured 2 wickets. He had the tourists guessing all the time. Play after lunch took a sensational turn, as in the course of 4 overs Barnes took 4 more wickets at a cost of just 12 runs. World famous West Indies batsman L.N.Constantine had a brief but merry innings and he delighted the crowd by scoring a six and two fours in one over. The crowd were sorry to see him out from a skier, caught by none other than Mr Barnes. Barnes bowled magnificently throughout the West Indies innings taking 7 wickets for 57 runs. In addition to Constantine's wicket, the crowd gave him a wonderful ovation when he came off the field.

A prospective crowd-puller, 2,500 people had attended the first day of play. A crowd of 10,000 had been present at a match previously in the North of England against the West Indians in spite of a depression in that area and it was felt amongst North Walians that 2,500 was a little disappointing.

Wales before lunch on the Friday triumphed over the West Indies by winning the match by 8 wickets. This was another personal triumph for Barnes. Despite the fact he had many catches missed from his bowling during the West Indies second innings he came out with the fine record of 13 wickets for 118 runs for the match. The tourists paid tribute to Barnes, stating that he was the finest bowler they had met on the tour. However, much to the delight of the crowd Constantine during his second innings hit a beautiful ball off Barnes onto the pavilion roof, breaking one of the tiles. He batted at number seven and scored 24 in his first innings and 16 in his second innings. Barnes was also hit for six by Rea who sent a ball out of the ground and into the nearest tennis courts.

West Indies first innings		Wales first innings	
G.Challenor lbw b Barnes	50	N.V.H.Riches c Roach b Constantine	12
C.A.Roach c Ryan b Barnes	4	D.Boumphrey b Francis	6
W.H.St Hill lbw b Barnes	20	C.A.Rowland b Constantine	6
R.K.Nunes b Ryan	25	C.N.Bruce run out	10
O.C.Scott b Barnes	7	A.Ratcliffe b Neblett	71
C.R.Browne b Barnes	0	V.A.Metcalfe c Rea b Neblett	18
L.N.Constantine c Barnes b Ryan	24	S.T.Jagger Neblett b Francis	30
E.A.Rae c Ryan b Barnes	0	C.E.Dolman c Neblett b Browne	35
E.M.Neblett b Barnes	17	S.F.Barnes not out	25
C.V.Wright not out	16	W.H.Rowland b Browne	0
G.N.Francis b Ryan	3	F.P.Ryan c and b Browne	0
Extras (21b, 11lb)	32	Extras (6b, 6lb, 4nb)	16
Total (all out, 60 overs)	198	Total (all out, 63.5 overs)	229

Wales bowling	West Indies bowling
Barnes 7/51, Ryan	3/68 Browne 3/26, Francis 2/70, Constantine 2/44 Neblett 2/54

West Indies second innings		Wales second innings	
G.Challenor lbw b Barnes	26	N.V.H.Riches c Browne b Francis	4
C.A.Roach c Ryan b Barnes	30	D.Boumphrey b Constantine	4
W.H.St Hill c Ratcliffe b Ryan	7	C.A.Rowland not out	52
R.K.Nunes b Barnes	17	C.N.Bruce not out	42
O.C.Scott c Ryan b Barnes	4	Extras (4b, 1b)	5
L.N.Constantine c Jagger b Ryan	16	**Total (2 wickets, 22.5 overs)**	**107**
E.A.Rae b Ryan	11		
C.V.Wright c Riches b Barnes	1		
J.M.Neblett lbw b Ryan	2		
G.N.Francis not out	0		
Extras 917b, 3lb, 2nb)	22		
Total (all out, 41.1 overs)	137		

West Indies bowling
Francis 1/29, Constantine 1/15

Wales bowling
Barnes 5/67, Ryan 5/17

The West Indies team continued their tour with drawn matches following against Leicestershire, Somerset, Glamorgan and Gloucestershire.

The West Indies in the early days were still dominated by English ex-pats and the team's success was patchy. The real turning point came in the 1950s and 1960s when players like Gary Sobers, Wes Hall, Frank Worrell and Everton Weekes came through the ranks to establish the team's identity as a mixture of powerful stroke play and ferocious bowling. The reputation was further enhanced in the 1970s and 1980s when the fast bowling attack, spearheaded by players like Malcolm Marshall, became feared around the world for short-pitched bowling on hard surfaces. Meanwhile, batsmen like Viv Richards were demonstrating the fearsome art of aggressive batting that would make the West Indies the number one side in the world in the mid-1980s. Although the team's fortunes have dipped in the past 20 years they have continued to produce some of the world's greatest cricketers, most notably Brian Lara, who still holds the record for the highest score in Test match cricket of 501 runs.

Wilfred Wooller (1912-1997), an ex-Glamorgan captain and born in Colwyn Bay, North Wales, commented that Barnes had a habit of making a deep impression on any batsman who encountered him for the first time. He said that he did bat against him when he was a schoolboy playing for a Denbigh side, and had never forgotten it.

"As a character," Wooller said, "Syd Barnes was an awe-inspiring figure to meet and play against. He was quiet, morose, and entirely dedicated to removing batsmen from occupying the crease. He had little use for anybody or anything that stood in his way. I got runs against him twice as a schoolboy. I found it a most edifying experience. I was beaten on average twice an over and never once was certain which way the ball was moving. Syd had no sympathy for my efforts and one felt he could clearly have removed me by any means within or outside his power. He has mellowed and maybe so have I, but I look back still with awe at the skill of the man with the ball."

Lancashire v Wales 1928

A compliment was paid to Welsh cricket by the Lancashire County Club in playing practically their full team in this 3-day match played at Stanley Park, Blackpool over a weekend on 25/27/28 August 1928. One would have thought in the present state of the English County Championship, Lancashire would have rested some of their players. The compliment in return had been duly appreciated by the Welsh Cricket Union.

Barnes, as expected, opened the bowling for Wales. Lancashire had won the toss and decided to bat. In the first day's play he caused havoc amongst the Lancashire batsmen taking 6 wickets for 58 runs excluding a catch taken off Jagger's bowling. If it hadn't been for Hallows the Lancashire side would have cut a sorry figure. The pitch was slow throughout the day but they did manage a total of 200 runs. It was 25 years since Barnes had played for Lancashire and 16 years since he played for England but he proved that he was still a bowler to be feared. His perfection in this match in length, leg break and variation of pace had all the batsmen in difficulties which resulted in well-deserved excellent figures. Wales were abruptly skittled in their first innings for 86 and only managed 131 in their second innings. This was after Lancashire declared on 97 for 3 in their second innings. Barnes took a further 2 wickets for 29 runs.

The match did finish with Wales losing by 80 runs. Comments were made of the fine performance put up by Wales against a very strong Lancashire side.

Lancashire first innings		Wales first innings	
F.B.Watson b Mercer	13	J.T.Morgan lbw b Sibbles	4
C.Hallows b Barnes	114	W.E.Bates st Farrimond b R.K.Tyldesley	14
G.E.Tyldesley c and b Barnes	26	C.A.Rowland c Watson b Hopwood	15
J.W.H.Makepeace lbw b Mercer	4	M.J.L.Turnbull lbw b R.K.Tyldesley	3
J.Iddon c Jagger b Barnes	0	N.V.H.Riches b Hopwood	0
J.L.Hopwood st Hills b Barnes	12	D.Davies lbw b Hopwood	33
L.Green c Bates b Jagger	0	J.J.Hills lbw b Hopwood	12
F.M.Sibbles c Hills b Barnes	2	S.T.Jagger b R.K.Tyldesley	0
W.Farrimond c Morgan b Barnes	2	S.F.Barnes c Watson b Hopwood	5
R.K.Tyldesley not out	4	J.Mercer b Hopwood	0
E.A.McDonald c Barnes b Jagger	0	F.P.Ryan not out	0
Extras (16b, 4lb, 3b)	23	Extras	0
Total (all out, 81 overs)	**200**	**Total (all out, 51.2 overs)**	**86**

Wales bowling	Lancashire bowling
Barnes 6/58, Jagger 2/26, Mercer 2/57	Hopwood 6/20, R.K.Tyldesley 3/35, Sibbles 1/1

Lancashire second innings		Wales second innings	
F.B.Watson lbw b Mercer	6	J.T.Morgan c Farrimond b McDonald	14
C.Hallows c Ryan b Barnes	10	W.E.Bates c Sibbles b McDonald	44
G.E. Tyldesley not out	44	C.A.Rowland lbw b McDonald	0
J.W.H.Makepeace lbw b Barnes	0	N.V.H.Riches retired hurt	6

Extras (12b)	12	M.J.L.Turnbull c R.K.Tyldesley b Hopwood	19
Total (3 wickets declared, 32 overs)	**97**	D.Davies c R.K.Tyldesley b Iddon	7
		J.J.Hills not out	24
		S.T.Jagger c Green b Iddon	3
		S.F.Barnes b Hopwood	4
		J.Mercer c Watson b R.K.Tyldesley	4
		FP.Ryan b R.K. Tyldesley	0
		Extras (4b, 2lb)	6
		Total (all out, 51.2 overs)	**131**

Wales bowling	Lancashire bowling
Barnes 2/29, Mercer 1/41	McDonald 3/28, R.K.Tyldesley 2/15, Iddon 2/38, Hopwood 2/40

Sussex v Wales 1929

Wales put up a fine show in a game which ended in a draw. Only 19 wickets fell at the Hove, Sussex ground in a 3-day match on 29/30/31 May, 1929. There were plenty of runs to suggest it must have been a perfect batting wicket. Altogether 1,136 runs were scored by both sides. Barnes only took 1 wicket. Sussex batted first and made 294 runs.

Wales followed, scoring a magnificent 555 for 6 declared (J.T.Bell 157, Lord Aberdare 134, J.J.Hills 120 no. Barnes did not bat). The match ended with Sussex, in their second innings, managing 287 for 3.

The Welsh team as they appear on the page (below) – they are: N.V.H. Riches, M.J Turnbull, J.T. Morgan, C.A. Rowland, S.T. Jagger, D. Davies, W.E. Bates, S.F. Barnes, J. Hills, J. Mercer, F. Ryan.

Wales v South Africa 1929

The South African cricket team toured England in the 1929 season to play a 5-match Test series against England. England won this series with victories at Headingley (3rd Test) and at Old Trafford (4th Test). The 1st Test at Edgbaston, 2nd Test at Lord's and 5th Test at The Oval were drawn. In first-class matches overall (including Wales) South Africa won 9 games and lost 7, with 18 being drawn. There were 3 other matches; 2 of them ended in South African victories, the other was drawn.

At 56 years of age, Barnes put up two marvellous pieces of bowling against the South Africans. After taking 8 wickets for 48 in 32 overs for the Minor Counties he followed it up a few days later with 6 for 28 for Wales. In three innings against the full strength of South Africa his analysis read: 68.4 overs, 21 maidens, 131 runs, 18 wickets for an average of 7.27 runs.

The Rydal School at Colwyn Bay was the venue for the Wales match against the might of the South Africans, over 3 days, commencing on 10th July, 1929. South Africa batted first and scored 192. Wales followed in their second innings with just 33 runs off the South African total. South Africa had batted steadily in their second innings totalling 262 and giving Wales a chance chasing 273 runs. In a close finish Wales fell short by just 10 runs.

South Africa first innings		Wales first innings	
R.H.Catterall c Bruce b Davies	117	J.T.Bell lbw b Ochse	0
I.J.Siedle c and b Davies	33	W.E.Bates c Vincent b McMillan	23
J.A.J.Christy c Jones b Davies	7	J.M.Jones c McMillan b Ochse	9
B.Mitchell lbw b Barnes	11	C.N.Bruce b Ochse	2
H.W.Taylor b Barnes	1	A.Ratcliffe b McMillan	17
E.L.Dalton c Davies b Barnes	5	D.E.Davies b Mitchell	53
H.G.Deane b Barnes	8	C.A.Rowland b Ochse	16
Q.McMillan b Barnes	1	T.Arnott c McMillan b Mitchell	15
C.L.Vincent b Barnes	0	S.F.Barnes not out	6
E.A. Van der Merwe b Davies	0	J.Mercer b McMillan	7
A.L.Ochse not out	3	H.E.Edge c Vincent b McMillan	0
Extras (b4, 1b1, nb1)	6	Extras (b7, 1b4)	11
Total (all out, 49.4 overs)	192	Total (all out, 60 overs)	159

Wales bowling	South Africa bowling
Barnes 6/28, Davies 4/27	Ochse 4/28, McMillan 4/82, Mitchell 2/25

South Africa second innings		Wales second innings	
R.H.Catterall c Jones b Davies	35	J.T.Bell c McMillan b Vincent	68
I.J.Siedle lbw b Mercer	45	W.E.Bates c McMillan b Vincent	102
B.Mitchell b Barnes	44	J.M.Jones b Mitchell	34
H.W.Taylor b Mercer	2	C.N.Bruce b McMillan	7
E.L.Dalton st Jones b Barnes	1	A.Ratcliffe b Vincent	16
H.G.Deane lbw b Mercer	64	D.E.Davies run out	2
Q.McMillan b Barnes	0	C.A.Rowland c McMillan b Vincent	3
C.L.Vincent b Barnes	8	T.Arnott c Ochse b Vincent	17
E.A.Van Der Merwe not out	5	S.F.Barnes lbw b McMillan	5
A.L.Ochse b Mercer	0	J.Mercer not out	1
J.A.J.Christy absent hurt	0	H.E.Edge b McMillan	0
Extras (b18, 1b16, nb1)	35	Extras (b1, 1b4, nb2)	7
Total (all out, 67.5 overs)	**239**	**Total (all out, 82.3 overs)**	**262**

Wales bowling	South Africa bowling
Barnes 4/62, Mercer 4/67, Davies 1/21	Vincent 5/70, McMillan 3/93, Mitchell 1/25

"You have to be fit to play cricket, don't you?"

"You certainly do," muttered Barnes. "I get up at five, run for two miles, come back and do four hours of exercises."

"How long have you been doing it?"

"I start tomorrow," he said, with tongue in cheek!

MCC v Wales 1929

Barnes was unable to secure a victory for Wales on this occasion. This first-class game was played at Lord's, London over 3 days on 21/22/23 August, 1929. Barnes received a wonderful reception from the Lord's crowd. Every time he was put on to bowl he was greeted with applause. He did not let them down. He took 3/36 in the first innings followed by 4/63 in the second innings excluding two fine catches. Wales batted first and scored 249 and at the end of their second innings set the MCC 296 to win. At the close of play MCC needed 40 runs with 2 wickets to fall. Very early in his innings Mayer was dropped at mid-off and went on to top score with 89 runs. If he had been caught the match would have probably been won by Wales. Match drawn.

Wales first innings		MCC first innings	
N.V.H.Riches c Hill b Meyer	18	S.H.Martin b Barnes	42
H.G.Symonds c and b Meyer	17	G.D.Fenner c Arnott b A.N.Morgan	42
C.F.Walters c Martin b Hill	2	E.A.E.Tremlett c Barnes b Raikes	4
W.G.Morgan c Buckston b Meyer	9	G.L.O.Jessop c W.G.Morgan b A.N.Morgan	10
A.Ratcliffe c Bowes b Wheatley	73	J.B.Wheatley run out	1
C.A.Rowland b Hill	1	J.W.H.T.Douglas b Arnott	38
T.Arnott c Meyer b Bowes	43	R.J.O.Meyer c Ratcliffe b Arnott	5
S.F.Barnes c Douglas b Martin	23	R.T.Stanyforth c W.H.Rowland b Arnott	9
K.C.Raikes b Bowes	50	R.H.R.Buckston b Barnes	2

A.N.Morgan c Tremlett b Bowes	3	D.V.Hill c Ratcliffe b Barnes	0
W.H.Rowland not out	0	W.E.Bowes not out	8
Extras (1b, 8lb, lnb)	10	Extras (9b, 2lb, 2w, 5b)	18
Total (all out, 98 overs)	**249**	**Total (all out, 89.4 overs)**	**179**

MCC bowling	Wales bowling
Meyer 3, Bowes 3, Hill 2, Wheatley 1, Martin 1	Barnes 3, Arnott 3, Morgan 2, Raikes 1

Wales second innings		MCC second innings	
H.G.Symonds b Hill	50	S.H.Martin lbw b Barnes	16
A.Ratcliffe b Meyor	4	G.D.Fenner c Barnes b Raikes	1
C.F.Walters b Bowes	9	E.A.E.Tremlett b Barnes	5
W.G.Morgan run out	55	G.L.O.Jessop c Walters b Barnes	29
T.Arnott c Stanyforth b Bowes	24	J.B.Wheatley c Raikes b Barnes	16
C.A.Rowland b Bowes	5	J.W.H.T.Douglas c Riches b Arnott	41
N.V.H.Riches b Bowes	4	R.J.O.Meyer lbw b A.N.Morgan	89
S.F.Barnes c Wheatley b Meyer	17	R.T.Stanyforth c Barnes b Raikes	17
K.C.Raikes c and b Meyer	21	R.H.R.Buckston not out	10
A.N.Morgan c Buckston b Meyer	9	D.V.Hill not out	5
W.H.Rowland not out	1	Extras (11b, 101b, 6nb)	27
Extras (19b, 41b, 2w, 1nb)	26	**Total (8 wickets, 100 overs)**	**256**
Total (all out, 63.3 overs)	**225**		

MCC bowling	Wales bowling
Meyer 4, Bowes 4, Hill 1	Barnes 4, Raikes 2, Arnott 1, Morgan 1

Wales v Minor Counties 1930

The victory by Wales over the Minor Counties was well-deserved. This was a 3-day match on 18/19/20 June, 1930 at the Penrhyn Avenue, Colwyn Bay C.C. ground. Wales won the toss and batted first, scoring 278. Minor Counties followed with a total of 324 (G.S. Butler 121). Wales replied 349 (W.E. Bates 146) for 8 declared. Minor Counties struggled in their second innings against some aggressive Welsh bowling with only three batsmen reaching double figures. They conceded defeat to Wales by 177 runs.

Barnes had very little luck bowling during the Minor Counties first innings. Time after time he was edged through the slips. He made the ball turn either way and had all the batsmen in trouble. On the first day he had a bowling spell of one and a half hours and on the second day he bowled 7 overs and had only nine runs scored from him. The Minor Counties team was a very strong one, which included county players from Surrey and Kent who had batting averages of about 50.

Wales first innings		Minor Counties first innings	
W.E.Bates c Walters b Hartley	12	H.W.F.Homer c Wilcox b Bates	27
J.T.Bell b Hartley	12	G.S.Butler c Wilcox b Barnes	121
T.Arnott st Inge b Stroud	54	E.D.Dynes b Ryan	27
N.V.H.Riches c Stroud b Dynes	73	H.S.Squires c and b Barnes	25
D.Davies b Dynes	25	W.T.Cook st Wilcox b Ryan	35
C.A.Rowland not out	51	C.Walters b Ryan	25
C.P.Woods c Cook b Dynes	5	T.K.Dobson b Arnott	5
SF.Barnes c Hartley b Stroud	18	E.G.Stroud b Arnott	17
S.C.Wilcox c and b Stroud	6	G.S.Watson c Wilcox b Arnott	3

J.Mercer b Stroud	9	F.Hartley c Arnott b Ryan	2
F.P.Ryan lbw b Stroud	1	W.W.Inge not out	6
Extras (b10, lb2)	12	Extras (b13, lb9, nb9)	31
Total (all out, 84.1 overs)	278	Total (all out, 92 overs)	324

Minor Counties bowling	Wales bowling
Stroud 5/60, Dynes 3/53, Hartley 2/72	Ryan 4/43, Arnott 3/62, Barnes 2/74, Mercer 1/47

Wales second innings		Minor Counties second innings	
W.E.Bates c Inge b Hartley	146	H.W.F.Homer c Bates b Ryan	35
J.T.Bell st Inge b Stroud	64	G.S.Butler c Arnott b Mercer	4
T.Arnott c Butler b Dynes	49	E.D.Dynes run out	6
D.Davies c Dobson b Dynes	39	H.S.Squires c Bates b Mercer	10
C.A.Rowland c Cook b Stroud	18	W.T.Cook b Ryan	2
C.P.Woods b Dynes	4	C.Walters c Barnes b Mercer	8
S.F.Barnes c and b Dynes	2	T.K.Dobson b Ryan	5
S.C.Wilcox not out	1	E.G.Stroud b Mercer	6
J.Mercer c sub b Dynes	8	G.S.Watson c Arnott b Mercer	0
Extras (b17 w1)	18	F.Hartley lbw b Mercer	13
Total (8 wickets declared, 96.3 overs)	349	W.W.Inge not out	9
		Extras (b17, lb9, nb2)	28
		Total (all out, 40 overs)	126

Minor Counties bowling	Wales bowling
Dynes 5/64, Stroud 2/104, Hartley1/54	Mercer 6/58, Ryan 3/23, Barnes 0/9

MCC v Wales 1930

Barnes played in this 3-day match for Wales against the MCC at the Lord's ground on 20/21/22 August 1930. Whilst in London, Barnes was asked how he would have liked to have had a go at Donald Bradman. He laughingly replied that had he been 15 years younger, nothing would have given him greater pleasure. There were many critics who believed that Barnes would have been able to skittle the Australians out as old as he was then.

The MCC won the toss and elected to bat first and scored 265, which was enough to win the match. There was no play on the first day because of rain. Barnes took 2 for 57 and caught the wicket of Nawab of Pataudi off the bowling of Arnott. In the end it was the batting that let Wales down, losing by an innings and 44 runs.

MCC innings	
W.A.C Wilkinson run out	20
A. Jeacocke c Sadler b Arnott	6
Nawab of Pataudi c Barnes b Arnott	105
S.H Martin lbw b Barnes	26
W.E Astill c Mallalieu b Barnes	5
J.W.H.T Douglas lbw b Arnott	1
S.J. Brown c W.H Rowland b Sadler	21
R.J Covill c Ratcliffe b MacNab	13
R.H.R Buckston not out	20
S.J Pegler b Sadler	22
H Pickthall b Sadler	6
Extras (b12, lb3, w1, nb4)	20
Total (all out, 76 overs)	265

Wales Bowling		
Barnes 2/57, Arnott 3/94, Sadler 3/55, MacNab 1/16		

Wales first innings		Wales second innings	
A. Ratcliffe lbw b Pegler	14	b Pegler	32
A.R Howard b Astill	6	b Pegler	22
H.R.J Rhys b Martin	7	lbw b Pegler	0
A.E Mallalieu b Martin	0	b Pickthall	0
T. Arnott b Astill	17	not out	45
C.A Rowland b Pegler	5	c Pataudi b Pickthall	21
A.E Hodges lbw b Astill	8	c Astill b Pegler	3
S.F Barnes b Pegler	1	b Pegler	0
M.R MacNab lbw b Astill	1	c Brown b Pickthall	2
T.W Sadler not out	1	b Pegler	17
W.H Rowland st Buckston b Pegler	1	b Astill	0
Extras (lb 6)	6	Extras (b10, lb2)	12
Total (all out, 36.2 overs)	67	Total (all out, 58.2 overs)	154

MCC bowling first innings	MCC bowling second innings
Astill 4/26, Pegler 4/14, Martin 2/21	Pegler 6/62, Pickthall 3/16, Astill 1/56

Barnes was given a warm welcome at the London Press Club on one of the nights he was in town. He took part in some interesting discussion with those conversant with the big part he played in English cricket in the years previously. Barnes had a good memory for the leading incidents of the tours he made in Australia and could tell many a good yarn. Some against himself!

Cricket on the Somme

'Taffy' Thomas had a story to tell when he returned to his home in Llandudno, North Wales from the First World War. It was of his friend and colleague 'Spider' Webb:

'Spider' Webb was a Cockney – from Stepney, I believe – who was with us on the Somme in 1916. He was a splendid cricketer.

We had had a very stiff time for six or seven hours and were resting during a lull in the firing. Then suddenly Jerry sent over five shells. After a pause another shell came over and burst near to Spider and his two pals.

When the smoke cleared I went across to see what had happened.

Spider's two pals were beyond help. The Cockney was propping himself up with his elbows surveying the scene.

"What's happened, Webb?" I said. "Blimey! What's happened?" was the reply. "One over – two bowled" (and, looking down at his leg) – "and I'm stumped."

Then he fainted.

Other Matches 1924-1947

Denbighshire v Staffordshire 1930

Some background to this match is necessary because Barnes was playing for Staffordshire and not for the Welsh county, Denbighshire. It was at the end of the playing season in 1930 when he left Colwyn Bay and moved back to Staffordshire and continued to play for the English county in the Minor Counties Championship. Barnes never played for Denbighshire. It was in 1930 the Welsh county joined the Minor Counties Championship, but because the opposition was too strong, disbanded after the 1935 season. They missed the 1932 season. The side suffered poor results and in its final season lost all of its eight matches, six of them by an innings and so many runs. Every season they competed they finished bottom of the championship table. This was not surprising as the Denbighshire players had only had experience at North Wales club level and were up against top-rated players, including professionals with first-class experience. There were also teams they played against that were equal in strength to many of the first-class counties. For example the Lancashire and Nottingham second elevens, had players who did play in the county first eleven sides who were just waiting for their chance to get a regular place in the first team. Cheshire and Staffordshire were also teams that were equal in strength to many of the first-class counties. During the time in the Minor Counties, Denbighshire played their home games on grounds at Marchwiel, Chirk and Brymbo, but the majority were played at the Penrhyn Avenue ground, Colwyn Bay.

This particular match showed up the level of standards between a good club player and a first-class county player, which represented a yardstick in comparison. It also showed an astonishing man of Barnes' stature, at 57 years of old, still up there with the greatest players of the day. As the averages revealed in 1930, in addition to another sensational bowling record for Staffordshire, he had done so much better in batting for some years that he easily headed that table as well.

Batting				
Innings	Runs	Not-Out	Highest Score	Average
10	252	2	63	31.50

Bowling				
Overs	Maidens	Runs	Wickets	Average
165.1	56	293	51	574

Minor-Counties-League-Table-(up-to-22-August,-1930)					
	P	W	L	No-Res.	Pts	Percentage
Durham	8	6	1	1	34/33	94.28
Surrey-II	11	7	1	3	40/30	75.00
Lancs-II	10	7	2	1	45/32	71.11
Buckingham	10	6	2	2	40/28	70.00
Oxfordshire	9	5	2	2	35/23	65.21
Cornwall	9	4	2	3	30/19	63.33
Wiltshire	8	5	2	1	35/22	62.35
Hertfordshire	12	7	3	2	50/30	60.00
Cheshire	8	4	3	1	35/20	57.14
Staffordshire	**10**	**5**	**3**	**2**	**40/22**	**55.00**
Bedfordshire	9	5	3	0	45/20	44.44
Cambridgeshire	7	2	3	2	25/11	44.44
Berkshire	9	3	5	1	40/17	42.50
Notts-II	8	4	4	0	40/17	42.50
Kent-II	9	3	6	0	45/15	33.33
Devonshire	10	3	4	3	35/11	31.42
Dorset	8	2	5	1	35/11	31.42
Lincolnshire	8	2	5	1	35/11	31.42
Yorkshire-II	8	2	6	0	40/10	25.00
Northumberland	6	1	4	1	25/06	24.00
Norfolk	7	1	4	2	25/06	24.00
Monmouthshire	8	1	6	1	35/06	17.14
Denbighshire	**8**	**0**	**7**	**1**	**40/01**	**02.50**

It was at Colwyn Bay's Penrhyn Avenue ground on 28th August 1930 that Staffordshire played their last game of the season against Denbighshire. This 2-day Minor Counties match opened with Denbighshire winning the toss and electing to bat under beautiful climatic conditions. The heat of the sun being tempered by a welcome breeze would in most unqualified eyes be considered a perfect batting wicket.

The Welsh county side, not surprisingly, failed to rise to the occasion. The bowling of Barnes, Taylor and Lockett was far too good for them. The opening bat, C. Morris, scored 20 and Startup managed 10 but they were the only players in the side who reached double figures. It was a pitiable sight, the dismissal of batsman after batsman in quick succession and their return into the pavilion was an expression of grief failing to keep their ends up with any show of distinction. The innings opened at 11.30am and finished at 1.10pm for just 69 runs.

Denbighshire first innings		Denbighshire second innings	
C.Morris c Wilkie b Taylor	20	C.Morris b Taylor	10
B.D.W.Sykes lbw b Taylor	7	B.D.W.Sykes b Barnes	2
W.Wooller st Cross b Barnes	1	W.Wooller lbw b Taylor	5
Capt. Bibby b Barnes	6	C.A.Rowland not out	1
C.A.Rowland lbw b Lockett	5	Extras	9
S.T.Jagger c Ellerker b Taylor	10	Total	27
G.Startup b Taylor	8		
Capt. Andrews b Taylor	0		
D.C.W.Lowe c Barnes b Taylor	0		
H.E.Edge not out	2		
J.Lewis lbw b Locket	0		
Extras	10		
Total	69		

Staffordshire bowling
Taylor 6/32, Barnes 2/17, Lockett 2/8

Staffordshire bowling second innings
Taylor 2, Barnes 1

Staffordshire innings
P.C.Yates c Lowe b Edge 17
Lockett c Morris b Jagger 12
A.D.Wilkie b Jagger 9
S.F.Barnes b Edge 45
H.W.Homer lbw b Lewis 54
E.Mayer c Lewis b Jagger 14
W.H.Ellerker b Lewis 12
A.Smith b Lewis 0
A.B.Hollowood c Andrews b Lewis 5
E.P.Cross not out 3
Taylor b Jagger 7
Extras 11
Total 189

Denbighshire bowling
Jagger 4/44, Lewis 4/37, Edge 2/37

A comfortable win for Staffordshire.

Denbighshire v Staffordshire 1931

The following year Denbighshire lost to Staffordshire again at the Penrhyn Avenue ground, Colwyn Bay in a 2-day match 24/25 August, 1931. On this occasion by 221 runs. At 58 years old Barnes was still bowling magnificently for his county by taking 7 wickets for 18 runs in this match. This was the fourth successive win over the home county and Barnes had brought

173

his aggregate against Denbighshire in 3 games to 25 wickets for 91 runs.

The match was favoured by excellent weather. The gate for the two days amounted to £12. Staffordshire batted first, scored 147, and Barnes opened the batting and scored 25 before being clean bowled. Denbighshire followed and were all out for a miserable 54 runs. Barnes captured 5 wickets for 8 runs. Denbighshire did a little better in their 2nd innings, scoring 88. Barnes took 2/10.

Staffordshire first innings		Denbighshire first innings	
S.F.Barnes b Barlow	25	B.D.W.Sykes b Barnes	0
P.C.Yates c Edge b Davies	5	L.A.Taylor lbw b Barnes	5
E.Mayer c Morris b Barlow	27	J.H.Mitchell b Lockett	12
W.H.Ellerker b Davies	6	W.Wooller lbw b Barnes	1
H.W.F.Homer c Sykes b Edge	17	F.Morton b Lockett	15
S.Crump run out	15	D.L.Hughes c Cross b Lockett	0
H.A.Sedgwick c Taylor b Barlow	2	C.R.Morris b Barnes	5
A.Lockett b Davies	9	A.Barlow b Lockett	4
W.E.Bourne b Barlow	26	H.E.Edge c Crump b Barnes	0
R.Smith not out	3	D.C.W.Lowe not out	0
E.P.Cross b Barlow	0	E.Davies b Lockett	0
Extras	12	Extras	12
Total (all out, 61.4 overs)	147	Total (all out, 27.4 overs)	54

Denbighshire bowling	Staffordshire bowling
Davies 3/64, Barlow 5/42, Edge 1/29	Barnes 5/8, Lockett 5/23

Staffordshire second innings		Denbighshire second innings	
S.F.Barnes lbw b Davies	8	B.D.W.Sykes b Barnes	0
P.C.Yates b Davies	14	L.A.Taylor c Homer b Barnes	3
E.Mayer b Davies	16	J.H.Mitchell b Sedgwick	2
W.H.Ellerker c Wooller b Morris	16	W.Wooller lbw b Crump	17
H.W.F.Homer c Mitchell b Davies	24	F.Morton c Crump b Ellerker	1
S.Crump lbw b Davies	27	D.L.Hughes b Crump	22
H.A.Sedgwick run out	26	C.R.Morris b Ellerker	12
A.Lockett hit wkt b Barlow	41	A.Barlow c Ellerker b Crump	3
W.E.Bourne lbw b Edge	0	H.E.Edge b Ellerker	5
R.Smith b Davies	27	D.C.W.Lowe not out	4
E.P.Cross not out	3	E.Davies b Crump	14
Extras	14	Extras	5
Total (all out, 95 overs)	**216**	**Total (all out, 44 overs)**	**88**

Denbighshire bowling	Staffordshire bowling
Davies 6/54, Barlow 1/65, Edge 1/35, Morris 1/6	Crump 4/17, Ellerker 3/26, Barnes 2/10, Sedgwick 1/18

It was in this year that Staffordshire asked Denbighshire to reconsider their proposed withdrawal from the Minor Counties competition. They pointed out that if the decision was final they were afraid that they would not be able to get their quota of games to enable them to remain in the competition. Cheshire and Lincolnshire were affected in the same way.

North Wales XI v Empire XI, 1942

This was the game that packed the ground at Penrhyn Avenue, Colwyn Bay to witness the clash between two great players of the day – 69 year old Sydney Barnes (North Wales) and 42

175

year old Learie Constantine (Empire XI). This was a one-day match played on the 12th July, 1942. The Empire XI won the toss and elected to bat.

The aged Barnes did not bowl in this match. The picture below is of the North Wales XI with Barnes sitting on the ground between Clifford Roach and Maurice Leyland. He did bat but scored just one run after being caught by Constantine off the bowling of Townsend. This innings might have possibly been his last ever innings at any level of cricket. The player standing at the left end in the back row is S.W. Newnham who played for Colwyn Bay and Surrey during his career. (Author's Uncle Stanley.) Next to Uncle Stan is another Colwyn Bay player Ted Lewis, and to this day there is a Ted Lewis trophy which is awarded to the member whom it is considered has made an outstanding contribution to the club. A very prestigious trophy.

North Wales XI

Not surprisingly, the 'Clash of the (aged) Titans' did not surface between these two players of gone-by days. The crowd had to contend themselves to just witnessing both players in opposition on the field of play, and of course were not disappointed.

Barnes was only tenth in the batting order but managed to get his name on the West Indies innings scorecard by getting opener Paynter out, caught off Leyland's bowling. Constantine took more of an active part by scoring a creditable 31 and had bowling figures of 0 for 39 runs off 8 overs. He must have been pleased when he got his name on the North Wales innings scorecard by getting counterpart Barnes out caught off Townsend's bowling.

Empire XI innings		North Wales	
E.Paynter c Barnes b Leyland	67	J.L.White b Pope	22
W.Place b Leyland	60	N.C.Nicholson b Martindale	2
N.Oldfield st Roach b Leyland	60	W.Barber b Martindale	2
L.F.Townsend st Roach b Leyland	21	M.Leyland st Duckworth b Wilkinson	41
G.H.Pope not out	78	R.C.Blunt b Wilkinson	46
L.N.Constantine c White b Leyland	31	C.A.Roach c Hallows b Wilkinson	0
R.H.Parkin not out	0	S.W.Newnham b Wilkinson	2
C.Hallows did not bat		F.M.Sibbles b Wilkinson	12
E.A.Martindale did not bat		W.E.Lewis st Duckworth b Wilkinson	3
L.L.Wilkinson did not bat		S.F.Barnes c Constantine b Townsend	1
G.Duckworth did not bat		E.W.Holt not out	10
Extras (9b, 2lb)	11	Extras (8b, 2nb)	10
Total (5 wickets declared, 34 overs)	**328**	**Total (all out, 29.3 overs)**	**151**

North Wales bowling	Empire XI bowling
Leyland 5/142, Newnham 0/42	Wilkinson 6/33, Martindale 2/9,

Not that he was always rude about batsmen. In 1932, when Barnes was 59, a 16-year-old got 69 not out against him, and Barnes said he was one of the best young cricketers he'd seen. Len Hutton said many years later that he still regarded that 69 as one of the best innings he'd ever played.

"Barnes was one of those bowlers you never knew how to take. He was over 50 when I first played against him, but he struck me then as the most difficult bowler I have ever had to tackle. He used his head. If you got a four against him, you had an uncomfortable feeling that he gave you that ball and would send down another which looked just the same – but wasn't – and would go up in and easy catch if you played the same stroke. So you went at it gingerly – and then perhaps you got caught just the same because Barnes' psychology had foreseen each thought that entered your mind and bowled accordingly."

Barnes secretive about his age

An interesting article appeared in the North Wales Weekly News on 11th August 1949 written by "Vigilant" and triggered by the news that Barnes had been elected an honorary member of the MCC that year. North Wales cricketers had welcomed the news because they remembered him as a one-time resident of Colwyn Bay during the 1920s.

"Vigilant" remembered Barnes as always reticent about his age. It was known that whenever his age was revealed, he was not very pleased about it. He was very critical of newspaper reporters for declaring his age and accused them of stopping him from making a living:

"Who will engage me now," muttered Barnes. "Who will engage me now they know I am so old....?"

His age made very little difference because he continued to make a living by playing cricket for many years afterwards.

The story of how his age became known is worth telling. It happened when he made his first appearance for Wales at Lords – following his "differences" with the MCC. After the first day's play "Vigilant" recalls he happened to be in the London Press Club and was called over by Stewart Caine, who was editor of Wisden at the time. Said Caine:

"What is this about your friend Barnes? I find that he is a few years older than the age given in a Wisden publication."

Someone had been to Somerset House!

Sydney Barnes is recognised as the greatest bowler ever by people who know the game. In Tests he took 189 wickets at 16.43. Half the time he did not play Test cricket because he could earn more in the leagues where he took 4,069 wickets at 6.03. In Minor Counties for Staffordshire he took 1,141 at 8.15. That is a total of 6,229 wickets with not more than three hours' coaching.

Geoffrey Boycott OBE

1922 Carlton Cricket Club

In 1922, the Carlton Cricket Club's captain Dr N.L. Stevenson invited Barnes to play for them in a special 2-day match against Western Union in celebration of their 60th Anniversary (Diamond Jubilee). Barnes accepted. The match was played in June of that year at their home ground at Grange Loan, Edinburgh.

In the first innings Western Union fared badly against Barnes' bowling. He finished with 7 wickets for 31 runs in 10 overs. Western Union were all out for 61 whilst Carlton replied scoring 216 for 7 declared. Barnes returned total figures of 12 for 45.

He was invited again in 1923 and played again for Carlton in 2 matches that year.

Dear Doctor,

At last I am able to give you our fixtures for the season 1923. On any other dates but those mentioned I shall be willing and pleased to assist you, the afternoon the better. I shall never forget my first visit, and can honestly say I am looking forward to playing with you again. After reading the book you so kindly sent me I can appreciate the spirit in which you play your matches – splendid. And I can also appreciate the great hospitality you extended to me last June – tremendous.

The MCC team in South Africa are not doing so well as I expected in the Test Matches. Several of the members whom I thought would be huge successes have done next to nothing. Perhaps it is the case of too many festive gatherings. Two teams should be sent, one for cricket and another to attend to the social functions.

Well I trust I shall have the pleasure of playing for the "Carlton" again.

With my best wishes I remain
Yours faithfully
S.F.Barnes

It was in 1922 that Barnes was playing in the Bradford League for Saltaire and in July had strengthened their position at the top of the league. Barnes was again in wonderful form, taking 8 wickets for 22 runs and in the process getting 4 men out with just 5 balls, including the hat-trick. In three matches in ten days Barnes had captured 26 wickets and his record for the season was 94 wickets at a cost of 4.16 runs each.

W.S.Young, a former Forfarshire and Scotland opening batsman, was speaking at a luncheon and presenting cricket trophies at the Kinnear Restaurant in Dundee in October, 1954. He said that one of the outstanding memories of his cricketing career was when he first fared up to Barnes in a match. Barnes bowled him in the first over. Young recalled that in the dressing room afterwards Barnes had given him a few playing hints which proved very useful later in his career.

1937

St Annes Cricket Club

Barnes at 62 years of age and professional at the St Annes Cricket Club was in 1937 considered to be a remarkable man playing the game at his age and yet showing no signs of weakening. By July of that year he had taken 46 wickets at a cost of only 11.4 runs each. He had scored 149 runs.

Barnes had proved to be a Box Office draw at St Annes where the gates were £15 in comparison to gates of less than £5 for many seasons past.

The disgruntled batsman stormed into the pavilion and flung down his bat. Barnes had just clean bowled him, first ball.

"*Terrible,*" he shouted. "*I've never played so badly before.*"

His captain looked up. "*Oh, you've played before, have you?*"

In a tense game, a batsman was given run out, a decision with which he obviously disagreed. He paced up and down outside the pavilion until the umpires came in.

"I wasn't out, you know," he said to the umpire.

"Oh no? Look in the newspapers tomorrow!" said the umpire.

Two boys were playing cricket in the street. This always annoyed the man outside whose house they were playing and he ran out and accosted the one who was bowling.

"How many times do I have to tell you? I don't want you playing cricket outside my house! Do you understand?"

The boy said nothing.

"I said do you understand?"

The boy remained silent and walked away.

The irate householder turned to the other boy. "He's not much of a talker, is he?"

"He's not much of a bowler either. He just put the ball through your window!"

1938

Bridgnorth Cricket Club

Barnes moved to Bridgnorth in 1938 and at 66 years of age he was still taking lots of wickets. In 18 games he had played for Bridgnorth, the Shropshire club, he took 102 wickets at an average of 6.8 runs. His stamina was considered remarkable. He had played every day in one week and on two of the days bowled unchanged.

Alec Bedser, bowling for England against Australia at Trent Bridge in June 1953, took his 190th Test wicket and thus broke the English record held by Barnes.

Barnes was in those days not an easy man to handle on the field of play. There was a fiendish aspect about him. He didn't play cricket out of any green field starry-eyed idealism. He rightly considered that his talents were worth estimating in cash values. In his old age he mellowed, yet remained humorously cynical.

An advert in the Yorkshire Evening Post on Monday 22 February, 1937. Sydney Barnes still wants to play cricket professionally, at the age of 64. "Engagement wanted for season 1937 – matches preferred. S.F. Barnes, Stafford."

Sports Writers XI v News Agencies
Wembley August 21st, 1938

L-r back row: Duncan Barnes, H.Martin, ---------, A.Gee, E.Hook, A.Dickinson, EM.Wellings, ----------(umpire).

L-r front row: AR.V.Barker, Arthur Brierley, L.V.Manning, B.J.Evans, D.R.Jardine, G.Duckworth, S.F.Barnes

1938 Barnes interview
with A.W. Ledbrooke

It was during the 1938 Australian tour and Test series against England that Barnes got into conversation on two occasions with the cricket correspondent, A.W. Ledbrooke. The conversations discussing England's position during the first and second Tests were recorded by Ledbrooke, and give a clear picture of Barnes' interesting and rare opinions of the game of cricket then, and the state of play in both these matches.

The stage was set. England were playing Australia in the first Test at Trent Bridge, Nottingham. This was a 4-day match 10-14 June, 1938. England had won the toss and decided to bat. And batted they did, and magnificently, enough to annihilate the Aussies with the score at 658 (E.Paynter not out 216, C.J.Barnett 126, Denis Compton 102, Len Hutton 100) for 8 wickets declared. Australia's answer to that was a decent score of 411 due mainly to the magnificent, intelligent and patient innings of one man, S.J.McCabe's 232, who was at the crease for almost four hours.

Their conversation was at the close of the third day's play. Australia had failed to avoid the follow on and were well into their second innings. J.Fingleton, had opened the batting and was out for 40, caught Hammond, bowled Edrich. Sir Donald Bradman, batting at number three, had joined W.A.Brown and had scored 3. Brown had reached his half-century on 51. The Australian score was 102/1.

Ledbrooke – *Well, you were about the only man in England who said the match wasn't as good as won on Saturday night and you were right. You said Australia might find a batsman capable of making 200, and they did.*

187

Barnes – *And what an innings! McCabe was in tremendous form and it was in every way a great feat of batsmanship. His footwork was so neat, so economical, that he made every stroke look easy and without a risk in it. I don't know of any batsman in the past thirty-five years who could have played this innings. He is certainly the finest stroke player in the world today, and equally certain is it that none of the old masters were better equipped. I do think, however, that when he was attacking Wright near the finish of his innings the ball should have kept up to him. That would have limited him at any rate to a certain extent the scope of his scoring shots and would have made him fight for his runs. Still, I am not going to be too critical of Hammond or of his bowlers. McCabe put the ball where he wanted it.*

Ledbrooke – *Although he scored so many runs I could have watched him all day. The size of the score never gave one the sense of "too much of a good thing" as it sometimes does.*

Barnes – *That's true. Yet, in this case figures are necessary to show how he dominated the match. He made his 232 out of 300, and while the Australians were taking the total from 194 to 411 the only help he got was Barnett's 22, O'Reilly's 39, McCormick's 2 and Fleetwood-Smith's 5. He made the rest. Mind you the tail-enders played their part much better than I expected they would. I don't think anybody expected they could defend so patiently or so well.*

Ledbrooke – *A great performance after going in with 658 up against them.*

Barnes – *Wonderful. The value of McCabe's innings is made all the greater by the fact that he must have been aware that one mistake by him would cost his side the game.*

Ledbrooke – *The pitch played pretty well or was that because McCabe played well?*

Barnes – *I noticed that just before he went off for the last time, Wright bowled a beautiful leg-break which turned a lot. That makes me think that it was McCabe's mastery which concealed some of the difficulties.*

Ledbrooke – *I didn't like the barracking because I thought it was ungrateful after all that had gone before, but all the same I did not like to see the cricket halted.*

Barnes – *I don't think Fingleton was justified in refusing to play. In my mind the barracking was very mild. There was no shouting only handclapping. In fact I thought it would be a gentle reminder of home to him. It was not to be compared with the sort of barracking I heard out in Australia in my playing days. I once refused to bowl while the row was going on, but in that case objectionable remarks were shouted. All that was over in a minute or two and that finished it. The slow play in Australia's second innings today was quite justified by the state of the game. If possible Brown and Fingleton wanted to avoid a new batsman coming to the wicket for an awkward half-hour.*

Ledbrooke – *The bowlers looked tired round about 6 o'clock. Perhaps that was why Bradman himself came in and took the risk of losing his priceless wicket.*

Barnes – *Well if he sent in Hassett or Badcock either may have been affected by the failure of the first innings and the light was still pretty good, not wonderfully good as one could expect for this time of the day without the sun actually shining.*

Ledbrooke – *I wonder what will happen tomorrow?*

Barnes – *Everything depends on the first two hours. If Brown sticks and Bradman gets going it will be odds on a draw, but another quick wicket or two will make it a good position for England. Indeed, it has come back to the position where we started the match – it all depends on Bradman.*

On the 4th and final day it was Brown (133) and Bradman (144 not out) who had frustrated England with their fine batting. England had failed to bowl out the Australians in an exciting finish, needing just 2 wickets for victory. Bradman had batted all day for his 144 not out and even in this high scoring battle, today he would have been a strong contender for the Man of the Match award. Barnes' forecast that the game would end in a draw if Brown and Bradman kept going, was correct.

England first innings		Australia first innings	
C.J.Barnett b McCormick	126	J.H.W.Fingleton b Wright	9
L.Hutton lbw b Fleetwood-Smith	100	W.A.Brown c Ames b Farnes	18
W.J.Edrich b O'Reilly	5	D.G.Bradman c Ames b Sinfield	51
W.R.Hammond b O'Reilly	26	S.J.McCabe c Compton b Verity	232
E.Paynter not out	216	F.A.Ward b Farnes	2
D.C.S.Compton c Badcock b. Fleetwood-Smith	102	A.L.Hassett c Hammond b Wright	1
L.E.G.Ames b Fleetwood-Smith	46	C.L.Badcock b Wright	9
H.Verity b Fleetwood-Smith	3	B.A.Barnett c Wright b Farnes	22
R.A.Sinfield lbw b O'Reilly	6	W.J.O'Reilly c Paynter b Farnes	9
D.V.P.Wright not out	1	E.L.McCormick b Wright	2

K.Farnes did not bat		L.O.Fleetwood-Smith not out	5
Extras (1b, 22lb, 4nb)	27	Extras (10b, 10lb, 1w)	21
Total (8 wickets, declared, 188 overs)	**658**	**Total (all out, 130.3 overs)**	**411**

Australia bowling	**England bowling**
Fleetwood-Smith 4/153, O'Reilly 3164, McCormick 1/108, McCabe 0/64	Farnes 4/106, Wright 4/153, Sinfield 1/51, Verity 1/36, Hammond 0/44

Australia second innings (following on)	
J.H.W.Fingleton c Hammond b Edrich	40
W.A.Brown c Paynter b Verity	133
D.G.Bradman not out	144
S.J.McCabe c Hammond b Verity	39
A.L.Hassett c Compton b Verity	2
C.L.Badcock b Wright	5
F.A.Ward not out	7
Extras (5b, 16lb, 5nb)	26
Total (6 wickets, 184 overs)	**427**

England bowling
Verity 3/102, Wright 1/85,Sinfield 1/72, Edrich 1/39, Hammond 0/15, Barnett 0/10

It was the second Test at Lord's a couple of weeks later when they met again to discuss the state of play in this 4-day match on 24-28 June, 1938. Australia were batting and at the close of play at the end of the second day were 299. W.A.Brown had opened the batting with Fingleton and was still there on 140 with B.A.Barnett on 6. Five wickets had fallen. They were chasing England's first innings total 494 (W.R.Hammond 240, E.Paynter 99, L.E.G.Ames 83) all out.

Ledbrooke – *We are not be able to force Australia to follow on but we are well on top now.*

Barnes – *Yes, that final thrust of Wellard's was a great piece of work for England. Just before 6 o'clock I remarked that two more wickets would be useful but I didn't see who was to get them. Within a few minutes both Hassett and Badcock had gone, and if Barnett could have been got rid of, we should have been laughing now. Yet I don't know that Hammond would forget the follow-on even if he had a chance. If the pitch is still good and the weather fine it is policy in a 4-day match to bat again and to get the side taking fourth knock. Still, in my opinion, Australia will save the follow-on, although of course we can look forward to a useful first innings lead.*

Ledbrooke – *A lead of a 100 or more should give the whole team the encouragement to go in determined to score solidly and to set Australia the task of saving the game on Tuesday.*

Barnes – *I feel more optimistic than I was when we had scored over 600 at Nottingham. There is more life in the pitch and the side are playing with some zest. At Trent Bridge on the Saturday we got three Australians out for 138 after we had declared. So that, on the score, they have done better this time. But the Lord's conditions are different, and we can say that there is a decent chance of a finish even in fine weather. Australia can't very well win, and I think we shall see them struggling to avoid defeat on Tuesday afternoon.*

Ledbrooke – *The record crowd had a great day's cricket to watch. It was a tremendous struggle even to the seasoned watcher.*

Barnes – *It has looked more like Test Match cricket than anything we saw – except McCabe's batting at Nottingham. The bowling and* *fielding were good yet the batting kept a high level too. Brown with his straight bat and watchfulness played very well although 100 in three hours and a quarter does not seem very exciting. The Australian total was then 231 in the same time which was quite satisfactory in view of the state of the game.*

Ledbrooke – *There was a general spirit of attack about the English side which I would like to have seen in the first Test. Farnes and Verity or Farnes and Wright always looked a dangerous combination.*

Barnes – *Even so, I think the selectors will still have to look around for another bowler. Wellard did magnificently when he bowled himself right out in that last spell, but up to then he had been giving away too many runs on the off-side. We shall have to wait and see whether he can produce another burst of inspired stuff in the second innings before we say that he has made sure of his place.*

Ledbrooke – *Although Farnes was really the big man of the attack, everyone had a hand in the good work and the score doesn't do justice to the cricket of the fielding side. In my opinion.*

Barnes – *Wright bowled a lovely leg-break to get Fingleton out just when the first two Australian batsmen were looking dangerously solid. Bradman came in and Hammond took Wright off – a move I mentally criticised but Verity did the trick, so that criticism is stifled. You can't criticise any captain whose moves, however obscure they may be, are successful. Possibly Hammond had in mind the fact that Verity has got Bradman's wickets as often as any English cricketer. Bradman was looking for runs which was quite good tactics on his part. Brown looked set and the captain's job was to get going while the wicket and weather remained good. But on looking around for scoring openings he picked the wrong ball did Bradman when he went for a cut and chopped the ball into his wicket because it came into him swinging a little. It was clever bowling by Verity who did extraordinarily well on this wicket. Brown played Verity best of all. Although he is not out,* *we can't expect fireworks from him like we got from McCabe in very similar circumstances at Trent Bridge.*

Australia went on to score 422 (W.A.Brown 206) all out. England scored 242 (Denis Compton 76 not out) for 8 declared in their second innings leaving Australia needing 315 to win the match. By the end of the final day Australia were 111 runs short which meant the game ended in a draw. Sir Donald Bradman played a well-deserved plucky century innings scoring 102 not out in Australia's second innings total of 204 for 6 wickets at the close of play.

England first innings		Australia first innings	
C.J.Barnett c Brown b McCormick	18	J.H.W.Fingleton c Hammond b Wright	31
L.Hutton c Brown McCormick	4	W.A.Brown not out	206
W.J.Edrich b McCormick	0	D.G.Bradman b Verity	18
WR.Hammond b McCormick	240	S.J.McCabe c Verity b Farnes	38
E.Paynter lbw b o'Reilly	99	A.L.Hassett lbw b Wellard	56
D.C.S.Compton lbw b O'Reilly	6	C.L.Badcock b Wellard	0
L.E.G.Ames c McCormick b Fleetwood-Smith	83	B.A.Barnett c Compton b Verity	8
H.Verity b O'Reilly	5	A.G.Chipperfield lbw b Verity	1
A.W.Wellard c McCormick b O'Reilly	4	W.J.O'Reilly b Farnes	42
D.V.P.Wright b Fleetwood-Smith	6	M.L.McCormick c Barnett b Farnes	0
K.Farnes not out	5	L.O.Fleetwood-Smith c Barnett b Verity	7
Extras (1b, 12lb, 10nb, 1w)	24	Extras (1b, 8lb, 6nb)	15
Total (all out, 137.3 overs)	**494**	**Total (all out, 121.4 overs)**	**422**

Australia bowling	England bowling
McCormick 4/101, O'Reilly 4/93, Fleetwood-Smith 2/132, McCabe 0/86, Chipperfield 0/51	Verity 4/103, Farnes 3/135, Wellard 2/96, Wright 1/68, Edrich 0/5

England second innings		Australia second innings	
C.J.Barnett c McCabe b McCormick	12	J.H.W.Fingleton c Hammond b Welland	4
L.Hutton c McCormick b O'Reilly	5	W.A.Brown b Verity	10
H.Verity b McCormick	11	D.G.Bradman not out	102
W.J.Edrich c McCabe b McCormick	10	S.J.McCabe c Hutton b Verity	21
E.Paynter run out	43	A.L.Hassett b Wright	42
W.R.Hammond c Sub b McCabe	2	C.L.Badcock c Wright b Edrich	0
D.C.S.Compton not out	76	B.A.Barnett c Paynter b Edrich	14
E.G.Ames c McCabe b O'Reilly	6	A.G.Chipperfield did not bat	
A.W.Wellard b McCabe	38	W.J.O'Reilly did not bat	
D.V.P.Wright not out	10	M.L.McCormick did not bat	
K.Farnes did not bat		L.O.Fleetwood-Smith did not bat	
Extras (12b, 12lb, 4nb, 1w)	29	Extras (5b, 3lb, 1nb, 2w)	11
Total (8 wickets, declared, 72 overs)	242	Total (6 wickets, 48.2 overs)	204

Australia bowling	England bowling
McCormick 3/72, O'Reilly, McCabe 2/58, Fleetwood -Smith 0/30	2/53, Verity 2/29, Edrich 2/27, Wellard 1/31, Wright 1/30, Farnes 0/51

Barnes' bowling arm

(age 61)

Barnes as a Batsman

Barnes possessed a very good knowledge of the technique of batting. He knew all the strokes and could demonstrate for the benefit of aspiring young batsmen how to play them. He often was seen going through the whole range of stroke production with a walking stick and an 'easy to understand' verbal explanation. Sometimes in the private room of a hotel in the evening during a match for Staffordshire with young batsmen from both opposing sides looking on. When he was at the wicket he looked the ideal batsman, standing up to his full height, swinging a perfectly straight bat and his forward strokes were said to be a joy to watch. Hard, low driving was his forte, but he could cut and glance too and push the ball to the on-side with little effort. In first-class cricket he was never called on as a batsman, but occasionally the needs of the side demanded an effort from him and on such occasions he surprised everyone.

At Melbourne in January 1908 when England were set to make 282 in the fourth innings to win the second Test match of the tour, Barnes stepped in and obliged. With 8 wickets down for 209 England still required 73, and the batsmen left to get them was Barnes, Humphreys (the Derbyshire wicket-keeper) and Fielder (the Kent fast bowler). It appeared to be a win for Australia. But Barnes and Humphreys added 34, and Barnes and Fielder scored the 39 to win the match by one wicket. Barnes made the winning hit, and scoring 38 not out at that critical stage, and gave some indication of what a great batsman he might have been. But that was only an exception to the general rule, especially in first-class cricket, for his batting was discouraged in the interests of his bowling and no doubt, rightly so.

His highest score in such cricket was 93, made during that same tour against Western Australia at Perth. In 1903 he had batted well on one or two occasions for the Players team against the Gentlemen, notably scoring 56 and in 1914 he scored 25 not out and 35 for the same team. The truth was he never had a batting average in first-class cricket that had any relation to his ability. But in Minor Counties and League cricket it was different. He played some fine innings for Rishton including more than one century, once hitting a quick 77 runs in 22 minutes. He made centuries also for Church including 113 not out at Bacup in 1904. Saltaire, Castleton Moor, Rochdale and Rawtenstall also derived great benefit from his prolific bat as well as from his dominance with the ball. Alas, his age and the passing years in his long career would, as expected, have a detrimental effect on him sighting the ball correctly when in flight. Yet a batting average of over 23 for Keighley in 1934, at the age of 61, would more than satisfy most men who were primarily bowlers, even at half his age. It seems strange that he batted four times for Staffordshire and scored just one run. Perhaps some blame should be considered by reports that the wickets at Wigan and Walsall were crumbling and unplayable when he made his mark at the crease.

A young admirer is taken notice of by his hero!

Barnes on Coaching

As well as being a professional coach during his 55 years as a professional cricketer, he did write a few articles on coaching. The following two articles was written by Barnes more especially to benefit young cricketers, but he stressed would also be equally interesting to non-players.

Fielding in relation to bowling

"In the first place I will endeavour to prove the great value of a good fielding side to a bowler. No matter how good the bowler may be he cannot hit the stumps when he likes, even though he is bowling well, so he must bowl to the field. This applies more to perfect batting wickets rather than damaged or sticky ones, because on wickets that you cannot get an inch of break or unless the ball swerves, it is not of much use simply trying to bowl a man out, for most of the straight balls are then put to leg. On such wickets always bowl as close to the off stump as possible, and then if you keep a good length you will always get wickets. It is this particular ball one bowls for catches in the slips. If you can make it go away a little it is a very deadly ball and the slip fielders, so that if the batsman does edge one, they will be ready to accept the chance. It is on these perfect wickets that a dropped catch generally proves disastrous to a side. So the fielders should be on the alert to every ball that is bowled. But even then catches are missed. I remember seeing in a match last summer one fielder dropping four catches within an hour and he is regarded to be one of the finest fielders in his position, but luckily for his piece of mind his side won the match. It matters not if a side has good bowlers and batsmen, if the fielding is not good they cannot expect to win matches.

Take the wicketkeeper. He has to always do his work neatly, no needless appealing to umpires such as one hears too often. He needs to get to know the batsman's weakness, for he needs to watch for this. As much as the bowler does, and on occasion dropping a hint to the bowler. Very often does him and his side a great service.

Next is the ideal slip fielder. A fast bowler would want nothing better than for the wicket to have a little 'life' in it. If the batsman did manage to edge one anywhere near to the slip fielders it would be a case of "all Lombard street to a gooseberry" and he would be smartly walking to the pavilion. The position of ''Point' is thought by many to be a very nice and easy one, but I can assure you from experience that there are better places on the field. Just fancy fielding there to a fast bowler who is a trifle short and the batsman can cut, well, I've been there so you know. The ball whizzes past you before you know where you are. Of course if it hits you it's "well fielded"! No, it is not the place where one can indulge in forty winks. To excel here, in fact in any position, you must have a knowledge of the batsman's style of play and watch the bowler deliver the ball. You can tell then if he will play forward or back and if he does play back you can move a little, but if he plays forward, hits or cuts, it's quite as well to stay back, then with long-fielders a slow-bowler can always 'feed' a batsman knowing that the first one he balloons and if it can be caught, one of them will be sure to catch it. The long-fielder should be a good thrower and able to return the ball so that the wicketkeeper receives it on the first bounce.

The fielder at Cover Point is required to gather the ball and return it in one action. When there is an Extra Cover fielder you never see a batsman take liberties when the ball is played anywhere near him. I have seen good Extra Cover fielders take catches that seemed to count for a four, but he has shot out his hand as the ball was passing and the bowler counts another victim instead of a boundary being booked against him.

When there is a good fielder at Mid-Off a bowler can always rest assured that anything that is possible to be stopped or caught will be dealt with. It would not require a genius to capture wickets. They keep their eyes open, watch every ball bowled down and they know by the stroke of the batsman when a ball is being played in their direction, or likely to be, for very often the ball goes where not intended, through the slips for instance and if they are not on the alert a chance is missed.

I think every player should be a good fielder providing he takes an interest in it, because it is so very natural to stop and pick up a ball, and with grounds in perfect condition there is no excuse not to collect the ball cleanly. The only way to become good fielders is to practise assiduously. A very good plan is for one to take a bat and the others to spread themselves out on the field and then the batsman to hit catches. At the same time having the wickets pitched a few yards wide of him and the wicketkeeper in his position. The fielders can also practise returning the ball as smartly as possible. A very good plan of having slip-fielding practice is for fielders to form a circle a few yards apart, and then throwing the ball about from one to the other trying to take each other by surprise. By constantly practising this you soon get out of that common bad habit of grabbing at the ball in your hands before closing them otherwise you will have some very bruised fingertips. For club cricketers to have half-an-hour of this every day there would soon be an improvement in their fielding and consequently the bowler's average would benefit accordingly.

Unfortunately players themselves do not, as a rule, pay enough attention to fielding although it is a well known fact that officials, when choosing a side, take into consideration a man's fielding abilities, and it very often is the case that a good fielder is selected instead of a decent bat. They know quite well in the truth of the old saying that it is sometimes easier to save runs than it is to make them.

It is always wise not to become used to fielding in one position alone. For occasions arise frequently when it is necessary for the captain to change the field and then it would be very awkward if all the side could only field in their own particular position. But everyone should know which position suits them best because I am sure every player can field in one position better than another. I will close now by giving a word of advice to fielders and bowlers.

To the bowler – Always bowl well within yourself and do not sacrifice length and accuracy for speed. In other words it is the same old saying that is handed down from one generation of cricketers to the next - "Bowl with your head".

To the fielder – Keep your eyes on the game. Watch the bowler for he may wish you to move to the right or to the left, to move back or come forward and in doing so without the batsman knowing. Always trust your captain implicitly and obey him without demur.

Good examples of fielders at their best. Tyldesley. Take the wicketkeeper first. An aspirant for the position could not possibly watch a better man than Lilley. Always does his work neatly. No needless appealing to the umpire such as one hears too often. And besides being a great wicketkeeper he soon gets to know the batsman's weakness for he watches this as much as the bowler does himself. And occasionally drops a hint to the bowler very often does him and his side a great service. Then Braund at slip is second to none and can well be taken as an ideal slip fielder, in my opinion the best I have seen. With him, A.C. McLaren and R.E. Foster together a fast bowler would want nothing better than for the wicket to have a little 'life' in it. If the batsman did manage to edge one anywhere near this trio it would be a case of the long walk to the pavilion."

My victims and how I get them

"When I stand at the wicket, with bat in hand, the thing which always strikes me is the amazing variety in the attack to which I am opposed. In fact, it almost seems as though there are about as many different types of balls as there are of bowlers. Of course in a general way we can sum up the kinds of bowling met with today under a very few headings. In doing this we should include as distinct types the fast pace man, the medium pace man, the slow bowler, the swerver and the googlie merchant. In those five you might well find nearly all the bowlers, as a batsman, you are met with today. As I say, however, such a summing up would but be a general one for it seems as though each type can be divided and sub-divided into many other different classes.

I sometimes wonder what some of the cricketers of old would say if they could look to one of our big matches. In those days, a hundred years or so ago, the only sort of bowling known then was underarm or lobs if you like. Round arm bowling was undreamed of and if some of these cricketers could be recalled to stand up against the varied attack of the present day I am quite sure they would be somewhat surprised. That cricket is all the better for the changes which have taken place I do not think anyone will deny that the greater variety in batting or bowling, has definitely created a greater charm in the game.

But while it is true that there are all sorts of ways of getting the batsmen out, it is equally true that now and then we strike a period when it seems as though one particular type of bowling was in favour. Not so long ago it was the googlie which came to the front. Everybody wanted to bowl this mysterious ball and at first nobody wanted to hold the bat against it. But the day of the googlie seems to have passed for the moment – it may come again.

Further back still, in the days of Richardson, Mold and Lockwood, it was a terrific bowler, the express man, who was in most demand and who seemed to get most of the wickets. Today, where are the really fast bowlers? We have a few, it is true, but there are many county sides who would like to find one and cannot do so. Today I think we can safely say is the day of the medium pace bowler. Such a large measure of success has attended various medium pace bowlers of late that at the moment this type of bowler is looked upon as being very necessary and useful on all sorts of wickets. Possibly the craze, if I may call it so, will vanish ere long. Whether that be so or not we can for a few moments think of some of the reasons for the success of the medium pace bowler and some of the methods employed as it is my type of bowling. I shall explain some of my own particular methods. It is understood of course that in so doing, I am not out to tell anybody that to copy me should be their aim or that it will bring success. Every bowler must bring individuality to bear on his deliveries remembering always that he is not a machine. This is one of the secrets of bowling success and the reason why there are so many failures.

Too many bowlers just keep sending down over after over, ball after ball, leaving the hand at the same pace and the same length or as near as they can make it. To study the batsman's weak points and to play up to them never seems to enter their heads. They may get some wickets by this mechanical bowling but they will certainly not get as many as they would like without using their brain to help them with their attack.

The first secret of success in all bowling is accuracy of length but this is more important to the medium pace bowler than to any other. A fast ball may get a wicket by sheer speed even if the length is not as good as it was intended. But to the medium pace bowler it might almost be said that length is well-nigh everything. Without something like accuracy in this direction he cannot hope to prove successful. When I prefer to accuracy of length I do not mean that every ball should be pitched on the same spot or within six inches of it. If I tried I could I suppose send down a whole over and pitch each ball within a circle of six inches but in actual play I should not dream of doing so. What I mean by accuracy of length is control of the length of the deliveries. This is the thing the young bowler should practise first of all. Never mind the speed and never mind the twist. Learn to pitch the ball where you want it – have control where you want to pitch it and have control over the length of your deliveries. When you have mastered the length you can get on with the other things.

There is another reason for whatever success I have achieved in bowling. Some batsmen I have chatted with declare that the thing about my bowling which makes it difficult to read so far as they are concerned is the height of which I deliver the ball. I am not tall. My height is like my bowling – medium. But when I deliver a ball my fairly long arm is stretched to the uttermost above my head and from this I get every bit of value there is to be got from what inches I possess. Undoubtedly the higher the bowler delivers the ball the greater his chance of success with it. Even to the non-playing man the reasons for this must be obvious. The greater the height at which the ball is delivered the greater the difficulty the batsman finds in judging the flight of the ball. Because of its height it seems likely to go much further than it actually does and many of my wickets have been obtained by batsmen who have thought they had a full-pitched ball to play when in fact it has dropped short before reaching the bat a foot or so in front.

The knack of making the ball increase in pace as it comes off the pitch is another valuable asset. In fact it might also be said that it is well nigh indispensable to the medium pace bowler. I am quite certain that Frank Foster, the Warwickshire player, who was so successful in the last Australian tour owed much of his success to this increased pace of the ball from the moment it came in contact with the pitch. Many of my own wickets have been obtained by the batsman playing too late.

Now we come to another important aspect of this medium pace bowling and that of the break. I do not claim to be able to make the ball break yards. I do not think it is at all necessary for a bowler to make it break sufficiently so that when the batsman makes his stroke the ball glances off the edge of the bat into the hands of one of the waiting fielders from off to leg or from leg to off. I can make the ball do a bit and I am always striving to change the direction of the break without any physical show of action which may inform the batsman of my intention. To deceive the batsman is a trick of the trade which every bowler should cultivate.

Summing up then, we may take it that the secrets of success for the medium pace bowler are the control of length, the increased pace of the pitch and sufficient break to beat the bat and with a high delivery as a valuable asset. In addition to all this there is a brain to be put into the bowling too. Then there are the fields men to be utilised and the batsmen's weak points to be discovered. There is the bowling for different types of wickets too. But these are big subjects of which we can only touch the fringe here. However, so far as the wickets are concerned did not somebody once say that any fool could get victims on a sticky pitch but on a good wicket a true bowler is required. If that be so then we may take it that the bowler who gets victims on a good wicket with fair regularity will reap harvest when the pitch is 'made' for him by the elements."

Barnes was introduced to an Arab sheik who boasted that he had eighty three wives. The bowler retorted, "You only need two more and you're entitled to a new ball."

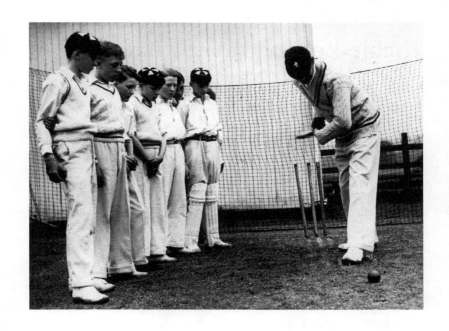

Richie Benaud salutes Barnes

Richie Benaud in his book 'My Spin on Cricket' names Sydney Barnes in his All-Time Greatest Cricket XI:

J.B.Hobbs (England)
S.M.Gavaskar (India)
D.G.Bradman Australia)
I.V.A.Richards (West Indies)
S.R.Tendulkar (India)
Gary Sobers (West Indies)
Imran Khan (Pakistan)
A.C.Gilchrist (West Indies)
S.K.Warne (Australia)
D.E.Lillee (Australia)
SF.Barnes (England)
12th Man: K.E.Miller (Australia)
Manager: F.M.M.Worrell (West Indies)

Richie Benaud wrote:

"Leading the attack is Sydney Francis Barnes, a bowler I met but never played against but one who, from the time I talked about cricket to older and more experienced people in Australia and England, is said by them to be the finest bowler of all time. I met him in 1953 at Stoke-on-Trent where the Australians were playing the Minor Counties. He bowled the first ball of the match. He had turned 80 years of age a couple of months earlier and the ball he bowled landed on a good length and the batsman bowled it defensively. Even then he was a tall straight-backed man with big hands, very long strong fingers and a firm handshake. Ability to swing the ball with great control and cut it off the pitch made him a formidable proposition. Barnes' record in Test cricket, at a time when the Australians had a splendid team, very strong in batting, and South Africa, the other nation of the time were very good, was astonishing.

He played only 27 matches, a mere ten of which were in England over a period of 13 years up to the start of the First World War. He took 189 wickets. When he went to Australia in 1911-12 he was up against the cream of Australian batting including Trumper, Bardsley, Hill, Armstrong, Kelleway, Ransford and the young Macartney. He took 34 wickets at almost 40 years of age on short-front pitches. He must have been some bowler!

When Barnes made his debut in a three-day Test at the Sydney Cricket Ground during the 1901-02 tour, he took 5/65 and 1/74. He took 13 wickets in the next Test, which was played at the Melbourne Cricket Ground, but damaged his knee two weeks later in Adelaide and played no more cricket on the tour. Melbourne was a favourite ground for Barnes and ten years after his Test debut he routed the Australians pre-lunch on the first day, taking 5/6 from 11 overs. Those present said he was close to unplayable as could be imagined. England won by eight wickets with Jack Hobbs included in my All-Time Greatest Cricket XI."

Barnes played in his first first-class match for Warwickshire in 1895; his last, for Wales, in 1930, when he was 57. Yet in that entire period of thirty-five years, he played only two full seasons and six odd games, in the County Championship, 44 matches altogether: he made more appearances than that for English touring teams in Australia and South Africa. But perhaps the most surprising comparison is that a man who played only 44 Championship games, played in 27 Tests.

Even if he had been an indifferent performer, the length of his cricketing life alone would make him remarkable. He played his first cricket match with adults for the third team of the local club in his native Smethwick in 1888: his last match was for Stone, in wartime Staffordshire league cricket, in 1940. That season, at the age of 67, he had such figures as 6 for 32 and 4 for 12 against Great Chell, 5 for 43 against Leek, and 5 for 22 against Caverswall.

More than six feet tall – he was still dominantly erect at ninety – with high, wide, rugged shoulders, deep chest, long arms and strong legs, he was perfectly built to be a bowler. There was virtually no cricket in his family, and he was never coached. But he had a natural aptitude – and avidity – for the game, and, by application and determination, he made himself into a right-arm, fast-medium bowler with the accuracy, spin and resource of a slow bowler, whose high delivery gave him a lift off the pitch that rapped the knuckles of the unwary and forced even the best batsmen to play him at an awkward height.

Stephen Brenkley's Top Ten Bowlers

In 2015 the well-known, highly-respected and knowledgeable cricket journalist Stephen Brenkley, of The Independent on Sunday newspaper and often seen on television and heard on radio, gave his list of the world's all-time greatest top-ten bowlers.

Before listing the names in order he explained how difficult it was to justify Barnes at number one since he had not bowled a ball in international cricket since 1914. (Brenkley can be forgiven for not remembering that Barnes played international cricket for Wales 1927-1930). It's true that the point he made was no-one who saw him is alive today. But, in his opinion, everything about him, the descriptions of his action, style, character approach, the figures alone make him a natural. He also writes that he was an independent-minded professional, a bowler before his time.

He mentions Sir Ian Botham and Sir Alec Bedser, whom he thinks might be rated too high. In true journalistic spirit he blames forces of nature that cannot be judged by normal standards when yeomen gladiators like the former should not be underestimated.

He considered that Fred Truman's legend precedes him because he remains what every young fast bowler should want to be. Of the spinners, his personal hero, Derek Underwood, he remembered was looking like breaking every record known to man when he took 100 wickets in his first season at 17 years of age.

Probably, in truth, he admits that Jimmy Anderson is too low. Also that John Snow, the thinking man's fast bowler who was the key in wins against the West Indies in 1968 and Australia in 1970-71 should have been included, but isn't.

Sydney Barnes – Perhaps greatest of all bowlers. Picked and chose matches, still took 106 Ashes wickets, prominent in the great 1911-12 series. A character as austere as medium-fast bowling was to being parsimonious.

Sir Ian Botham – For five years, utterly irrepressible. Often overlooked how markedly he declined – his first 202 wickets cost 21 runs each, the next 181, 36 – but what a compelling performer.

Harold Larwood – For the Bodyline series alone deserves his place. Won the series, carried can but also had key part in two previous Ashes. A great fast bowler.

Fred Trueman – The legend became almost greater than the bowler. Not quite. A seriously skilful, initially genuine speed merchant, with boundless charisma and a beautiful, durable action.

Hedley Verity – Illustrious left-arm spinner in what was an enduring English production line. His 14 wickets in a day at Lord's against Australia in 1934 will never be surpassed.

Sir Alec Bedser – Line and length bowler with immense stamina and resolve. Took 39 wickets in the victorious 1953 Ashes, still a record for an England seamer.

Jim Laker – For his deeds in 1956 alone will always be remembered. He took 46 wickets in the series. 19 in one match, his off-spin was the template for all.

Derek Underwood – Had breakaway tournaments and rebel tours not intervened would probably have set a record still to be beaten. Unique left-arm spinner who offered control and penetration.

Jimmy Anderson – Operating on the sort of pitches he often likes, his record is remarkable. True match-winning displays but his longevity, his ever increasing skill, a joy to behold.

Brian Statham – Under-rated, probably under-capped Lancastrian, should have been Trueman's foil much more often. *"If they miss, I hit,"* he said – and he was right.

An interesting point of view

Sydney Barnes was regarded by the Establishment and by some of his fellow professionals as an impossible human being whose genius simply wasn't worth the hassle. Inspired more by financial reward than status he gave up county cricket in 1903. He was content to slum it in the Lancashire/Yorkshire leagues earning a pretty penny. However, he was named Wisden Cricketer Of The Year 1910. He remains the only man to be picked for England whilst playing league and minor county cricket. He took 1,432 wickets for Staffordshire at less than 9 runs each and played for the county until he was over 60 years of age.

Why was he so good?

Like most small boys even today, Sydney Barnes wanted to bowl fast, like his hero Tom Richardson. At 15 when he started playing for Smethwick in the Birmingham League their professional, Billy Bird of Warwickshire, thought he saw something in the lad and insisted in him joining his net for practice.

Billy bowled medium paced off-spin and the young tearaway who also batted and kept wicket was persuaded to give off-spin a go. The compromise was fast-medium off-breaks.

A tall fellow of 6 ft 1in, Barnes bowled with a high action – he later spoke of hooking up with the sky as he delivered – and brought the ball down from a considerable height.

Today these positions are called 'the set up', 'the unfold' and 'the delivery'.

He must also have soon developed a huge amount of action on the ball because those who faced him describe how he got the ball to move away from the right hander before breaking back into him and others describe how the ball dipped late on them so that they would misread its length. These are descriptions of the Magnus Effect at work.

He was not an instant success either at club level or later when playing for Warwickshire in three matches, but he was obviously difficult to get away even if he wasn't taking wickets. Those wickets may well have fallen at the other end, as a result of the pressure he was putting on batsmen at his end.

After his selection by MacLaren to tour Australia in 1901/02 he told the captain that, in the cricket he had played in the Lancashire League, he felt that he had to get results on any kind of wicket. If the wicket took spin he did not bowl his heart out with fast stuff, but if the wicket was good and firm he did bowl faster.

Most cricketers and students of the game belonging to the period in which Barnes played were agreed that he was the bowler of the century. Australians as well as the English voted him unanimously the greatest. Clem Hill, the famous Australian left-handed batsman, who in successive Test innings scored 99, 98, 97, against MacLaren's England team, told me that on a perfect wicket Barnes could swing the new ball in and out "very late", could spin from the ground, pitch on the leg stump and miss the off. At Melbourne, in December 1911, Barnes in five overs overwhelmed Kelleway, Bardsley, Hill and Armstrong for a single.

Hill was clean bowled by him:

"The ball pitched outside my leg-stump, safe to the push off my pads, I thought. Before I could 'pick up' my bat, my off-stump was knocked silly."

Barnes was creative, one of the first bowlers really to use the seam of a new ball and combine swing so subtly with spin that few batsmen could distinguish one from the other.

Although successful in Australia, the experience of playing at Melbourne in the second Test after the wicket had dried out (with the help of the ground staff using blankets and rollers overnight) and two similar experiences trying to take wickets on a flat Oval track he started to work on a leg break.

Apparently it took some time and work in the nets, but once he had gained the skill he found it easy to accomplish.

Again, with his long and strong figures he must have been able to impart considerable turn on the ball because opponents now spoke in awe of the in-swinging ball that pitched on or even outside leg stump, but which broke across them to hit the top of the off-stump or find the end to the wicketkeeper or slip cordon. This was further evidence that there were enough revs on the ball to get the Magnus Effect (often called the Magnus force and named after its 1852 discoverer, is a lift force of tremendous importance to all bowlers who want to bend the flight of a ball) to give the ball sideways momentum. The leg break was also bowled out of the front of the hand. The third and small finger of the right hand is held under the side of the ball and that the spin is imparted by these fingers flicking upwards.

Barnes was described as "perfectly built to be a bowler" because of his straight posture with wide shoulders, deep chest, long arms and strong legs. His remarkable figures were a simple testament to a top-class bowler from a golden age. While he played in just 10 home Tests, the remainder (13 in all) were played in Australia and the other 4 in South Africa. Barnes was always clever at hiding his pace in the pitch and could produce deliveries that were both faster and slower than his ordinary fast-medium ball. He lacked the personal charm that might have enabled his less striking character traits to be overlooked but he was treated with respect and he would give back by working hard and being loyal.

Many bowlers can form a good idea of the kind of ball needed to test a batsman's weak spot, but few can actually bowl the right one at will. Barnes very quickly combined a quick insight into a batsman's methods and inclinations and a rare judgement of the kind of ball required to find his weakness, with the ability to deliver exactly the ball he wanted to bowl. A remarkable foresight as to what precisely the batsman will do with it. Another outstanding ability was to bowl for long spells without the slightest loss of either sting or accuracy.

His skill with which he could probe a batsman's individual characteristics was an asset which increased in value as his experience and his keen insight developed. When placing his field there had been criticism that his slowness in not getting on with it, was a means of a design to impress when he was bowling. Some players, as well as spectators, were irritated by his flicking finger when monitoring a fielder a yard or two this way or that. Many a voice was heard from the crowd to "get on with it" only to reveal a combination of impatience and ignorance. This showing was not in the least irritating to fielders who knew him. They were very much aware of his intense mental concentration in the business of getting the batsman out and of his exceptional faculty of calculating a batsman's stroke. It was not assumed then but the statistics have proven that he did not rely mainly on his fielders for his wickets. A large proportion of them had been clean bowled. It's probably true that no bowler has completely beaten the bat and narrowly missed the wicket as many times as he did. His speciality was the 'flashing' leg-break which, ball after ball, just beat the off-stump or rose an inch or two over the bails.

He had the perfect physical advantages for a bowler. With 6ft of stature, an exceptional reach, a supple and athletic frame, not an ounce of superfluous flesh, and great powers of endurance, he was ideally built for a bowler. Perhaps his most important physical feature consisted of his long and strong fingers, made for spinning a cricket ball. In delivery he used a run of moderate length with just two or three big springy strides in it. He made full use of the impetus gathered to getting his arm high and straight and able to 'whip' the ball down. So, out of clear thinking, great will power and the fullest use of remarkable physical advantages, he was able to produce a comprehensive repertoire, appropriately and affectionately called the 'Barnes Ball'.

What was the 'Barnes ball'?

In his own words:

"My idea was to deliver the leg ball from the same height as the one from the off, thereby, instead of tossing it up, as most leg-break bowlers do, to whip it down, and this, in my opinion, is the chief virtue of this particular delivery."

Some cricket observers came to the conclusion that Barnes used his third finger for leg-break, much in the same way that the first finger is generally used for off-break. An opinion was that it is not a case of turning the hand over the ball to obtain leg-spin. It appeared that the ball was held in exactly the same way in three fingers for the leg-break, as of the off-break, the second finger being over the top and the first and third spread on either side. The delivery being the same with the ball being whipped down from the full height of his reach, whether he is delivering off-spin, mainly with the first finger, or leg-spin, mainly with the third. The effect of this was that the batsman was left in doubt until the ball actually left the hand as to which way it was going to spin, and even then it was not by any means easy to be sure. Also the batsman's difficulty was enhanced by the fact that there was little change in flight and pace to differentiate the leg-break from the off-spinner.

The 'Barnes ball' was considered to be ineffective without accuracy. His ability to bowl a spinning, fizzing ball, and mix it with off-breaks and swingers, and almost every variety of ball (except a googly he regarded a little scornfully not to use for some reason), to apply all different speeds of the ball from really fast to slow-medium all the time was very rewarding. His marvellous accuracy and a unique leg-break was in the opinion of many what made him the greatest bowler of all time.

A Cricket Story

At a cricket match in Yorkshire in 1904 an appeal was made against the batsman for obstructing the field. The visiting side were not quite sure which umpire should be asked so some asked one and some the other. Umpire No.1 said, "Out". Umpire No. 2 said, "Not Out". Consequently a dispute ensued. At last Umpire No.1 stalked up to Umpire No.2. "Have you shaken hands with Lord Hawke?" he demanded imperiously. "No," said No.2. "Well I have – Out" came the reply. That settled it and the batsman sheepishly left the field.

An audience with David Frith
(Cricket author and journalist)

"What do you want?" A nice greeting, I must say, to a pilgrim who had just driven for three hours all the way up to Cannock, Staffordshire. It was not as if my visit was unscheduled. Sydney Barnes had agreed to it by telephone. He was now 94, and still ferociously sharp mentally. And here I was, looking up into that gaunt face framed in the doorway, and wondering if I was ever going to be invited in.

Maybe he was playing games, teasing, provoking? The history books tell of how difficult he could be to captains, committees and opponents. Now he even refused to sign a book because I had only a ballpoint pen. His copperplate handwriting with a fountain pen – or was it a quill? – was renowned. "I'm not going into the office for you just to get my pen," he croaked. It was a Saturday, so the council office in Stafford where he worked part-time would be locked anyway.

He took some warming up. Then the stories began to flow, though I can't recall a real smile throughout that awesome session in the living room – a faintly evil grimace, yes.

Animatedly he talked me through his first morning spell against Australia at Melbourne in the 1911-12 Ashes series: bowled Bardsley with his first ball, had Kelleway lbw, bowled Hill, then had Armstrong caught by his Warwickshire wicketkeeper Tiger Smith: 4 for 1 in seven legendary overs. Having Minnett later caught by Hobbs gave him 5 for 6, all quality wickets, and England were on their way to sweeping the series after the first Test had been lost. That'd show that vain captain, J.W.H.T. Douglas, that he should use the new ball with Frank Foster.

Barnes revealed that the man who brought a bottle of whisky to him in his room the night before, after word had circulated that he was sick, was none other than the Australian veteran, little Syd Gregory, who was not playing. It made all the difference next day. "SF" was fiery as ever, shocking Australia with that 11-over spell, later flopping to the turf when he was barracked for slow field arrangement, resuming only when it stopped.

Did he cut the ball like Underwood? *"Cut* it!" He glared, and again I wondered if he might hurl something at me. "I *spun* the ball!" Those long, gnarled fingers gyrated around imaginary leather. He bowled a brisk medium, but applied spin, with excruciating accuracy. No wonder he was regarded as the greatest bowler of all by most thoughtful judges. His bag of 34 wickets in South Africa in 1913-14 is still a series record. And he missed the fifth Test! The official reasons were hazy, but Barnes now explained: they wouldn't pay for his wife's accommodation. That marked the end of his erratic Test career: 189 wickets at 16.43 in 27 Tests. He was 40. Had he played as many Tests as Shane Warne (as yet unborn when we met), Barnes might have finished with around 1,000 wickets, though covered pitches would have cut him back a little (my view, not his).

Like most old-timers, he had a distant look in his eyes as he recalled long-ago incidents and events: England's one-wicket victory which he pulled off with Arthur Fielder at the MCG in 1908, and his feigned injury when the fee offered for playing in the Lord's centenary match in 1914 was reckoned inadequate. Money drove him beyond most other considerations.

He went from league club to league club because the pay in county cricket fell short. He had as little respect for committees as for opposing batsmen. This theme saturated his reminiscences. Years later the great South African off-spinner Hugh Tayfield passed on to me some extreme advice that Barnes had given him: "Don't take any notice of anything anybody ever tells you!"

It was slightly demanding as well as pleasurable to be in Barnes' company. A nonagenarian he might have been, yet his brooding countenance gave a vivid taste of what it must have been like to be an opposing batsman. He wasn't all malevolence: as I was leaving, he relented and signed my book."

David Frith is a famous cricket journalist and author. He was born in London in 1937. In 1973 he became editor of The Cricketer. He founded the Wisden Cricket Monthly and in 1988 won the Sports Council's British Sports Journalism award as Magazine Sports Writer of the Year. He has written dozens of books on both cricket in modern times and cricket of the past. His book the *Bodyline Autopsy*, won Wisden's book of the year in 2003 and, in January 2010, it won Cricketweb's award for "book of the decade". He is the only author to win the Cricket Society's annual book award three times. He has been honorary vice-president of the Cricket Memorabilia Society since its foundation in 1987.

In 2013 he was awarded honorary life membership of the Association of Cricket Statisticians and Historians, and wrote a further book, 'Guildford's Cricket Story', which revealed his adopted home town's unique claims to being the 'cradle of cricket'.

In association with the National Film and Television Archive, he presented an annual archive cricket film evening at the National Film Theatre in London for 30 years.

He could also play cricket too. During the 1960s he played first-grade cricket in Sydney, Australia where he lived for a while.

David Frith at home

Barnes (90 years of age) presenting the end-of-season prizes to the players at Stafford Cricket Club on 13th July, 1964.

Letter to John Arlott

Barnes received a letter from John Arlott in October, 1962 inviting him to a celebration lunch for Sir Jack Hobbs' 80th Birthday. The following is a photocopy of the original reply which he wrote in the style of his handwriting as a skilled calligrapher.

> Coppice House
> Teddesley
> Penkridge
> Nr Stafford
> 5 Nov. 1962

My Dear John,

Thanks for yours of the 31st October. As for coming to London for Jack's 80th I am sorry to say I cannot promise to be at the lunch – even if I do a short journey in the car, I have a giddy turn when I get out. So a long journey is out of the question – please give him my best wishes.

As to John Bridges coming to see me and get my views on Jack's batting, I shall give him to the best of my ability what I think and what I always thought.

I note you are writing an article for The Cricketer in the Spring.

For my abode forget Penkridge, I am 4 miles away, come to Cannock and I am on the Cannock to Stafford road. At Huntingdon you will come to a dual carriageway of a length of about 1 mile from the end of the said dual CW. About half a mile further on towards Stafford you will see on your left some farm buildings standings some 100 yards from the road. The house is among these buildings – in fact it is the first building on the left after leaving the dual CW.

Perhaps I shall hear further from (you).

Yours sincerely, *Syd. (S.F.Barnes)*

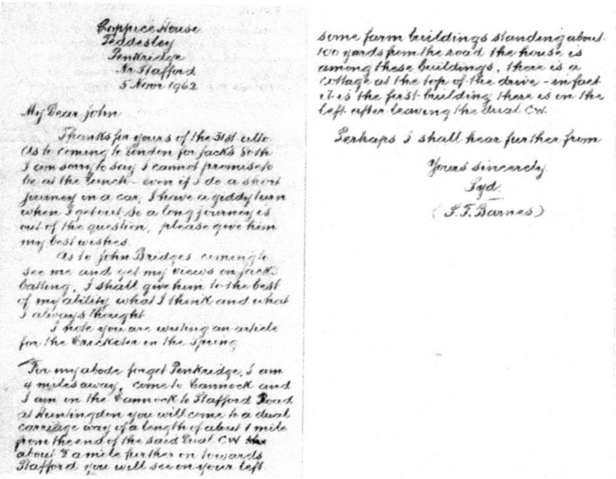

[handwritten letter reproduced]

John Arlott (Leslie Thomas John Arlott OBE, 1914-1991) was an English journalist, author and cricket commentator for the BBC's Test Match Special. He was also a poet and wine connoisseur. With his poetic phraseology, he became an iconic cricket commentator noted for his "wonderful gift for evoking cricketing moments" by the BBC.

Sir Jack Hobbs (1882-1963) played for Surrey from 1905 to 1934 and for England in 61 Test matches between 1908 and 1930. Known as "The Master", he is regarded by critics as one of the greatest batsmen in the history of cricket. He is the leading run-scorer and century maker in first-class cricket, scoring 61,760 runs and 199 centuries. A right-handed batsman and an occasional right-arm medium pace bowler, Hobbs also excelled as a fielder, particularly in the position of cover-point.

He was the first cricketer to be honoured with a Knighthood in 1953.

Sydney Barnes - cricket's living legend

In 1963, John Arlott paid tribute to Barnes as follows:

"The living legend of cricket, that is Sydney Francis Barnes, became ninety years old on April 19, 1963. Those who played with or against him, over a period of almost three normal cricketing lifetimes, had no doubt that he stood alone – the greatest bowler that ever lived. He played county cricket before the Boer War; he was still returning amazing analyses in club games during the Second World War. Yet he was perhaps the least seen of all great players.

He played in his first first-class match for Warwickshire in 1895; his last, for Wales, in 1930, when he was 57. Yet in that entire period of thirty-five years, he played only two full seasons and six odd games, in the County Championship – 44 matches altogether: he made more appearances than that for English touring teams in Australia and South Africa. But perhaps the most surprising comparison is that a man who played only 44 Championship games, played in 27 Tests.

Even if he had been an indifferent performer, the length of his cricketing life alone would make him remarkable. He played his first cricket match with adults for the third team of the local club in his native Smethwick in 1888: his last match was for Stone, in wartime Staffordshire league cricket, in 1940. That season, at the age of 67, he had such figures as 6 for 32 and 4 for 12 against Great Chell, 5 for 43 against Leek, and 5 for 22 against Caverswall.

His usual pace was about that of Alec Bedser, with a faster ball and a slower one, in well-concealed reserve, and the ability to bowl a yorker. He himself is content that he was essentially a spin bowler, that his movement through the air was, in modern technical language, swerve – obtained by spin – rather than 'swing', which derives from the 'seam-up' method. Certainly he made the ball move both ways through the air, and with a first and second-finger application rather similar to that of Ramadhin – he bowled both the off-break and the leg-break. Indeed, he could bowl the googly at about slow-medium pace and where, in exceptional conditions, the pitch dictated it, he could be a fine slow bowler.

This is such technical equipment as no one in the history of the game has excelled. Barnes added to it a sustained hostility and remarkable stamina, which were reflected in constant, unrelenting probing for a batsman's weakness and then attacking it by surprise, each ball fitting into a tactical pattern.

A striking example of this aspect of his cricketing character comes from the 1913-14 tour of South Africa, where his combination of lift and spin was virtually unplayable on the matting wickets and he set up a record for any series by taking 49 wickets, although, because of a financial disagreement, he did not play in the fifth Test. H.W. Taylor was the only South African batsman who really resisted him, though Barnes took his wicket in five of the eight Test innings Taylor played against him. In the Fourth Test, Barnes, convinced that he knew how he might beat Taylor, bowled on and on at him: Taylor, content merely to defend against Barnes (32 overs for 88 runs and 7 wickets) scored 93 before Barnes had him lbw – as he had said he would do.

Both Sir Jack Hobbs and Wilfred Rhodes thought this was one of Barnes' finest bowling spells, though they were both playing two years earlier when, on a perfect, hard Melbourne wicket, he produced his epic opening spell against a strong Australian batting side. Starting the bowling with F. R. Foster, he put out the first four Australian batsmen – Bardsley, Kelleway, Hill and Armstrong – for one run. He had Minnett's wicket, too, and after eighty minutes, his figures were 11 overs, 7 maidens, 6 runs, 5 wickets.

It is hard to believe that a player of such quality could be allowed to stay out of county cricket in modern times. As a straightforward fast bowler of nineteen, he was promising enough to play for Warwickshire in a two-day match against Cheshire, then an immensely strong Minor Counties side: he did not bowl in the first innings: in the second he was one of ten bowlers used by Warwickshire while Cheshire built up a big score: his eight overs cost 27 runs and he did not take a wicket. Still raw, he played in one match for Warwickshire in 1895 and two in 1896.

Three wickets at an average of 75 runs apiece, was the extent of his cricket with Warwickshire before he went to League cricket with Rishton from 1895 to 1899 and then for two seasons with Burnley. He played twice in the Championship for Lancashire in 1899 (4 for 161), and then, in 1901, A. C. MacLaren put him in the Lancashire team for the last match of the season-against Leicestershire at Old Trafford.

Rain spoilt the last day but, in the first Leicestershire innings, Barnes took 6 for 70. Immediately afterwards MacLaren announced that the unknown bowler – with a first-class record of thirteen wickets, spread over seven seasons – would be in his team to go to Australia. Barnes began the tour with five wickets in the match against South Australia, twelve against Victoria and five against New South Wales. He was picked for the first Test, 5 for 65, and 1 for 74; in the second he had 6 for 42 and 7 for 121. Then he broke down with a knee injury but, although he himself believes he was still far short of his best, he had established himself as a world-class bowler.

He spent 1902 and much over-bowled in1903 with Lancashire: but then he left them because of a dispute about winter employment and became, for the rest of his career, a professional in League cricket and for Staffordshire in the Minor Counties competition. He was proud of the profession of cricketer and while he believed, uncompromisingly, that the labourer was worthy of his hire, it would have been foreign to his nature to shame it by giving less than his best.

But that best, outstanding on international level, was killing when directed at league players. Small wonder that many of them found themselves shaking at the approach of this glowering near-giant in physique, utter giant in ability. His professional honour, however, was satisfied by the fact that every league club that ever engaged him won its competition.

His first league engagement was in 1895, his last in 1938: in those 43 years he earned his wages with over four thousand wickets for an average of about seven: seventeen thousand runs at roughly 25 an innings. For Staffordshire, in twenty-three seasons between 1904 and 1935, his record is 1,437 wickets at 8.04, and 5,254 runs at 22.45.

He continued to play for England, on and off, until 1914: in eight series (seven, if the Triangular of 1912 is counted as one) he played in 27 Tests, all against Australia or South Africa, and took 189 wickets, at the rate of one every seven overs for an average of 16.43. In eight matches for the Players against the Gentlemen he took 45 wickets at 15.26: no other bowler in this century has taken so many in that fixture at so low cost. Otherwise his first-class cricket was confined to appearances for Staffordshire, the Minor Counties or Wales, usually against the touring side. In 1929, his figures in two matches against the South Africans were 8 for 41 and 1 for 19 (for Minor Counties) and 6 for 28 and 4 for 62 (for Wales). That year, at the age of 56, he was fifth in the first-class bowling averages.

His last season as a professional was for Bridgnorth in 1938. He was 65 years old; he played on every day except Friday of August week and finished top, not only of the club's bowling (126 wickets at 6.94), but of the batting as well (314 runs at 28.55).

Five wickets in five balls in a league match: four in four four times (including the first four of Durham in 1907): an uncounted number of hat-tricks but including two against major batsmen: one in a Test Trial another in Gentlemen v. Players: and, once, two in an innings: all ten at least a dozen times.

Durham seem to have been his favourite victims: in 1909 he took 14 of their wickets for 13 runs in a single day: the next year, 8 for 16 and 8 for 30: in 1911, 9 for 37 in the first innings, 8 for 46 in the second-and he himself scored 136 in his only innings of the match. In 1908, when the Minor Counties competition was arranged in four groups and played off between the four leaders in knock-out form, Barnes won it for Staffordshire with 24 wickets at 3.25 each in their semi-final and final matches.

In all cricket he took over 6,300 wickets at an average of 9. But one could go on and on quoting bewildering figures for him: and no one can hazard a guess at the number of times, even against the greatest batsmen and on good wickets, that he beat the bat and missed the stumps.

But certainly, with his peerless, flashing leg-break alone, he must have done so more often than anyone else in all cricket. So often the batsman could not even edge a catch. Hence the classic Sydney Barnes story of the day when two tail-enders were playing at him and missing or, occasionally, snicking, and he stalked away at the end of the over with the comment 'They aren't batting well enough to get out.'

It is an essential aspect of his cricket, however, that in the second Test of 1907-08 against Australia, when he put on 34 for the ninth wicket with Humphries and 39 for the last with Fielder, his batting won the match for England by one wicket.

Indeed, there is good evidence that he could have made an extremely capable batsman if his captains, MacLaren in particular, had not been so anxious to save him for his bowling that they even told him not to take batting practice!

On the 1907-08 tour of Australia, when the M.C.C. side was troubled with injuries and Barnes himself was only partly fit, A. O. Jones asked him, half-jokingly, to 'play for his batting' against Western Australia. After Hobbs, Fane, Hardstaff and Rhodes had all gone for less than 120, Barnes made 93, second highest score of the innings and his own biggest score in first-class cricket, and with George Gunn, put on over 200 for the fifth wicket. In League cricket, too, he often made runs at crucial stages of matches, batting very correctly and, from his appreciable height, getting well over pace bowling.

He was one of those fortunate athletes who, although very strongly built, never tended to run to fat. He kept himself sternly fit because he was deeply concerned always to bowl well: that guiding light to his life is important, for it explains the fact that no one records him bowling untidily, nor – amazingly – ever having an 'off day'. Even now, at ninety, his essential strength and co-ordination are reflected in an impeccable, copperplate handwriting and in his unhurried, but unwavering, movements at an age when most men are at least somewhat shaky.

Nowadays, among cricketers, it is a memory to cherish – like having bowled to W. G. Grace – that one batted against Barnes. It is sad, though, that he was so little seen. He did not play twenty first-class matches in the south of England and barely a hundred in all England. Yet the evidence is overwhelming, in South Africa, Australia and England, that he was the greatest of all bowlers.

His bowling in 1913-14 made the South African batting look abject: but it should not be forgotten that they had beaten England in the preceding series over there. In fact, too, more than half Barnes's seven-hundred-odd wickets were taken in representative games.

Simply to see him bowl – and he was over sixty on the only occasion I ever watched him in action – was to make the instant impression of majesty, hostility and control. This was, without doubt, a born bowler, who lived to bowl.

No batsman even dared to claim that he was Barnes' master. Asked which of them he found most difficult he answers `Victor Trumper'. Who next? `No one else ever troubled me.'

No cricketer who played with or against him has any doubt that Sydney Barnes was the greatest bowler the world has ever seen. Had Warwickshire, in 1896, or Lancashire, in 1903, thought differently and kept him in county cricket, the history of the game would be markedly different – and richer."

Remembering a Super Star by Bill Keleghan

"In my time, the bell indicated the end of the school day at "four ten", the year that the Romans left Britain as we were often reminded in both History and Latin classes. Coincidentally, the bus to Doxey (a district in Stafford) was timed for ten-past four and, as a result, there was often a sprint from the entrance in Friars Terrace to the bus stop in Newport Road which, on occasions, culminated in a leap onto the platform of a moving vehicle. Buses are a lot less fun than they used to be. On other days, I caught later buses and, consequently, spent lengthy periods standing outside the school.

Sometimes, I would see an erect, elderly, slightly gaunt gentleman boarding the bus to Lichfield from the opposite pavement. This was Sydney Barnes, one of the finest cricketers who ever played the game. He was then in his late eighties and still working as a calligrapher for Staffordshire County Council.

I was first aware of Sydney Barnes when, in 1953, my father took his seven-year-old son to a game to mark the eightieth birthday of the great man. This featured some of the finest players of the day, including Denis Compton and Cyril Washbrook. Barnes initiated the event, attended by 5,000 people, by bowling a maiden over.

That was my first visit to The Hough where, in later years, I was to represent both the school and Stafford Cricket Club (but never in front of so many spectators). Who remembers carrying the communal kit, stored in the Cloisters, to and from The Hough on match days? It was one of those character-forming tasks that no-one liked but which had to be done.

Sydney Barnes was the most prolific bowler in the history of Test Matches, averaging 7 wickets per match and taking 189 wickets for England, a figure that was not surpassed until thirty years after his final appearance. To put this achievement into context, only Dennis Lillee, Sir Richard Hadlee and Muttiah Murilitharan have reached 5 wickets per match in modern times. Barnes stands second on the all-time list for wickets per over (nowadays termed Strike Rate). In an age when cricketers were either Gentlemen (amateurs) or Players, Sydney Barnes was a dedicated (and reportedly forthright) professional, spending most of his career in local leagues. His appearances in County Cricket amounted to a few games for Warwickshire and two seasons at Lancashire, but he took 1,441 wickets for Staffordshire in the Minor Counties competition, a record that will never be surpassed. He played competitively until he was well into his sixties and his prowess was undimmed. At the age of 58, he took 115 wickets for Rawtenstall in the Lancashire League at a cost of only 6.3 runs per wicket.

Sydney Barnes joined Staffordshire County Council in 1939 when he was 66 years old, an age by which the majority of Old Edwardians have retired. At the Shire Hall, he was able to exercise his second great gift, a talent for copperplate writing that he developed at school. The County Council marked his ninetieth birthday with a hamper of food and wine. As a lad, I was aware that Sydney Barnes had been a great cricketer and, even then, I found it remarkable that he could go about his business not in any way harassed and largely unrecognised. That would never happen today. However, it was not until recently, while pontificating about great sportsmen of the past to a young colleague, that I discovered the full extent of his exploits via the internet.

Sydney Barnes was born in Smethwick, which was then part of Staffordshire. Alongside Stanley Matthews, he must rank as one of the county's greatest sporting heroes and should never be forgotten. Comparisons serve little purpose but, at a time when, in my opinion, the standard of batting in English cricket is extremely low, I suspect that a reincarnated Barnes would be as successful today as he was in the distant past. He played much of his cricket in the days before motor cars, let alone aeroplanes, and yet he toured Australia on a number of occasions and claimed a record 49 victims in only four Test Matches in South Africa in 1913/14.

I have many memories from my schooldays, recalling masters, fellow pupils and occasional transgressions, but none is more vivid than my recollection of seeing Sydney Barnes going quietly about his business. He was a true sporting superstar."

"*We don't understand you,*" Lord Hawke had said when he was trying in vain to persuade Barnes to go to South Africa. "*You only play when you like.*"

"*And that is what I intend doing. I have a life besides cricket and I am looking after it. Cricket is a secondary consideration,*" replied Barnes sternly.

A Barnes postcard

A postcard sent to a Mrs A.Bennett of Northampton from Howard. The postmark is dated 24th September 2004 and was sent from Accrington.

The message reads:
    "Hope to hear from you soon. I think the S.F.B photos are a treat don't forget to send, Howard"

Testimonial Match

At 80 years of age Barnes bowled the opening over at his birthday Testimonial match.

"Did he take his usual run?" asked a cricket reporter. *"He did and his arm was high as ever"* was the reply.

At the age of 80 in April 1953 he had just bowled an over in his own Testimonial game on the Stafford ground. There were names like Norman Yardley, Bill Edrich, Dennis Compton, Reg Simpson, Cyril Washbrook and Wilfred Robins and other famous England players on the scorecard, but it was Barnes' day. He was the man that 5,000 people wanted to see. Clad in immaculate white and choosing to wear his old, faded, green cap with the famous Staffordshire knot from the dozens of other cricket caps he could have worn, he bowled six good balls to John Akin, the Lancashire and England batsman, who was still 17 years off being born when Barnes was first getting wickets for England in Test matches.

Then he walked briskly off the field and the crowd, which included the Duke of Devonshire, cheered him and cheered him again. Back in the pavilion Barnes' only comment was:-

"Glad I could make the ball reach the other end."

Former Test match cricketer R.W.V.Robins said he was struck not only by the height of Barnes' arm but also by the nonchalant way he caught the ball as it was thrown to him. *"Might be bowling every day,"* added Robins.

Actually Barnes had not had a ball in his hand for twelve years. Then he had played in a full afternoon's club game – at the age of 68! Barnes, incidentally, it has already been mentioned in this book, was getting Test players out with his bowling and still accepting fresh League engagements when he was well over 60. On this day he was loath to let his swansong end, he stayed in his whites posing for a photograph here and there, chatting to old friends and still making new, and some of the time watching the cricket with his young grandchildren Peter and Penelope. Once he remarked wistfully:

"I wish I was a player now – they tell me batsmen's wickets are easier to take than they used to be."

A short speech of thanks to the crowd at the end of the game. He disappeared into the pavilion in his white flannels, probably for the last time.

(kindly supplied by Peter Barnes)

The teams:-

England XI
W.J.Edrich (Middlesex and England)
D.C.S.Compton (Middlesex and England)
J.Robertson (Middlesex and England)
J.A.Young (Middlesex and England)
L.Hutton (Yorkshire and England)
N.W.Yardley (Yorkshire and England)
H.E.Dollery (Warwickshire and England)

A.Spooner (Warwickshire and England)
S.Surridge (Surrey and Minor Counties)
R.V.C.Robins (Eton)
R.Simpson (Nottinghamshire and England)

Sydney Barnes XI
R.M.V.Robins (Middlesex and England)
C.H.Palmer (Leicestershire)
C.Goodway (Warwickshire)
D.M.Haynes (Stone and Staffordshire)
N.B.Browning (Stafford and Bedfordshire)
D.H.Wadham (Stafford and Staffordshire)
C.Washbrook (Lancashire and England)
J.T.Ikin (Lancashire and England)
E.Hollies (Warwickshire and England)
C.Grove (Warwickshire)
J.Goodwin (Leicestershire)

The testimonial fund for the 80 year old amounted to £685. After paying entertainment duty of £145 Barnes received £50. A crowd of 5,000 watched the match and although rain was forecast it stayed dry throughout the game. The game played out in April sunshine but with a chill wind.

The Barnes XI batted first and scored 240 for 4 declared. The England XI followed and scored 289 for 6 and were declared the winners but all agreed at the end of the day it was Barnes who was, undoubtedly, the outright winner!

England XI Innings		S.F.Barnes XI Innings	
J.D.B.Robertson b Hollies	56	J.T.Akin sp Spooner b Young	43
R.T.Simpson b Goodwin	64	C.Washbrook sp Spooner b Young	40
W.J.Edrich b Goodwin	18	N.E.Browning c Spooner b Perks	29
D.C.S.Compton c Haynes b Hollies	52	C.H.Palmer not out	83
N.W.D.Yardley c Haynes b Hollies	51	R.M.V.Robins b Perks	15
H.E.Dollery b Robins	9	D.M.Haynes not out	22
R.T.Spooner not out	21	T.D.Goodwin did not bat	0
R.V.C.Robins not out	6	C.C.Goodway did not bat	0
R.T.D.Perks did not bat	0	C.W.C.Grove did not bat	0
J.A.Young did not bat	0	W.S.Surridge did not bat	0
S.F.Barnes did not bat	0	W.E.Hollies did not bat	0
Extras	12	Extras	8
Total (6 wickets)	**289**	**Total (4 wickets declared)**	**240**

S.F.Barnes XI bowling	England XI bowling
Hollies 3/73, Goodwin 2/61, Robins 1/35	Barnes 0/0, Perks 2/54, Young 2/28

STAFFORD CRICKET CLUB 616

S. F. BARNES TESTIMONIAL MATCH
S. F. BARNES' XI
v
AN ENGLAND XI
SUNDAY, 26th APRIL, 1953
at
THE HOUGH, LICHFIELD ROAD, STAFFORD
Commencing at 11-30 a.m. Gates open at 10-30 a.m.

Admission to Enclosure 4/- (Inc. Tax)

This ticket is purchased on the understanding that play is not guaranteed, and that no money can be refunded in any circumstances.

S. F. Barnes

THE SYDNEY BARNES CRICKET SOCIETY
1965

—

Sixth

Annual Dinner

NORTH STAFFORD HOTEL

STOKE-ON-TRENT

TUESDAY, 15th APRIL, 1975

—

President : J. T. IKIN, Esq.

Joint Secretaries :

J. BRADBURN, Esq.   J. D. SCHOLFIELD, Esq.

Barnes (80 years of age) Testimonial Match on Sunday, 26th April, 1953 at Stafford. Cyril Washbrook with bat looking on.

Barnes – man or beast

It was said Barnes was not an easy man to handle on the field of play. There was a fiendish aspect about him. He didn't play cricket out of any green field starry-eyed idealism. He rightly considered that his talents were worth estimating in cash values. In his old age he mellowed, yet remained humorously cynical.

Put him at the wrong end and he would "scowl and sulk and develop mysterious physical disorders, sprains and strains". He also intimidated team-mates. One was heard to say:

"I was frankly afraid of his scowling displeasure, his ferocious glare, his crippling silences and his humiliating verbal scorn."

It was repeatedly said that he was too old to resume his Test career in 1921, and yet he was a year younger than Wilfred Rhodes, when the Yorkshireman was recalled in 1926. Unfortunately, Barnes already had three criticisms against him: he'd rejected the accepted path to national selection by trading in first-class cricket for the leagues; he wouldn't take orders; and he frowned colleagues as much as opponents.

Barnes certainly knew his own mind, but it was not surprising that some people found him difficult. A reason perhaps it was unusual in those days for a professional to speak so firmly and indeed bluntly ("the hand that fed him" comes to mind) but Barnes was never one for mincing words when he felt strongly about something.

There was a story heard, within the confines of the corridors at Old Trafford, that Barnes left Lancashire because his fellow professionals threatened to go on strike if he did not toe the line. If there was a missed catch or a shoddy piece of fielding he would in his rage let the player know about it. Barnes the perfectionist could not stand it. When he bowled, he bowled all out. In the field he could not relax and cricket six hours a day and six days a week was not his idea of a sporting life.

Barnes and MacLaren had their difficulties. There was an occasion when Barnes had one of his few disagreements with his captain when playing for Lancashire. They had discussed a situation with field placing. MacLaren thought otherwise to Barnes' suggestion. Barnes was quoted as saying:

"Usually he left the placing of the field to me, but on this occasion he moved the men into positions on the boundary, especially on the leg side. I told him quietly that I did not want the field like that, but he did not give way so I said to myself, If I can't have the field as I like, I'll bowl as I like, so I did. With the greater part of the fielders on the leg side I bowled down the off for the slips and enjoyed seeing the fours shooting off the bat past point and down through the covers. I could sense MacLaren glaring at me without a word but I would not look at him. After a time the batsman commented to me, what's the matter. I just said, oh, nothing just get on with your batting. MacLaren did take me off soon afterwards. It was later when the batsman asked me why I didn't pitch the balls up. I decided not to let him know for I felt sure he would have a dig at MacLaren and this would not have done me any good."

In 1903 Barnes, surprisingly, was not selected to play for England to go to Australia with the team led by the captain P.F.Warner. It seems Warner left him out because he thought he could not bowl an off-break. Barnes thought this rather strange in view of the fact that he had been bowling them for years. After the team had been announced and before the team sailed for Australia, Lancashire met Middlesex at Lord's which gave Barnes a glorious opportunity of proving to Warner that he was mistaken. In his own words Barnes commented:

"I was bowling to Mr Warner from the nursery end which meant that an off-break had to go slightly uphill. I had been bowling balls that went away from him when I whipped one down just outside his off stump which broke in and knocked back the leg wicket. As Mr Warner was walking back to the pavilion, I turned to the umpire and said,

"I'm as pleased as if someone had given me a fiver." "Why?" asked the umpire. *"Is there bad blood between you?"* "No," I replied, *"only he said I couldn't bowl an off break."*

That demonstration was not sufficient to cause Warner to issue a belated invitation to Barnes but he remembered it years later though his recollection differed from that of Barnes as to the type of ball it was.

He never spared himself on the field and always expected others to do the same. A typical situation occurred in a Festival match when a well-known celebrity came in to bat third wicket down to face him. As the batsman took guard the captain came over to Barnes and said:

"Go easy with him. He was at a party and didn't go to bed until 4 o'clock. The crowd have come to see him play."

"Oh," Barnes replied. *"If he's in that state he's no business on the field. The pavilion's the place for him."*

And to the pavilion he went, out first ball! Barnes believed that it did not pay to be nice to anyone, especially the opposition.

As a rule, Barnes spoke little on or off the field, unless he was spoken to. It was this perhaps which gave rise to the view he was unfriendly and unapproachable. Most often than not his fellow players did consider he did have a sense of humour even though it might have been grimly mocking, business-like humour. He was always business-like on the field and on an instance in a league match he wholeheartedly showed this to be true. The story goes that in a match when an incoming batsmen appeared on the field his captain advised him to put another man out at backward point because he was strong on the off-side.

"No," replied Barnes in a loud voice for the batsman to hear, *"leave the field as it is, he can't cut especially against me."*

He bowled two balls just outside the off and both found the boundary for four. The third ball was faster and a fuller length which dipped in to the off and middle stumps. The batsman missed and was given out LBW. Barnes was heard to say:

"It was comical to see him try to change his stroke and cover up much too late."

His captain thought otherwise and scolded Barnes:

"Two fours in his first two balls," he said. *"And leaving that gap open for him. What's the idea?"*

"Plain arithmetic," replied Barnes with a grin on his face. *"Two fours make eight, he generally makes fifty."*

Another story comes from his years residing in Colwyn Bay. A local builder asked him to play in a charity game:

"I will do you a favour and play," he said to the builder, *"if you will do me a favour and build me a house."*

Needless to say that was one match he didn't play.

His humour sometimes would lighten the tension of a situation. In one instance for example he placed a fielder just a yard from the bat only to see an easy catch dropped with the words:

"Save the one, mate."

This incident sent both players and spectators into reams of laughter.

Off the field and away from the business of the day he could relax with pipe and a drink and to be very entertaining. At a Minor Counties match at Colwyn Bay he was sitting on the grass relaxing and watching the game. A courting couple outside the ground were enjoying each other's company on a rise above the sight-screen which had distracted the batsman and the couple had failed to understand the umpire's yells and gestures. Barnes thought this very funny, got off the ground cupped his hands round his mouth and shouted in a loud voice for all to hear:

"Down on her, man! Down on her!" with the funny Ha! Ha! chuckle.

Wilfred Rhodes found him to be a good, genuine companion and friend. He said that he had strong character and was not afraid to pass his opinion and did not always agree with you in order to be polite. He said you could depend upon him to stick up for his rights and that he would not be pushed around.

I wonder what Barnes would have thought about this? I am sure he would have welcomed this. There has never been a more conventional aspect of the game of cricket than umpiring. With technology being used more and more these days for the benefit of the men in the white coats, the ICC have had the task of bringing umpiring into the 21st century. Their skills are being monitored in international matches so there can be regular assessment of their performances. Amongst the list of technologies are included:

A snickometer: A difficult decision for any umpire. Did the ball come off the bat? The pad? Neither? Both? Often it's very hard to detect by sight alone. The sound can often provide more than a clue. Using microphones in the stumps, the snickometer can study tell-tale noises and can illustrate them on screen. An edge is shown by a long thin line extending almost from top to bottom of the snickometer box. Ball hitting pad is a much more 'chunky' picture.

Hawkeye: Six cameras around the ground track the path of the ball as it is bowled. The data goes into a computer and emerges with a prediction of where it would have finished. It has turned out to be a valuable coaching tool for umpires and players.

An Alsager Community Theatre Play

How much more of an accolade can be bestowed on a man who was one of England's greatest cricketers? How many great sportsmen or women have had a play written about them and re-enacted on stage? To name just one – Sydney Francis Barnes.

Written and directed by Keith Plant, and performed by actors from the award-winning Alsager Community Theatre, he presented the premiere of 'Nothing To Do With Cricket' – the story of Staffordshire born Barnes at the Bank Corner pub in Lawton Road, Alsager on 17th November, 2016. Keith wrote the play to show how Barnes rose from Victorian poverty to challenge the Establishment.

"It's also meant for the play to hopefully introduce Barnes to a new generation," said Keith. "The show runs for about 45 minutes and promises fast-moving entertainment that will open your eyes about how to survive in sport and why breaking records was less important than providing for your family for a man born into the filth and grime of Victorian poverty.

"It's funny, it's gritty, and in the end it's very touching – and it's a fantastic story which is guaranteed to warm the hearts of cricket lovers. He was a man years ahead of his time and in many respects he brought professionalism to sport. Sydney Barnes was a working class lad who believed cricket was dominated by essential 'amateur toffs'. He had to challenge the Establishment which gives the play its dramatic energy. I hope we entertain people most of all. I also hope the play is stimulating and provokes some thoughts on the challenges we can face. Barnes was not an easy man, but he had to challenge social conventions. This is a hugely entertaining piece about the life and times of the greatest bowler the world has ever seen. Barnes was a sublimely talented but difficult man who challenged authority and changed the nature of sport forever. The play bristles with drama about class, status and the evolution of 20th century sport."

Keith goes on to say:

"I have liked the story of Barnes because it is a remarkable story and because I played for the club where he had his Benefit match in Stafford. I have always known the legend of the man and I think unfairly he has been sadly neglected in terms of fame in world sport. His achievements are absolutely unbelievable and it's good to bring that to a wider audience. 'Nothing To Do With Cricket' is and isn't a cricket play. Obviously Barnes is a cricketer and cricket is the backbone of it but it is much more than that because it spans the first half of the twentieth century. So it's the evolution of sport, the social history and most of all about a real human being, a challenging, difficult, multi-faceted man who juggled with Victorian poverty at the beginning of his life and who was determined that his own family was never going to suffer that. It is about how you prioritise things between the game that you love and the family you need to support. So it is something to do with cricket but a lot more than a play about cricket. Barnes was born in Smethwick, in the last quarter of the 19th Century. He was born into a real working class family. His father had worked in the smog and the grime at a metal bashers' factory for 63 years and he never had any pension or any reward and they lived in a squalid little slum of a house with a canal on one side and factories on the other three sides. And that's what drove Barnes because he was absolutely determined that his family were going to have a better life than the life he had. He was going to make certain that they weren't subjected to the sort of poverty at a time when there was no Social Security and State Pensions. It could easily have been a play about facts and figures because Barnes' statistics are truly amazing and it's about bringing it to life."

Keith is a keen cricketer himself and knew Barnes' story, but in the process of transferring the play from page to stage has learned a lot more about the man himself. He added:

"It has certainly been a journey of discovery. I grew up with the legend so I knew a bit about him already, but I've learned so much more in doing research on him for the play."

Actor Chris Garton from Alsager takes on multiple roles in the two-man play opposite Philip Jackson, who plays the part of Barnes. He says:

"It is good to have someone as venerated as Barnes as the subject for our play. Nothing particularly grabbed myself and Philip when we first read the play – it was full of facts and figures about cricket. But as we began to rehearse it, we realised it was a very moving story. It was a different world for Barnes back then. He was very special and he changed the world of professional sport. Without people like Sydney Barnes I don't think sport would ever have progressed the way it has. Barnes himself was in my opinion a good man. I mean he did have this bad press of being this kind of a grouchy, scary, kind of grim reaper figure but he really wasn't. He had a heart and I see him as someone with a strong sense of self-injustice who was doing a lot more than just being a sportsman. He was actually paving the way for working people to have a much better life."

(Author: Keith has asked me to make it clear that his play is copyrighted and any performances require permission from him.)

'Nothing To Do With Cricket'

A Play written by Keith Plant

Voice: (it's a middle aged grown up with the voice of a child)

When I passed my eleven plus, and not many people did in those days, it was really important. I mean, I could go to a school with a proper cricket pitch rather than play with a tennis ball on the tarmac.

My heroes were Trueman and Compton and Statham and sometimes we were allowed to go next door and watch them on television. Then somebody told us there was an even bigger hero and we could actually go and see him when he walked to work...

So one morning we skived assembly and went round the corner to the Shire Hall.

Everybody had told us that even though he was really, really old, he still went to work there. And he did. This bloke walked across the market square and up the steps. But he didn't look that old...he walked all upright and he strode in. He was dead smart, even if he was old fashioned...sort of square shouldered... a black overcoat and his tie was like ours should have been...except he had a pin that held it in place, fixing it against the collar. And his shoes were much better polished than ours – even if ours did come from the Clark's shop. We thought we might ask for his autograph, but he was so old he'd be getting a telegram from the queen soon, so we knew he wouldn't be able to write that much. And he had a face like a hatchet. And anyway we needed to get back for French.

We found out that he was 90 and took two buses to go to work and then walked from the bus station. We went back loads of times after that and he was always there looking the same. Except we realised that he had massive hands and really long fingers that could have gripped you round the throat. Some people said he was even older than Hitler would have been...and he was in our stamp collection. And he was dead.

J.L. NICHOLLS

Later on I had an English teacher who took us for cricket ...and we used to play proper games on a square (my dad thought you played on a pitch) and he thought I was a good bowler so he got me to go to our local cricket club to play for the juniors.

I'd never been good at anything before and suddenly I found myself playing for the second team because I could turn it a long way. And when we played our home matches the same old man used to watch. Always sitting on the same seat in front of the pavilion. Wrapped up warm. Smartly dressed. Never got excited. Of course, I found out who he was. He'd been even better that Trueman. In fact, everyone said he'd been the greatest bowler that had ever lived. Which meant, of course, that you didn't dare speak to him. In fact, it seemed to me that not many of the grown ups dared to speak to him either.

One day a mate of mine came down to watch and asked him for his autograph...gave him his book and a biro. But the old man wouldn't sign. He said he should come back with a proper fountain pen with a square nib.

When I was fifteen I got into the first team. That was a real achievement and my dad bought me a cap to play in. I had this dream debut and took five wickets. I thought I was going to be a Test cricketer. Of course that meant that the team stood back and let you lead them off the pitch. And as I walked up the steps the old man got up, (a smartly dressed older man appears and walks down to him – it's Barnes) sprightly as anything, and came down to me. He reached out to shake my hand (he does) and I thought 'this is it, praise from the greatest bowler there's ever lived, it doesn't get any better.' (Barnes reaches out his hand to shake it but looks at the hand instead)

Barnes: *You'll never make a spin bowler, your fingers are too bloody short.*

(the boy is shocked still, then turns and runs off almost in tears. Pause. Barnes stands still and upright).

Barnes: (calls) Boy! Boy! Come back here. (boy does, cautiously – keeps his distance).

Barnes: (more kindly) What's your name? William, isn't it?

Boy: Yes, sir.

Barnes: Don't call me sir. You're a cricketer now. I can't be doing with all that sir and madam nonsense.

Boy: OK,s... OK.

Barnes: And let me tell you something else...never...never...show deference to anybody unless they've earned it in your own eyes. You know what deference is?

Boy: It's what I'm supposed to show to teachers but I...

Barnes: But you don't until they've earned it...good boy! (long pause) Boy...
William...you seem to have something about you...

Boy:...even if my fingers are too short...

Barnes: Exactly! Sit down. I've been thinking for months now...I'm not going to be around much longer...and my boy...well he's only interested in taking photographs, not words...I need someone to share my story...

Boy: Weren't you born here?

Barnes: No...this is softee shoe making country. I was born in the Black Country. Smethwick, South Staffs. It was full of greyness, a ghetto, although we didn't know the word then...our little crowded *house (I'd got four brothers and sisters) was surrounded by factories on three sides and there was a filthy canal on the fourth.*

(William settles down to listen)

There was lots of love though… when our parents weren't too tired to give it and a lot of bloody hard work even for children. My dad worked for 63 years for the same metal bashing company and there was never, ever, any point at all when his bosses acknowledged his efforts or his loyalty or made any provision for his old age. And there were no pensions then…That made a big mark on me. It was not a fashionable idea then for a working class lad, in the 1800s, but I decided that nobody, nobody was ever going to take advantage of me like that, however important they thought they were. The buggers. Of course I was sent down to work for Muntz Metal too, but then something magical happened to me… One weekend I drifted down to the local cricket club at the back of the Galton Hotel to watch and I thought: 'I like this game.' And, of course I wanted to be a batsman, because every boy did. And I joined and I got picked for the third eleven…it was a great day for me… And I got runs and wickets. And I got picked for the second eleven. And I got runs and wickets. We had a professional.

William: *A professional?*

Barnes: *Which meant that he got money for playing for us…he used to play county cricket for Warwickshire…Billy Bird his name was… and he asked me to practise in his net. I wanted to bowl fast. I wanted to send stumps flying. But Billy said 'no' and he taught me how to spin the ball. That was pretty much the only coaching I ever had…there was no cricket history in the family, so I had to teach myself.*

And I got into the first team.

But, first match, it wasn't like it was for you…nobody asked me to bowl. And I was out first ball. When I got back to the pavilion I heard someone in a posh hat say 'you're no bloody good'. And I thought 'you bugger, I'll show you and all the other toffs'. But I was dropped. Then next time I scored a few and then, suddenly, there was a time when I was keeping wicket and the captain said 'Barnes, take off your pads and have a bowl', and I did and I took seven wickets for nineteen runs. And that was it. Before I knew it, they wanted me to play for Warwickshire. I said: 'But I've only had three hours coaching in my life', but at first they didn't seem to mind. Then I realised that it couldn't work – they wanted a bowler who was ready made. I was just promising and they weren't prepared to invest.

And I thought, 'Sydney, make this your chance, you might as well try to make a living from this too, if you don't want to go metal bashing like your dad'.

That meant moving away because the good money was all up north. The Lancashire League paid well and Rishton offered me £3-10s a week if I helped prepare the pitch, plus 7s.6d if I got 50 runs and another 10s.6d if I got six wickets. And beer was only three halfpence a pint! On top of that they had bucket collections when you'd had a good game.

And while I was there, I taught myself to bowl the leg break… not an ordinary leg break either. A fast leg break. (there's interaction with a cricket ball) I was snapping at the ball with these long fingers. (compares them to William's) I was like a violinist with a fiddle. Nobody else could swing, seam and spin the ball at the same time.

Swerve and curve. Curve and swerve. Straight balls never got wickets. I could tear pieces out of the turf. It changed my life.

So much so that I was asked to talk to Lancashire. But county cricket was stuffed full of amateurs and puffed up committee men who'd no need to understand what a pipe of baccy cost. Rishton was the same…I was taking more wickets so I wanted more money because I wasn't my father and I wasn't going to work for less than I was worth…so I went to Burnley.

It was 1901 and I got called for nets at Old Trafford to bowl to Archie MacLaren who was England captain at the time. I ran in and thumped him with one on the left thigh.

The next ball rose up from a length and hit his glove. 'Sorry, sir,' I said. (Barnes gestures him to stand up and join in the story. From now on William plays all the parts other than Barnes)

254

MacLaren: (posh) 'Don't be sorry, Barnes, you're coming to Australia with me!'

Barnes: And I did, and I didn't even play county cricket. I couldn't believe it (pause).
I had actually called him 'sir'!
Most of the team were amateurs....they could play for fun....and I knew I didn't fit in. I didn't want to fit in. But it was this amazing adventure sailing around the world.
No one else from Smethwick could have dreamt of it. Still, I had less respect for committees who ran it than I had for opening batsmen. I wouldn't doff my cap or tug my forelock for anyone... When we were crossing on the boat we hit a really heavy storm in the Bay of Biscay. And at the height of it I heard MacLaren...

MacLaren: At least if we go down, that bugger Barnes will go down with us.

Barnes: In my first Test I took five wickets and was 26 not out. We didn't need to bat again.

MacLaren: And straight away you got the world's greatest batsman out. Victor Trumper caught and bowled.

Barnes: I did.

MacLaren: But you caught it casually, in one hand, when you could have used two.

Barnes: Well, I caught it, didn't I?

MacLaren: Yes...but you might have missed it and he might have got 200!

Barnes: I bowled against him in 20 innings. I got him out 13 times. If he's the world's greatest batsman, what does that make me? (Barnes turns away).

(William becomes an Australian batsman.)

Australian: In the second Test he took 13 wickets. He'd carry the ball in his left hand as he ran up to bowl and only put it in his right at the last minute. So you couldn't even see how he was gripping the ball. And boy, did he let you know who was the boss. One Test, I was just closing the pavilion gate going into bat…

Barnes: Don't bother shutting it, lad, you'll be back soon.

Sid Gregory: And I was. But I'm bloody sure he cowed his own players as much as ours (demonstrates. There should be lots of opportunities for interaction, throwing around a cricket ball etc). They didn't dare drop a catch off Barnes. He had this ferocious glare. He'd humiliate players publicly so even his teammates were clearly afraid of him. That was good for our morale. Even his silences were crippling. By this time Australian mothers were using the word 'Barnes' to frighten their children to bed.

He bowled the leg break faster than anyone we'd ever seen. I remember him bowling against our finest player, the great Victor Trumper. After he got out, Trumper was staring into space in the dressing room and he shook his head and I heard him say to himself in disbelief: 'It was the sort of ball a man might see if he was dreaming or drunk!'

You know Barnes was over six foot with a very high action (Trumper said: 'My goodness you look ten feet tall.') The ball reared up at you, spinning like a gyroscope.

One night he had a fever and it looked like he wouldn't be able to play in the Test next day. So I took him a bottle of scotch and some blankets to sweat the fever out of him.

He played next day…he wasn't quite at his best…but he still took 5 of our wickets for 6 runs!

So we couldn't believe our luck when they didn't open the bowling with him in the third Test. Then we saw a different Barnes. Suddenly he'd scowl and sulk and he'd be rubbing his thigh and looking at his wrist and complaining about all sorts of mystery sprains and strains. He didn't even bat or bowl in the second innings. Of course we won the match. What can I say? He was not well known for his joie de vivre!

Barnes: When I got back home there was a bit of business that was far more important than cricket to sort out. We'd had to keep it under wraps for as long as we could. I'd met the lady I wanted to marry. I was in my late twenties so I'd waited long enough and I knew it was the right thing to do. I'd met her when I was playing in Lancashire and she was definitely the one for me. The only trouble was that she was married to someone else.

People didn't get divorced then. And when George, the husband, found out he was furious as you might expect. Now that was a test of character, even for me, because I was challenging conventions, but I knew what I felt was right, no matter what anybody else said, so I stood up straight to him – I could be an obstinate ass when I wanted something – and told him that I would let him name me as correspondent, if he gave Alice her freedom. And he did. And we proudly married on 23rd May 1903. I now had family responsibilities and I took them seriously. I wanted to offer a better life than I had known. There was no way I was to let the two of us live cramped up in a tiny room like my own family had. This was the 20th century and I expected us to have some comforts.

I decided I must be a businessman. That meant I had to make as much as I could out of the thing I excelled at. Too many professional cricketers were doomed to manage fourth rate beer houses, trading, as best they could, on their former glories. I wasn't going to have a fleeting career as a famous cricketer. I preferred business with pleasure!

1912 was a bad year for Britain. War was looming. The unsinkable Titanic had gone down. Robert Scott had been a talisman and his mission to the South Pole ended with everyone being frozen to death.

THE LEGENDARY CRICKET GENIUS SYDNEY F. BARNES

THE LEGENDARY CRICKET GENIUS SYDNEY F. BARNES

When I got back from Australia, men and boys needed a new hero. I'd brought the Ashes home! I was that hero...and a working class hero at that! I showed 'em what ordinary people could aspire to.

I could choose to work as a clerk in a colliery during the week. Or I could also play full time for Lancashire during the summer and get reduced winter pay in the off-season. I went to see the committee secretary... Mr Swire, I have a proposal that will save you money.

Swire: *(middle class Lancastrian) Go on, Barnes...But I'll bet it will make more money for you...*

Barnes: *Yes. You see, if you could help me to find paid work from some of your colleagues during the winter months when I'm not touring... you could keep my winter pay.*

Swire: *Barnes...you seem to forget that the committee here are busy men...they have business interests to take care of.*

Barnes: *But they could find me work in one of their businesses!*

Swire: *They can't be bothered with a few months' winter work from someone who won't risk damaging his fingers!*

Barnes: *I can do paperwork. I have beautiful copperplate handwriting. I've worked hard to perfect it. I could write documents for the King.*

Swire: *(laughs). Barnes! Did you hear what you just said, man? (pause) But I will tell you something. The committee has recently been discussing the remunerations of professional players. And very kindly they have proposed offering you the proceeds of a benefit match at the end of eight years' service.*

Barnes: *Right. But if you give me a match I shall choose it.*

Swire: *You're sadly lacking in...*

Barnes: ... then I won't bother you again about money. The match I want is Yorkshire.

Swire: We have never done that for anyone, and I cannot do it for you.

Barnes: Mr Swire, I'm afraid that if you cannot meet my very reasonable request, I will be forced to look after myself. Please accept my resignation from the county forthwith.

So I decided then and there that I would leave the county...knowing that that meant I might not play for England again.

In no time a league club offered me £8 a week, that's eight pounds, and a benefit match. And I could work during the week.

Swire: Work, Barnes, yes. But first you've got to learn to work alongside people.

You down tools more often than an East End docker. Nobody speaks to amateurs like you do – that's why they dislike you so much. You can't spend your life forever kicking against the pricks and quarrelling with the establishment...

Barnes: But I...

Swire: No, you're listening to me for once. Don't you realise there'll be half the Lancashire team glad to see the back of you. Some of them are actually afraid of you – your scowling, your ferocious glare...not to mention those crippling silences that turn grown men into ice. And you show no respect to umpires: that look of cold contempt you give them if they turn down your appeal is a disgrace. When it comes to proper cricketers, you're a just a social misfit – you'll be better off with the bloody mill workers in the leagues. (pause)

Barnes: (deep breath, re-gathers himself. Speaks quietly at first). By the time I was 10 I could read fluently unlike most of the boys at my school. I remember the first time I saw and read a newspaper...just *after the F. A. Cup final it was…Blackburn Olympics from over yonder against Old Etonians. And Blackburn whipped them.*

Working class professionals beat public schoolboys for the first time. I've never forgotten what the paper said: 'A victory for the manual working class over the sons of the best families of the upper class in the Kingdom.' I've had enough of members who don't know one end of the bat from another summoning me to bowl at them in the nets because they see me as a servant. Times are changing…people are saying there'll be motor cars in the streets soon…the jobs our fathers grew up with are fast disappearing. (pause) I think I'm paving the way for others just like Blackburn did…and you know what…I'll be happier with the bloody mill workers in the league – and richer!

Barnes: (regathering dignity. Speaks to audience) *After I left Lancashire, someone said: 'Syd, you can humble the greatest batsmen in the world. How can you be content to play league cricket?' But I'd already decided that I wasn't having a career as a famous cricketer that would be over before I knew it. Playing only once a week would keep me fresh so I could go on playing for longer and earning for longer. At Lancashire they made me earn my money. I used to take the new ball at half past eleven and would still be bowling at six o'clock unless I'd bowled 'em out.*

Swire was right, I loathed some of those toffee-nosed amateurs playing county cricket as much as I loathed the committee men. There was one occasion when they left me out of a second XI match. They said it was because the wicket was damp! 'That shows how little you know about the game,' I said. 'It's the first time I've heard that a spinner can't bowl on a damp wicket. But it's all right with me. If you're going to rest me you can rest me for all of the season as long as you pay me. It's a question of money. They didn't drop me again! (pause).

Once a so called fashionable amateur, I'll not mention his name, came in to face me and the captain came up to me and said: 'Go easy with him, Syd, he was at a party last night and didn't get in until 4 o'clock. The crowd have come to see him'. I said, 'If he's in that state, he's no business being on the field. The pavilion's the place for him.

When I'm bowling I am the captain.' And I bowled him first ball. Working class lads playing tough league cricket were so much more honest.

William: And you said Wisden wrote your obituary: (reads from Wisden)
    'Temperament is a great thing in cricket; and in this respect Barnes has always been deficient. If he had possessed the enthusiasm for the game that had characterised others he might have made a great name for himself.'

Barnes: But Wisden knew that if they had given in to my demands, it would have opened the floodgates: working class players would have taken over their glorious game. Men who took the game seriously instead of spending their nights drinking and gambling. I played cricket as I would approach any other job. My father worked from 8.00 to 6.00 in a factory. He wouldn't stay on and work until ten past for no more pay. Truth is that one of the few I really respected because he wasn't frightened to tell me how it really was, was Bert Strudwick who kept wicket for me and for England many times....

(actor becomes Bert, a southern voice)

Bert: Syd was playing only minor counties cricket for Staffordshire, yet he was still selected for our tour of South Africa. It was Syd's tour: Syd made all their batsmen look quite ordinary, beating them at least four times every over and took 10 wickets in the first Test. In the second, Wisden, the holy bible of cricket wrote: 'on no occasion was the great bowler seen to quit such advantage, proving quite irresistible on the last morning.' Understatement! It was Barnes' match. Never have I seen anyone bowl as he did in that match. Time and again he beat the bat only to see the ball go over the top, or just miss the side of the stump. Syd took 17 wickets. Only one man could stand up to him: Taylor. And they were fierce rivals. I caught Taylor more than once off Syd but the umpiring was 'less than ideal'. In one match he was eventually caught at second slip but stayed at the wicket. We were so angry none of us would appeal and we all sat down on the pitch. Then Taylor sat down too. Syd was furious: he threw the ball on the ground and said he would not bowl again, shouting: 'It's Taylor, Taylor all the time!' The crowd had never seen anything like it. Eventually someone appealed and Taylor had to come out. When I asked him about it afterwards he said: 'Oh I was giving the umpire another chance!' Syd said: 'Rot!' Rot or not he took 49 wickets in the first four tests and I swear I have never kept to a finer bowler.

His attitude was part of his stock in trade – he wanted to re-enforce his image as the batsman's bogey man. There was a touch of wickedness about him! Even on the sunniest day, there was a chill wind of antagonism blowing from him.

And he didn't play in the final match! Once again Syd was at loggerheads with the management – this time the South Africans.

I always thought he was the first player to have a manager – and the manager was S.F. Barnes. He'd taken his wife and boy out on the trip...Syd always said it was for health reasons and he'd been told that they would take the hat round if he did anything outstanding – and he'd taken 49 wickets in 4 games. A record. He felt he needed the money to pay for accommodation for his family, but they wouldn't keep their promise. Syd got mad. When Syd got mad he could be really mad, and an obstinate cuss as well. He thought that if he'd done something to lengthen the matches rather that shorten them, he would have been more popular. So he put his head down and refused to play in the last Test. And you know, cricket would have moved forward faster if there'd been more characters like S.F.B. He was far ahead of his time that people didn't understand him – neither his bowling nor his attitude.

Barnes: Cricket is a craft. A craft should never be devalued. And an artist can only give his best when circumstances challenge his virtuosity.

Bert: He held his hand out and said it was because he had spun the skin off his fingers. He'd bowled with his blood smearing the ball. He never played for England again.

Barnes: And what did Wisden say about the tour?

Bert: 'Barnes dwarfed all other bowlers...it would be hard indeed to praise him beyond his deserts. Everyone felt before he left England that he would do well, but his success exceeded all expectations. He was simply irresistible.'

Barnes: Wisden never loved me very much...though they were quite happy to use me to advertise their cricket balls. It was another pillar of the establishment. And it seemed to me that England resisted me quite easily. Even when we were being played off the pitch by Australia and used thirty players in a series, there was no place for S. F. Barnes.

William: Wouldn't you have liked to play against Bradman?

Barnes: Aye. A true great of course. But you know what...he was vulnerable to the ball that cut away outside off stump...and my leg-cutter, you know...(he mimes it with his hand)

William: Bradman got his own back though...he said you weren't the greatest bowler ever because you didn't have a googly.

Barnes: It's quite true. I never bowled the googly. (pause). I didn't have to.

William: Who was the greatest captain you ever played under?

Barnes: Me. When I was bowling.

William: Did you think you were too old for Test cricket once the war was over?

Barnes: It was a tough time for all sports then. So many young people had not come home...then of those that did come back the flu finished more of them off. Yes, I was old but fit as a flea. And if I was younger

I might have died on the Somme. Look at the figures, lad, look in the record books.

William: *But only for Staffordshire.*

Barnes: *To me Staffordshire was the finest. It was an honour to play for my own county. 'Barnes of Staffordshire', I became. I'd already got the record in 1906. Now you think you're a pretty fine young bowler. You've just taken five wickets. Listen to this (takes a notebook from his pocket). 375 overs, 100 maidens, 119 wickets...average 7.83...8 wickets for 10 runs against Bedfordshire...15 for 93 against Cambridgeshire...14 for 72 against Suffolk...14 for 29 against the Indian tourists...how long have you got, lad?...I remember them all. And they had ambition: they might have been a minor county – even though there were no major counties. They used to have four players padded up when Barnes was bowling. And because I looked after myself and didn't wear myself out playing every day, I was still bowling fast for them when I was 61! Even then, there was no shortage of people wanting me to play for 'em...*

Mayor of Castleton: *(Lancashire voice. A formal speech to a committee). Fellow Castletonians, I ask you to dig deeper into your pockets to secure the services of Sydney for another two years. Yes, his demand of £450 per annum will stretch the club to the limit...but his bowling has made us league champions, no less.*

Furthermore, no professional has enthused such loyalty into his players as Barnes has done these last three years. I wish to kill once and for all the notion which seems to have been broadcast that Barnes is a difficult man to get on with. He is a very reticent man, and like all geniuses, he has his way of doing things. But the boys adore him and will be very sorry indeed if he goes elsewhere.

Barnes: *But they couldn't afford me, so I went to Rochdale who could.*

Hayden Jones: Mr Barnes, I'm Hayden Jones of Jones Construction. I'm organising a charity cricket match next month, and since you're living in Colwyn Bay now, I wondered if you would turn out for my team?

Barnes: I'll tell you what: you build me a house for free and I'll play cricket for you for free.

Durnell: (Black Country voice) Syd, you're 53 now. Why don't you come back to your roots and finish your career with Smethwick? We can open together.

Barnes: Nothing would give me more pleasure. But can you afford me?

Durnell: I'll tell the committee that the rise in gate receipts will more than pay for your wages.

Barnes: In that case my fee will go up: I'll take a share of the gate receipts as well – I spend a pound a match on embrocation, these days.

Sir Ernest Johnson: Syd Barnes, they'll always remember you in Staffordshire. I was there when they gave a trophy at Porthill Park. You were never off the field throughout the match…you opened the batting and got 76 not out, then you took 10 for 12 with the ball. But this is today. This is a time when we need heroes more than ever before. We've pulled out of Dunkirk. The army's finished. Hitler'll be on our shores before we know it. This could be the last summer of cricket for a generation.

Come and coach the youngsters at Stone and maybe play a few games.

Barnes: I'll come and play and maybe coach a little. But there'll be no end to cricket here and no Hitler either. *(pause) (to audience) I was 57 years old. I took 28 wickets at 8.28 apiece. That made 6,229 wickets as a professional cricketer.*

William: *But you did bowl again, didn't you?*

Barnes: *It was my 80th birthday and they put on a marvellous day for me here in Stafford.*

Pat Wadham: *Syd, things are coming along nicely for your birthday match.*
Everyone wants to be there: Hutton, Compton, Edrich, Washbrook. Nobody I've asked has said no.

Barnes: *And I want you to play too, Pat. Someone born in Staffordshire who still plays for Staffordshire.*

Pat: *I'm very honoured, Syd. But I can't play against all those greats, I'm just an ordinary bloke.*

Barnes: *Pat, when I started off the world was full of Victorian so-called gentlefolk with their toffee-nosed ideas...I took 'em all on. When I played against Australia in 1902 I remember Hawke, Lord Hawke, say 'Pray God no professional may captain England: it was just before he dropped me after I took six wickets at Sheffield. The only Test they ever played at Sheffield, the only Test I ever played in England. And, as you know, no-one did until Len Hutton last year. I've always been for selection according to merit rather than class and privilege. Since then we've had two World Wars and women have got the vote. Maybe I was ahead of my time...some said I should have been a politician like Keir Hardie. And I am the rise of the working man. (pause). But perhaps it's enough to have changed the world of cricket just a bit. I watch you play here every week and you're plenty good enough to hold your head up with the best of 'em. Just like I was, am.*

Pat: *One more favour then. The committee would like to ask if you would bowl the first over.*

(pause, considers)

Barnes: I'll never retire. Once you retire your life's over. That's why I turn up at the Shire Hall everyday. (pause). I shall bowl the first ball, but I don't know about a full over. I can't really spin 'em now. I can cut 'em of course, but any bloody fool can do that. (pause) Shall I change into flannels? I don't know. And if I did bowl the whole over, it would rather spoil matters if I took the first six wickets! (pause) So you'd better give me an old ball because I don't want to spoil the match. But I'll wear my green Staffordshire cap.

Pat: *(to audience) He did wear his flannels. They hung pathetically loose over his sparse frame. We batted first and there were tears in my eyes when I watched him, tall and gaunt, but still as upright as ever, lead his men into the field, laughing and joking with them a little. He licked his fingertips, curved them lovingly around the ball and took a few steps to the wicket. Over came the arm as high – I swear it – as it must have in the olden days, brushing his right ear. He bowled six balls of immaculate length and direction. Dennis Compton, smoothing his Brylcreem, called him from mid-off: 'How are you getting on?' and Barnes said:*

Barnes: I shall be all right about four o'clock.

Pat: *He turned and walked back to the pavilion. The crowd of 5,000 clapped and cheered. It had been another maiden.*

Barnes: I received a cheque for £540 from the testimonial. My heart was too full for words.

Pat: *And no groaning or bickering that day, Syd.*

Barnes: You know, I think I was beginning to enjoy the fame that I'd so long been denied. In the twilight years... I was wined and dined and interviewed and feted and honoured and painted and presented...I was even loved at Lord's. I suppose I enjoyed the belated helping of jam on

267

my bread. (long pause) Perhaps, until then I'd thought that just me, me alone, had been aware of my genius.

Pat: If you'd been more prepared to fit in during your playing days, you might have had much more jam, much sooner.

Barnes: You mean accepting that I was the servant and they were the masters?

Pat: Perhaps.

Barnes: But don't you see...it was fighting the establishment that spurred me on to perfection. It was nothing to do with cricket. (he tosses the ball between his hands then throws it to William as a gift for the future as the lights dim.)

"S.F.Barnes, said by everyone that played against him in the grandiose of Australian batsman around about the time he played, that he was the greatest bowler who ever lived. He was fast-medium and he swung the ball and cut it off the 'concrete like' Australian pitches, uncovered pitches in those days too. And he did well against the South Africans but the things to look for with Barnes is the match scores and the score cards and see how the splendid bowlers who were in the side with him who did nothing, whereas Barnes did everything." Richie Benaud

A Staffordshire County Legend

Bernard Hollowood was a Minor Counties cricketer who played for Staffordshire from 1930 to 1946 and one of his team mates was Barnes. Born in June, 1910 he was from a very competitive cricketing family. His grandfather, Thomas Robinson, played for the Gentlemen of Staffordshire (1872-1888); his father Albert and his two brothers, Roy and Tom, and himself played for Burslem in the North Staffordshire League. His father also played for Staffordshire and opened the batting in that famous match against Durham in 1907 (highlighted in this book). This was the game Barnes took four wickets in his first four balls in his second over, took 12 wickets for 30 runs and captured his 300th wicket in the Minor Counties Competition. Bernard Hollowood was a scholar who graduated with a degree in Economics from the London University. He certainly had a zest for life and lived his life to the full. An economist, a writer, a self-taught artist and cartoonist, a contributor to the literature of the game of cricket in newspapers and magazines and at one time the editor of 'Punch' and assistant editor of 'The Economist'. He died on March 28, 1981. In 1970 he wrote about Barnes, naming him easily the greatest of Staffordshire cricketers:

"It was three years ago on the Saturday of a Lord's Test, I spotted him in the pavilion. He was alone, puffing at his pipe, and glaring out through the Long Room window at the sun-drenched arena. I had not seen him since 1935 and I was amazed to find so little change in him. He stood as straight as a guardsman, and was as lean and leathery as in his heyday. As I watched him I remembered the profound shock I had experienced on first seeing him strip for action at Birkenhead Park. He then had seemed indecently ancient, senile almost. One corner of the changing-room was roped off by his supports; and a fearful odour seeped from the clutter.

It was the smell of hospitals. I looked for formaldehyde and other embalming fluids, for crutches, wooden legs and scars of operations.

Barnes was already a legend in my family. He was a contemporary of my father's and because I thought of my old man as... well, old, I naturally enough considered Syd as having one and a half feet in the grave. But he was a spry old bird and kept himself in good condition by regular exercise, moderation in all things, an enquiring mind and steady application in his civilian job as clerk and calligrapher.

But that was more than thirty years go. Now, there he was, the same man, still glaring from furrowed brows, still stiff enough to suggest rigor mortis. After five minutes of nostalgic rumination I approached him.

"Mr Barnes," I said, "you won't know me, but..." His head jerked from the cricket, his eyes twinkled and his face broke into the familiar smile of truculent superiority.

"Hollowood," he said, "Bernard Hollowood, Albert's lad. How are you?"

We shook hands and I congratulated him on his state of preservation. He began to talk about my father, about what Albert would have done to the rubbishy bowling being served up by the Test idols in the middle, and then he was suddenly engulfed by fans, young codgers of seventy and eighty, who descended on him like a pack of cub reporters. And of course I lost him.

My father regarded Barnes as the greatest bowler of all time, though he invariably spoke disparagingly of him in other contexts than cricket. They had played together for Staffordshire during Syd's golden years and had battled against each other on numerous occasions in the League. Barnes, my father said, was as mean as they come, and 'difficult' – by which I understand him to mean that he didn't care very much for Barnes' brand of heavy sarcasm and bitter comment. But there was no doubt whatever about the genius. "Oh, yes, he could bowl 'em all, but he got his wickets with fast leg-breaks. Marvellous, absolutely marvellous, he was. Fast leg-breaks and always on a length." Others, Barnes included, have claimed that he bowled every known ball except the googly – swingers, off-breaks, top spinners, the lot. But undoubtedly his chef d'oeuvre was the leg-break. He took a long run, a bounding, springy run, and as his arm came over to a perfect action, mid-on and mid-off could hear the snap of his long fingers as they rolled and squeezed the ball into its revolutionary parabola. There has been no one like him. O'Reilly could bend them from leg, but not with Barnes consistency or devil: Douglas Wright could bowl fast leg-breaks, but not on the length that destroys and goes on destroying.

He was a strange man, a social misfit in the cricket scene of Victorian, Edwardian and Georgian days. He might have been a Keir Hardie or a George Lansbury or a Frank Cousins if he had turned his mind to politics, for he was forever kicking against the pricks and quarrelling with the Establishment. He considered himself undervalued by his employers, insufficiently recognised, and overworked, and he would down tools as readily as an East End docker. Throughout his long playing career he carried outsize chips on his shoulder, and not one of the many clubs he played for could ever be certain of his unqualified loyalty and co-operation.

He resented discipline not because he wanted complete freedom but as a matter of principle. At all levels of the game he had to be handled with kid gloves – by captains, colleagues and committees. Outspoken himself, he resented outspokenness in others and displayed acute sensibility to any word or deed that slighted his personal Bill of Rights. Put on to bowl at the 'wrong' end, he would scowl and sulk and develop mysterious physical disorders, sprains and strains. Time and time again his career was broken by some real or imagined injustice. He would be on top of the world, the master bowler wanted by his country, a dozen counties, scores of league clubs: and then he

271

would disappear from public view. At the height of his powers he dropped out of the England team for years at a stretch. He sampled county cricket, played a match or two and quit.

The most common reason for these surprising exits was finance. Cricketers are poorly paid today: in Barnes' time they scratched a living and unless they found jobs during the winter – which wasn't easy – those with family responsibilities existed only marginally above the subsistence line. The old pro of the sentimental school of cricket writers is a dear fellow, nut-brown and sultry-tongued, who reminisces cheerfully with pipe and pint with every opportunity. In reality, the majority of county cricketers who ended their careers before the Hitler war found their middle and old age blighted by poverty. There was no pension funds for them, no large lump sums from benefit matches, and only a handful, the spectacularly successful, picked up good money on the side from journalism, authorship, lecturing, advertising, coaching and sponsoring. There was no money in radio, and television was not yet in action.

The players had no union to protect them, so that they were more or less compelled to accept whatever wage their counties thought reasonable, and the counties were governed by autocratic amateurs who treated the professionals with the kindly condescension that they reserved for their domestic servants, gardeners and local tradesmen. And it was this that made Barnes see red. His trouble, at root, was that he demanded equality of opportunity and the abolition of class distinctions fifty or sixty years before the rest of the country, and at a time when a lot of the vast majority was docile servitude.

His take-it-or-leave-it attitude of no compromise was a new phenomenon in industrial relations – on the employees' side – and obviously it produced deadlock when matched by similar obstinacy from the bosses. Barnes asked for travelling expenses on top of his wage; the county told him that the wage

included the travelling expenses; Barnes said that if they didn't
meet his modest request he would leave the club; the county
said they couldn't be dictated to by players. End of contract.
Barnes retires fuming to his tent. He told the Lancashire
secretary that he expected the county to find him a decent
job during the winter and was rebuffed, the secretary saying
that he couldn't be bothered. Barnes was promised a benefit
match if he served the club dutifully and successfully for eight
years, Syd asked for the Roses Match, Lancashire v Yorkshire,
at Old Trafford on a bank holiday. The secretary explained
that the club had never done as much for other players and
couldn't make an exception for Barnes. So Barnes walked out.

On the field he was always a trier, always active mentally
and physically. He wanted the game to run his way and was
openly critical of almost every captain he played under. If his
advice was not heeded he grumbled and then retreated into
cold fury. He set himself the highest standards of play and
could not tolerate inefficiency in others. His masters paid by
results and Barnes sweated and schemed to achieve rewarding
figures, and anyone who reduced the effectiveness of his efforts
through slackness, inability or misfortune had to suffer the
consequences, scathing looks and words and a display of icy
scorn.

His colleagues admired his skills, but were terrified of
incurring his displeasure and found games with him a sore
trial. So there was no great outcry when the selectors omitted
the name Barnes, S.F., from their national elevens. I suspect
that on these occasions – and they were numerous – all the
more easy-going Players and most of the Gentlemen breathed
a sigh of relief...

Barnes was always certain that he knew better than the
umpire, and his method of registering displeasure with a
decision was to stare at the official hard and long, his lean
fingers loaded with disgust and contempt. These staring
sessions seemed to last for minutes on end and were acutely

embarrassing to everyone except Barnes. I was batting with him in his last match for Staffordshire at Castleford in 1935 when he was given out, lbw, to the Yorkshire fast bowler Hargreaves. From the other end he looked dead in front, but Barnes stood his ground and glowered at the umpire for so long that I honestly thought he refused to go. The fielders watched immobile, and fascinated, and the umpire looked distinctly uncomfortable. Then with the passing of aeons, old Syd turned and marched to the pavilion with the face like that of Mr Hyde.

Thirty years ago I wrote a piece for the Boy's Own Paper in which I described Barnes' method of psychological warfare against tremulous batsman.

All who have been fortunate to play with him... are agreed that as a bowler of length and spin, Barnes has no equal. Even one of our youngest cricketers, the record-breaking Len Hutton, has said, "One of my best innings was against Sydney Barnes when I was sixteen; I scored 69 not out." I remember that innings of Hutton's, and I recall the warm praise it received from Barnes. The master or the ' Maestro' as he is known in Staffordshire, turns the ball with equal facility from leg or off without ever losing a perfect length. His field placing is a work of art. It is not a matter of a 'bit deeper' or 'round a little'. When Barnes moves him a fieldsman must proceed to an appointed spot, mathematically determined, and stay there.

Denbighshire were batting and near 'stumps' on the first day had lost three wickets – all to Barnes. The game had been held up by rain and Staffordshire badly wanted another wicket before the close. The last over was called and the spectators moved to the gates. Barnes was bowling. The batsman defended stubbornly. Five balls were played carefully. Then in the middle of his long springy run for the last ball, Barnes stopped. He motioned to me at point (two yards from the bat). His long fingers made some sign which I did not understand, but I moved round to silly mid-off. After all, there was only one ball. Once again Barnes turned to bowl, and once again his eyes swept the field as he began his run up to the wicket. I was watching, my hands cupped. His delivery arm was almost over when he halted suddenly, and looked at me with a face as black as thunder. Then, while the crowd laughed derisively, he walked up the pitch and led me (almost by the hand) to the position he had in mind. "The old buffer," I thought, "How does he know what the batsman will do?"

By this time the poor batsman was in a terrible state. He looked hard at me, and I saw panic in his eyes. Barnes bowled. The batsman prodded forward and the ball popped, so gently, into my waiting hands. It was typical of the 'maestro'.

My last memory of him will always be of Barnes sitting late at night in the lounge of a Manchester hotel. He is surrounded by young Staffordshire players and we are begging him to reveal some of his secrets. We buy him drinks and he twinkles and chuckles. He rolls a ball in his long fingers and manipulates it like an Epstein fondling a clay bust. The top spinner like this, see! The leg-break like so. The out swinger, well hold the ball this way... it is obvious he considers the demonstration a waste of time. He can tell us what to do, but we couldn't possibly do it. There was only one Barnes. "Whatever you do," he adds "don't bowl outside the off stump. Don't wait for the batsman to get himself out – always attack, and always bowl at the stumps."

Finally, let me quote from Ian Peebles on Barnes. In his excellent book Batter's Castle, Ian writes:

Walter Robins was playing for Sir Julian Cahn's team, a very strong side, against Staffordshire at Stoke, and was amongst those shot out for less than 80 by the useful 60-year-old Barnes. The position was indeed parlous when they came in to bat again, well behind, and Sir Julian took desperate council of Walter who recommended one and all having a bash. To this suggestion Sir J. replied that he had better lead the way, so that Walter in due course took middle and leg and awaited his first experience of Barnes with the new ball. It was quite something; in fact, Walter recalls it was one of the most beautiful overs he has ever seen bowled. The first was the out-swinger, which just missed the off stump. The second was an in-dipper, and the defender pulled the umbilicus smartly out of the way as it shot over the leg stump. The next was a leg-break and, just to keep things symmetrical, this missed the off stump again; a yorker, an off-break and then the last ball of the over, another leg-break. Trying to smother it, the batsman just snicked it almost before it arrived in the wicketkeeper's gloves, all present appealed. To their astonishment, and that of the striker, the umpire said "Not out" and Walter lived to fight another day, or at least another over. Be it said for Julian, who liked to win, that on seeing his adviser in such a tangle he laughed until he cried. Meanwhile Walter had come to a powerful decision, and at the start of the next over, abandoning all thought of trying to parry this superb artistry, he rushed down the wicket and let the bat go. In the circumstances it was sheer vandalism, but it worked, and 16 runs came from the face, edges and back of the bat. This was too much for Barnes, who, with the temperament inseparable from genius, snatched his sweater and left the battle for less fry.

Comments Worth Mentioning

"Sydney Barnes believed that an incoming batsman was tense, keyed-up and at the most uncomfortable period of his innings. This was the time 'to get him'. Very early on, sometimes when the batsman had played only one ball, Sydney would move a fielder only a few inches to the left and then a few inches forward, then, still not satisfied, he would move him a few inches to the right and a few inches back. All this to unsettle the batsman." A Staffordshire supporter.

Simply to see him bowl and he was over sixty on the only occasion I ever watched him in action – was to make the instant impression of majesty, hostility and control. This was, without doubt a born bowler, who lived to bowl. No batsman ever dared to claim that he was Barnes' master. No cricketer who played with or against him had any doubt that Sydney Barnes was the greatest bowler the world had ever seen.
– *John Arlott*

'His most deadly weapon was the 'Barnes ball' which pitched on the stumps between leg and middle and then turned sharply to threaten the off-stump or find the edge of the bat by ceaseless application during those early years. Barnes had achieved the great dream of every bowler, the ability to deliver an accurate leg-break at true pace.' – *Benny Green*

Barnes supposedly taught George Pope the secret of his leg cutter (or leg spinner as he would claim) and Pope supposedly taught Alec Bedser who also had enormous hands.

One can also conclude that he was a terrible teacher, since neither Pope nor Bedser could deliver the Barnes ball. The "Barnes ball" was effectively the same as the ball with which Warne famously bowled Mike Gatting, except that it was delivered at 75mph. – *A.M.*

He will be mourned by cricketers the world over. He was the finest bowler there ever was and a magnificent personality after his playing days. – *Arthur Gilligan, President of M.C.C.*

The extraordinary thing about him was that all his contemporaries considered him the greatest bowler. There was never any doubt in their minds. This must have been unique. – *S.C. Griffith, Secretary of M.C.C.*

Barnes was a very fine medium-paced bowler, the best I ever played with. He had a lovely run-up to the wicket, carrying the ball in his left hand until he was only two paces from the crease and then transferring it to his right. He kept a perfect length and direction and, if you wanted to field close to the wicket say, at short leg, you could stand up to the batsman without any fear. He was quite a decent bat, far better than he was made out to be and too good for a number eleven. He was also a very good fielder. – *Wilfred Rhodes*

He was the greatest bowler I ever kept wicket to, for he sent down something different each ball of the over. He could turn it either way in remarkable fashion and I shall never forget keeping to him for the first time in a Gentlemen v. Players match at The Oval. His opening delivery pitched outside the leg stump and flew over the top of the off stump. I said to a team-mate: "What sort of bowler have we here?" I soon found out. Sydney could do almost anything with the ball. On matting wickets in South Africa where I toured with him, he was practicably unplayable. Barnes took 14 wickets for 13 runs, less than one run apiece, playing for Staffordshire against Cheshire in 1909. – *Herbert Strudwick, Surrey and England*

Test and First-Class records – Bowling and Batting

Test Career (1901-1914)						
bowling						
balls	mdns	runs	wkts	best	fig.	ave.
England	7873	356	3,106	189	9-103	16.43
batting						
England	27	39	9	242	38*	8.06

First-Class Career (1894-1930)						
bowling						
balls	mdns	runs	wkts	best	fig.	ave.
Overall	31,430	1,600	12,289	719	9-103	16.43
batting						
	m	I	n/out	runs	h/s	ave.
Overall	133	173	50	1,573	93	12.78

Record breaking bowling feats

A world record (at the time) of 17 wickets in a Test match. (Only Jim Laker in 1956 with 19 wickets has beaten this.)

4 Wickets for 1 run and 5 wickets for 6 runs at the opening of an Australian innings on a perfect wicket in Australia in a Test match for England.

A world record of scoring a century and taking 17 wickets in the same match for Staffordshire.

9 wickets for 1 run in an innings.

9 wickets for 0 runs – last man came in and first ball was dropped by Porthill fielder v Leek 1908. If caught would have been 10/1)

Taking all 10 wickets in an innings 9 times.

(1906 – Porthill, Leek Highfield 10/12, 1907–Leek Highfield,

1908 – Saltaire, 1915- Basildon Green 10/14, Bowling Old Lane 10/33, 1918- Keighley 10/36, 1924-Compton, 1925-Haywood 10/24.)

5 wickets in 5 balls once.

4 in 4 balls 4 times.

Numerous 'hat-tricks' including twice in 1 innings. One with three of the best bats in England and another for the Players against the Gentlemen match. A hat-trick for Staffordshire against Norfolk in 1913.

A record of 150 wickets in 24 league and cup matches in one season.

A record bowling average of 3.84 in the Bradford League and records in the North Staffordshire League for the highest number of wickets in a season and the lowest bowling average on more than one occasion.

Batting centuries in Minor Counties and League cricket (1895-1934)

	year	runs
Staffordshire	1906	100
	1911	150
Total runs for Staffordshire in 253 innings = 5,254		
Rishton	1898	106
	1899	100
Church	1904	113*
Porthill	1906	104*
	1907	116*
	1908	142*
	1910	129
	1914	120*
* not out		
Total runs in League matches in 171 innings = 15,456		

Photos of the man in his twilight years

A plaque erected outside a main gate at Edgbaston in 1973 inscribed that it was universally acknowledged in later years that Barnes was "The Greatest Bowler of them All." Barnes' grandchildren Peter and Penny are in the picture. The plaque has since been moved to the bottom of the Bell Tower. His ashes are kept at the top of the Bell Tower.

Index

Morgan, T.R. 135
Morgan, W.G. 163, 164
Morkel, D.P.B. 110,
Morris, A. 94
Morris, C.R. 172, 174, 175
Morton, F. 174, 175
Moston, F. 139
Mostyn, Lord Llewelyn Lloyd 146, 147
Murilitharan, Muttiah 233
Murlidharan, 78,
Nawab of Pataudi 167, 168
Neblett, E.M. 154, 155
Newnham, Stan W. 176-178
Nicholson, N.C. 177
Noble 47
Norman Mr. 130
Nourse, A.W. 139
Nunes C.K. 152
Nunes, R.K. 154155
Nupen, E.P. 139
Ochse, A.L. 161, 162
O'Keefe, Frank 89,
Oldfield, N. 177
O'Reilly, W.J. 188, 190, 191, 194, 195, 271
Orton Mr. 36, 135,
Osborn, G.F.A. 129
Owen-Smith, H.G.O. 110, 111,
Page, M.L. 149, 150
Pallett, Henry 35, 84
Palmer, C.H. 56, 238, 239
Parkin, Cecil H. 102,
Parkin, R.H. 94, 177
Parry, Dave 1, 128, 130, 131, 134,

Paynter, E. 177, 187, 190, 192, 194, 195
Pearman, Roger 31, 32
Peebles, Ian 275
Peel Robert 142
Peete Ted 142
Pegler, (South Africa) 167, 68
Pell, I. 135, 136,
Perks, R.T.D. 239
Pickthall, H. 167, 168
Pike, S. 94
Pilsbury Mr. 131
Place, W. 177
Plant, Keith 1, 247, 248, 250
Pope, G.H. 177
Pope, T. 30
Purdy, Councillor W.E. 129
Quinn, N.A. 111,
Rae, E.A. 154, 155
Raikes, K.C. 149, 163, 164
Ramadin Sonny 226
Ranjitsinhji, K.S. 46
Ransford, (Australia) 209
Ratcliffe, A. 154, 161-164, 168
Ray, E.N. 135,
Remnant, P.F. 110, 111,
Rhodes, Wilfred 39, 46, 57, 58, 62, 75, 226, 230, 242, 245
Rhys, H.R.J. 168
Richards, Viv 156, 208
Richardson, Tom 9, 34, 56, 85, 204, 214
Riches, N.V.H. 148, 154, 155, 158, 160, 163, 165,
Riley, L.A.R. 130

Bibliography

Sydney Barnes
Wilfrid F. White (E.F.Hudson)
S.F.Barnes – Master Bowler
Leslie Duckworth (Hutchinson & Co (Publishers) Ltd.)
Batter's Castle
Ian Peebles (Pavilion Books)
My Spin on Cricket
Richie Benaud (Hodder Paperbacks)
The Picador Book of Cricket
Ramachandra Guha (Picador)
Connie The Marvellous life of
Learie Constantine
Harry Pearson (Little, Brown)

Newspapers

North Wales Weekly News, Dundee Courier,
Staffordshire Sentinel, Pall Mall Gazette,
Yorkshire Evening Post, Western Morning Newspapers,
Burnley Express, Star Green 'Un,
Grimsby Daily Telegraph, St James's Gazette
Manchester Courier, Burnley News,
Leeds Mercury, Athletic Newspapers.
Aberdeen Press and Journal,
Staffordshire Advertiser,
Dundee Evening Telegraph,
Sheffield Evening Telegraph,
Lancashire General Advertiser,
Shipley Times,
Sunderland Daily Echo,
Hull Daily Mail,
Bradford Daily Telegraph,
Lancashire Evening Post

CPSIA information can be obtained
at www.ICGtesting.com
Printed in the USA
BVHW04*0205250818
525590BV00001B/1/P

9 781912 183531